IN THE NAME OF
ALMIGTY GOD.

Mysteries of Sufferings

Mohammad Reza Shayegh

Translated by
Mohammad Kazem Bagheri
Raziyeh Fallah

Title: Mysteries of Sufferings
Author: Mohammad Reza Shayegh
Translators: Mohammad Kazem Bagheri & Raziyeh Fallah
Editor: Leila Ghoraeizadeh
Publisher: Supreme Art, USA
ISBN: 9781942912934
For information contact; address www.Shayeq.ir

Table of Contents

Introduction i

UNIT ONE: *Preliminary Discussions* 1

Chapter One: Types of sufferings in a general perspective 3

   1.   General and permanent sufferings............................ 3

   2.   Sufferings that Encompass all but are not permanent 5

   3.   Sufferings that are Neither General nor Permanent 6

Chapter Tow: Types of sadness... 15

   1.   Sacred Sadness 15

   2.   Emancipating Sorrow 19

   3.   Feeling Sad for Unknown Reasons 21

   4.   Lovable Sadness 23

   5.   Blessed Sorrows 24

   6.   Good Sorrow, Bad Sorrow....................................... 26

   7.   Harmful Sorrows.. 29

   8.   The secret of the difference between endurances in hardships. 35

UNIT TWO: The Origin of Sufferings 37

Chapter One: Human Nature... 39

   1.   Ungratefulness... 39

   2.   Haste... 42

   3.   Avarice 44

   4.   Fret... 44

   5.   Niggardliness.. 45

   6.   Stinginess 46

   7.   Weakness 47

   8.   Superiority and Supremacy 48

9.   Love of the World.................................. 52

Start Edification from Yourself...........................55

Chapter Two: Painful Deeds................................. 67

1.   Heart-Breaking.................................. 67

Malice: A Deadly Characteristic 68

The Heart of The Faithful is More Sacred than the Mosque .68

2.   Tongue.................................. 70

Tongue is Called to Account Minutely 74

Loose Tongue, The Cause of Deprivation 77

Our Word Is Reasonable 79

3.   Breaking One's Ties of Kith And Kin 79

Reward of Respecting Ties of Kith And Kin 80

Do Not Make Friends with Them 81

Recommended..82

Modification of Luqman's Advice in the Holy Quran...........83

4.   Defaming the Believers 84

Disgraceful Media Behaviour...............................86

5.   Haggling with People to Please One's Self 86

6.   Bad Habits 87

Bad Habits Make a Bad Man...............................88

7.   Flattery 89

8.   Prayer (Dua').................................. 89

Relation between Traditions and Tranquility 90

Relationship between Abandoning Good Deeds and Sufferings 94

The Relationship between Corrupt actions (*Makruhat*) and *Sufferings* 99

Chapter Three: External factors of suffering 101

1.   People's jealousy 101

2.   Evil Eye 103

3.   People's Envy 104

4.   People's Avarice 106

5.   Laziness 108

Getting Into Trouble by Fearing the Trouble 114

Laziness and Decadence 115

Struggling For The Sake Of Comfort in This World Is Not *Jihad*

.... 119

Seek Comfort in *Jihad* 119

Chapter Four: Causes of Miseries (Calamities) 125

Do We Suffer Miseries Merely Because We Are the Elect? ... 126

Answering the Questionable Misconceptions 138

A Common Mistake Clarified By the Quran 148

UNIT THREE: The Effects of Sufferings 153

1.   The Factor of Soul Excelence (*Nafs*) 154

2.   TheHinder of Soul Decay (*Nafs*) 156

3.   Creating The Soul Sensitive 157

4.   The Factor of Motiontoward Perfection 160

Let's Not Be Afraid of All Sufferings 163

5.   Suffering Will Make a Man from You. 165

6.   Transforming Suffering to Treasure 167

7.   Suffering Strengthens Determination 174

8.   Sufferings Are Nurturing to The Soul. 187

9.   Sufferings, the Bitter Medicine of Shortcomings 190

10. Suffering Will Bloom Dormant Talents 192

UNIT FOUR: GUIDLINES 197

Chapter One Guidlines for Warding off Sorrows and Sufferings 199

1.   Patience 199

2. Belief in *Kismet* 200

3. Writting and Reviewing Blessings 208

4. It Could Have Been Worse. 209

5. Comparing Oneself with the Disaster Stricken Not the Comfort Seekers 210

6. *Adhkar* That Eliminate and Ward off Sadness............ 212

7. Cheering up People's Hearts 213

8. Rendering Relief to the Deprived........................... 219

9. Du'a 224

    Du'a for *Mu'minin* 225

10. Avoiding Deeds That Induce Sadness 227

Chapter Two: Guidlines for Quitting Unpleasant Habits 229

1. Being Open to Criticism.................................... 229

2. Inculcation.. 230

3. Finding a Suitable Substitute............................... 233

4. Gradual Quitting... 233

    Islam and Step-By-Step Training 234

5. Religious Vow 237

6. Display 237

Chapter Three: Guidelines for Repelling the Love of This World 241

1. Contemplation 241

    How to Look on the World................................... 244

2. Making the Hereafter Your Goal............................ 246

3. Recognizing the Real Nature of the World 249

    The Wealthy on the Day of Judgement 252

4. Contentment with Divine Guardianship 253

Introduction

Man, hedonistic by nature, escape sufferings and his perfection is rooted in this natural tendency, provided that he takes an appropriate path, does not go after chimerical desires, and does not escape sublimity for illusion of sufferings (as this nature deviation is the great problem of human world)

Innate allurements, the acme of which is the Most Sacred Being (Allah), all move man toward infinite impeccancy. «و أنَّ إلى

رَبِّکَ الْمُنْتَهی» **"That to thy Lord is the final Goal."** [1] The answer to all innate needs is but Him and since reaching Him is tantamount to reaching infinite joy and getting away from all sufferings, man's God-seeking nature tries to flee from anything having the hue of suffering and misery and demands pleasure.

In man, alas, unmindful to guidelines drawn by prophets (AS), these innate allurements go astray oftentimes. Most people fail to see interminable joys in enduring ephemeral pains and everlasting agonies in temporary gayety. They, regretfully, take fright from the former's looks and run away from them, and are beguiled by the nice facade of the latter and are pulled towards them and thereby get on the wrong track, cause scuffles, and buy themselves the miseries of this world and the world to come.

This book, through the *Ayahs* of the Holy Quran and traditions of the infallible Imams (AS) tries to lay bare the true nature of sufferings and their consequences. It also tries to elucidate the fact that man's way to perfection is possible only if he treads through sufferings, that happiness in this world below and everlasting bliss in the world high above is intertwined with suffering. It also teaches us how to turn the threat of sufferings into opportunities, a ladder to success and evolution, and the keys to the tressure happiness.

Special care is taken that the discussions proceed independant of the readers' likes and dislikes. Therefore, it is avoided to use attractive yet empty mottos, which are incompatible with the

---

[1] An-Najm, *Ayah* 42

i

realities of everyday life. The discussions are rather focused on applicable facts in order to be of utmost use to everyone especially those facing a disappointing impasse and help them find a way out. And this is possible only with the permission of the Almighty God.

Praise is to Allah who is the Beginning and the End.

Mohammad Reza Shayegh

UNIT ONE
Preliminary Discussions

Chapter One:
Types of sufferings in a general perspective

1. General and permanent sufferings

General and permanent sufferings are kinds of pain that all people suffer from and that no one is an exception. They are consistent, for when the birth happens, man opens his eyes to that suffering, lives with that, and dies in it. Wherever he looks, he sees these sufferings; and since everybody is afflicted with them, they are not easily sensed. For example, if a person is born and lives in a prison, he never says why he is there. However, if they take him out, show him the city and its facilities, and then tell him to go back to the prison, he will get upset and complains, "Why should I come back?!" Because ever since he opened his eyes he was in prison and he has always lived there, also all the inmates around him have suffered the same, he fails to feel how bad the situation is. "Being held in confinement" is a kind of suffering that life in this world imposes on us. Do you know that you are captive in the place now?!

A kind of captivity is chaining the captive to a wall; this way he is prevented from any kind of movement. If he is confined in a three-by-four-meter room, he will have a bit of freedom, better than the previous. If he is imprisoned in a castle or a military camp, he will have more freedom to move around. Sometimes he is taken to another city where he is not allowed to leave but there is more room. Let's think the man in question is driven into exile, nothing can hamper his movement; but yet he is imprisoned. On a larger scale we are all trapped on the earth: of course with more room but with gravity takes over us. We really need to put a lot of energy into what we do. We are taken captive by the earth and its conditions. However, there are some people who are free from this kind of limitation, like some great men who are able to teleport

(Tyalarz) instantly from one place to another. As it is known, Sheikh Gholamreza Yazdi (Faqih Khorasani) had the power.

An Example of Imperceptible General and permanent Suffering

Imagine that you are conferred a power that allows you to be instantly present where you wish. With this power, you will not have the problems of commuting by car, train, plane, etc. Many problems will be taken out of your way and your time will not be wasted. Anytime you will, you can present anywhere and come back. No need to get the passport, visa, and ticket and no need to waste time and energy. If you have the power for a year and then you are returned to your normal state, can you live comfortably as before? If the answer is "No", then a second question is raised: how did you live before that magic power? Of course you say: this is an overwhelming suffering, should I capture in the place again?! Should I stand in line for a car and a train again?! They say: you didn't feel suffering before! The answer is "I was born in such suffering, everybody was associated in that, and then I didn't feel at all.

This is one type of human suffering, everyone is involved; but as it is general and permanent, nobody feel that till they leave that. There are a lot of sufferings which we live in, immersed in but don't feel them.

Another type is what "time" imposes on us. We are prisoners of "time" too. Do you know what will happen in an hour, what fate awaits you? Which one of these poisonous "arrows of time" will hit you? As you see we are unknowingly afflicted by time. We are also prisoners of ignorance. We don't know lots of things. Ignorance can have negative and debilitating effects on individuals. It can hurt. If someone comes up to give you some important news but suddenly fails to do so and leaves you in a state of ignorance, you will be hurt. If he says he will let you know about it the next day, expectation may not let you get a wink of sleep all night and if in the meanwhile he asks you some money, you will give him immedietly. Why?! Since you suffer ignorance. How much ignorance do we have about issues?!

In the Quran in *Surah* Al-Ballad, after taking a few vows, Allah says:

$$\text{لَقَدْ خَلَقْنَا الْإِنسَانَ فِي كَبَدٍ}^{\,١}$$

"Verily we have created man into toil and struggle."

The conclusion drawn from all this is the fact that man is born unto troubles and hardships. His life is full of sorrow and vexation,

---

[1] Al-Balad, *Ayah* 4

yet he doesn't feel them because they are integrated into his everyday life. However, if he is given a chance to step out of them, he will easily see them. For further explanation an anecdote about this suffering is expressed:

In a funeral procession the son of the deceased was wailing, "Dear Dad, you are being taken to a place where there is no carpet and pillow, no lights, no food and no water, a place full of insects, cockroaches and beetles". Upon hearing this, the little boy turns to his poor father and asks, "Are they taking him to our house Dad?" The boy has been in such a house since birth and thought that everywhere was the same.

2. Sufferings that Encompass all but are not permanent

People in declining years face this kind of suffering. Everybody likes to have a long life, but nobody wants to get old. However, growing old is an inevitable proces unless you die at an early age! If longevity is what you wish for, as a matter of fact you need to get old and suffer, more or less, the health problems this age group is afflicted with. Nevertheless, this kind of suffering does not go hand in hand with you all the time, simply because you are not old all the time. You are young, you are middle aged and then you are old. Suffering of this kind, therefore, is not permanent, but it is easily felt especially when old age is put next to another age group and seen in one frame. It is distressing to a senile old man who is suffering from arthritis to see a vigorous young fellow running vivaciously in the park, but it will console him to see some other old men in the park walking around with difficulty. It will equally make him feel better to think that the youth will grow old too (A black camel that kneels befor every door). Disaster, when widespread, will be more tolerable, as the saying goes.

«اِنَّ البليةَ إذا عمَّت طابت»[1]

General sufferings are temporary and are felt more than sufferings in the first category. Sufferings of the first category are not felt till the man leaves it. But the second ones are felt more with less pain as they are general.

---

[1] Bihar al-Anwar, vol. 32, page 261

3. Sufferings that are Neither General nor Permanent

These sufferings are not for all, nor are they permanent; they are, moreover, remediable like poverty. Although many people are desperately poor, many more are not, and secondly, poverty is not always everlasting. This group of sufferings, unfortunately found in abundance, is deeply felt as when the one who is stricken by poverty looks around, he clearly sees that others are not suffering from it. Yet the upside of the whole thing is that by trying hard you may find a way out of it. He is constantly limping to escape and looking for a way out.

Kinds of Suffering

1. Desirable sufferings: Those that would be welcomed, or in other words, they are "good sufferings" which are not followed by bad consequences.

2. Undesirable sufferings: It means that man suffers, but the result is bad or useless. Like someone who digs out the ground for a hidden treasure, but he gets none or even worse he gets bitten by a snake. This man has suffered in vain and this suffering is harmful. Most of the sufferings are the same.

3. Voluntary sufferings: Like a student who suffers to learn something or an athlete who takes systematic training.

4. Involuntary sufferings: Unwanted sufferings, such as illnesses, death, accidents etc.

5. Sufferings that result in comfort: Like troubles we face to obtain spiritual positions, worldly degrees and a comfortable life. These sufferings are the result of comfort which is gained after tolerance.

6. Sufferings caused by comfort: Like those of the people who say, when they are asked to do work and try, "let's have fun today!" These people will be caught in troubles later; the pain they suffer later is the effect of their previous indolence. Therefore, there are some sufferings that are causes of comfort and some are caused by comfort.

Note

The point, which should be explained here, is that suffering must be directed or let's say targeted. If you want to take a trip to a city you have never been before, first you need to find it on the map before getting on the road. Then the sufferings you are touched with on the way like tiredness or something won't be in vain. You are getting nearer and nearer to your destination. But if you err and take a different direction, the suffering you have to endure will yield no positive results, and you will get farther and farther away from your goal. So first the goal must be set up, its truth must be found out, and then suffer for it.

Differences between Sorrow and Suffering

"Sorrow" is a burden on the soul and mind, and "suffering" is a burden on the body and flesh. You get sad when you fall into thoughts. For example, you think about something you could have had, but right now you don't. This will give you a bitter feeling of sadness. Like when a disabled person whose legs have been amputated broods over the loss he cannot change. "What would I be like if I had my legs? How am I now with out them?!" he laments. This is sorrow

However, being legless is suffering per se, because he faces deprivation in his day-to-day existence. Someone who does not have a vehicle will have to suffer pain in his muscles due to the fact that he has to get around on shanks's pony, this is suffering. But, if he thinks that if he had a vehicle, he would be able to do his jobs more easily, a sadness or sorrow will take over his life. Therefore, suffering is different from sorrow. This explaines the fact that why some people are in sorrow while they are not suffering and many people are suffering but they are not in sorrow. This is because they have great patience and trust God. We have seen a lot of cases who live in suffering, but they live a happy life, because their soul is calm. They trust God and leave their suffering to Allah. They know if they show due patience they will be rewarded, so they are happy and content. If someone forcibly stops you and tells you he wants to insert a sharp needle into your vein, you will be hurt. Plus you will be upset because of incapability in defending yourself. But if a doctor or a nurse shows you his certificate and gives you the vaccine that prevents a fatal disease, you will readily pull up your sleeve so he or she can give you the injection with the sharp and pointed needle. You will get the pain with no sorrow. Therefore, body is the place of suffering and soul is the place of sorrow. Although when we suffer, a feeling of sorrow usually comes along with it. This sorrow is not ours, we can leave it.

A judicious man had very well understood the matter. He made an example and said: I had a glass to drink water from. Then it broke. The fact that something which was mine was gone and that I did not have it any longer, was an unpleasant suffering I had to face. But feeling sorrow about losing it is more than my fair share. Imam Ali (AS) has said:

$$\text{«المُصيبةُ واحدةٌ وَ إن جَزِعتَ صارَت اثنَتَين»}^{\ \text{١}}$$

"The adversity is one, but if you become anxious it becomes twofold."

One of these two can be thrown away.

Suffering is a deficiency. Deficiency is a lack of something that is necessary: lacking eyes, hands, etc. or any health problems, or even not having enough wealth. But sorrow is not a deficiency. Sorrow is the grief due to that deficiency. Sorrow is also the anticipation of the sufferings to come. If you told someone who does not have a car that he would get one in two hours, would he be still sad? If the answer is "No", is it necessary to grieve for the future that hasn't come yet, that does not exist now?

There is a distinction to be made between suffering and sadness. Suffering involves prevailing hardships; something that exist now. But sadness involves chimerical hardships; things that are nonexistent. Well pay attention to these words, these are key words. Poverty is suffering because it actually does exist. But it is anxiety and concern if you sit somewhere and brood all day what this prevailing poverty is going to result in. This suffering is imaginary.

In general; suffering leads to perfection and sorrow leads to deficiency. Many of the sufferings leads human to perfection. Suffering is a deficiency and lots of times deficiency activates human mind. It is said: "الْاحْتِياجُ أُمُّ الْاخْتِراعْ", **Need is the mother of invention**. It keeps you vigilant. If the Americans wanted to destroy us at the beginning of the Revolution, they should have

---

[1] Tasnif Ghurar al-Hikam wa Durar al-Kalim (Exalted aphorisms and pearls of speech), page 262

said: don't you lift a finger! We give you whatever you want. Then today we would have neither nuclear technology, nor auto industry and nor other achievements, but they left us no opportunity. They closed all the doors on us, which led our society to perfection. Instead of worrying and grieving, take your time and think of a way to find the right solution.

However, this point was expressed that most of the sufferings lead to perfection, not all of them. For example, an individual who is hearing impaired from birth is unable to learn language, to study or to be literate because a deaf person becomes dumb too and loses contact with society. In addition, sublime sorrows will bring perfection as well. Like sorrows for Saints of God .As the poet says:[1]

Alas, in vain my life spent, deprived of thy grief;
O would I, heretofore, get entangled with thy grief!

Feeling sorrow and grieving for Sayyid al-Shuhada (AS) is a high level of perfection by itself. In that state, your mere act of breathing will lead to perfection and will be rewarded as if you have been worshiping Allah (according to the traditions of the infallible Imams, AS). [2]We did not say sorrow is rejected utterly, this matter is exceptionable too.

Some sorrow is meritorious. It has rewards, for example, if you regret failing to attend the congregational prayer. This feeling of regret will probably make up for that failure. The mere sorrow you feel because of your mistakes in the course of life is a kind of self-reproach that expunges the mistakes and sins. The sorrow of missing an opportunity to do some good work has rewards too. It can be said, in conclusion, that spiritual sorrow will lead to perfection, whereas sorrow for material things will lead to deficiency.

It is possible to suffer pain and hardship without feeling any sadness. There are people who are happy and hopeful despite all

---

[1] Hilali Jaghtai

[2] Al-Shakh Al-Mufid, page 338: ‏قالَ الصّادقُ (ع):«نَفَسُ المَهمُومِ لظُلمِنا تَسبِيحٌ وَ هَمُّهُ

لَنا عِبادَهٌ»‏; The breath of someone who is distressed for the cruelty that has come

upon us is glorified and his distress is an act of worship.

the problems they have, simply because they are determined and high-spirited; because their cast of mind is right from the base.

Once a friend told me, "I got the chance to talk with the representative of the Red Cross in the camp of the Iranian captives in Iraq. He told me, 'I have been in many of the world's prison camps. It is strange that I have never seen captives like Iranians. After two or three months other prisoners of war lose their minds, suffer from depression, and start doing crazy things. Some of them even commit suicide. But Iranian captives have been here for eight or nine years and their spirit is still high.' One of the interpreters even told me, 'The Red Cross representative had said that he and his family were gathered together for Christmas. No matter how hard he had tried to make his family believe that in such a dire atmosphere the inmates are not only alive, but they are also happy and hopeful, they could not buy it at all.' Then I asked him, 'What do you think the reason is?' He replied, 'I don't know, I'm still lost in amazement.' I told him, 'The reason lies in our religious beliefs.'"

Yes! It is possible to suffer hardship without feeling sad, but sorrow without suffering is impossible as each sorrow is a suffering itself. If you feel sorrow you are a sufferer. Then the suffering without sorrow is possible but not the other way.

There is yet another difference: not all sufferings are optional. A stone comes down from nowhere, hits your head and breaks it. While crossing the street a car hits and injures you. These things are not done voluntarily. But sorrow, in most cases, is just a matter of choice. We can push away much of sorrow we are touched with. Imam Ali (AS) said to Imam Hussain (AS):

$$\text{«اُطْرَحْ عَنْكَ وَارِدَاتِ الْهُمُومِ بِعَزَائِمِ الصَّبْرِ وَ حُسْنِ الْيَقِينِ»}^{1}$$

"Ward off from yourself the onslaught of worries by firmness of endurance and purity of belief."

Often sorrow disposal is in our own hands. Hafiz says:
"Suffer not grief for the world: take not my counsel from thy mind:"
"For, from a wayfarer, I recollect this sweet saying:"
"Give contentment to that given; unloose the frown from thy forehead:"

---

[1] Nahjul Balagha, letter 31

"For, the door of choice is not open to me and thee"

Hafiz does not believe in fatalism. What he wants to say is: what God ordained has happened whether or not you feel sad. Since what is done cannot be undone, you'd better throw your sorrow away. Why do you endure half the great suffering? This is optional.

Suffering is for the present time and sorrow is for the past and the future. The suffering of a person who does not have a vehicle is the pain in the muscles he feels due to walking long ways. But his sadness, the fact that he does not have a vehicle and why he cannot go to different places more quickly, is not limited to the present. It stretches back to all the past days or years he did not have one and also for all the upcoming years for which there is no prospect of buying one. But what the suffering is?! Suffering is what we feel now. A poem attributed to Imam Ali (AS) says:

$$مَا فاتَ مَضى وَ مَا سَيَأتِيكَ فَأينَ$$

$$قُم وَاغتَنِمَ الفُرصَةَ بَينَ العَدَمَينِ ^1$$

What you lost is past, and the future has not yet come. Rise up and treasure the moment between two things that are nonexistent.

Would a wise man grieve for things that are nonexistent? Would he sacrifice the present opportunity for things that do not exist? Would he sacrifice present pleasure for the imaginary pleasure? People in the past used to say, "Such and such a person is used to making the most of the present time and giving little thought either to the future or to the past." He took the cash and released the loan. Present time is what counts. Sufis and mystics are said to have no consideration for the past or for the future. Enjoying the moment, they put very little trust in tomorrow. We are not like that. Now we say one minute later, next we say five minutes later and then we post pone it to tomorrow and future while the present is failed. Once we see that our life over and constantly we said tomorrow, the day after, etc. Some of us are always worried about the days to come, some of us live in the past and regret past mistakes and missed opportunities, and some have both worries. Saints of God, however, do not live in the past or in the future. They live in present.

---

[1] Ghurar al-Hikam wa Durar al-Kalim, page 222

أَلا إِنَّ أَوْلِيَاءَ اللهِ لاَ خَوْفٌ عَلَيْهِمْ وَلاَ هُمْ يَحْزَنُونَ [1]

"Behold! Verily on the friends of Allah there is no fear, nor shall they grieve"

Fear is related to future while sorrow is related to past. Both are painful. But Saints of God are from now. They have no fear of the future and no sorrow for the past. But of course, we need to take lessons from the past in order to have a better future. But wasting time on thinking what happened and what shouldn't happened is useless. It has no more losing the present time.

A Tale

The following story might help illustrate the issue. Someone had lent a man some money and now he wanted his money back. He kept asking the man for his six dirhams, but the man kept answering, "Get away and mind your own business. You want the money? Pigs might fly!" So he went up to Bohlool and asked him: you, who are better than me, can't you get my money back? He asked: what has happened? The man told the story. Bahlool said, "I will go and talk to him. While I am talking with him, you should come in and demand your money. If he refuses to give it back, just go out and after a while come back again." The man asked, "What will happen then?" Bohlool answered, "Don't worry. I will have him return the money." With this Bohlool went to the store of the debtor and said, "Mr. Shopkeeper, one day I went to a garden and I found a great treasure." The greedy shopkeeper pricked up his ears and said loudly, "treasure?" Bohlool said, "Do not shout! People may hear." The man got anxious, "Well, what happened next?" Bohlool answered, "Nothing! I tried to count them, but I couldn't. There was a countless number of them." The man who was more anxious by now asked, "What happened then?" Bohlool said, "I was looking for an honest man to share the treasure with when suddenly you came to my thought." The man said, "Does it mean that I can have part of the treasure too?" "Half of it; you can have half of the jewels and gold coins," Bohlool replied. All of a sudden the creditor came in, stood before the shopkeeper and said, "Give me my six dirhams back!" The shopkeeper said, "Leave me alone! Don't you see I'm talking to a respectable man?" Bohlool asked," What was that?" He answered, "Nothing. Please go on."

---

[1] Yunus, *Ayah* 62

Bohlool continued, "Yeah, I was saying that I was trying to find someone honest and trustworthy to share all the silver and gold coins with." The man asked, "How much was it?" Bohlool said, "Thousands." The man said, "Ok then, and you said share and share alike?" "Of course," Bohlool answered. "When and where should we go?" the shopkeeper said.

They were making plans when that fellow came in and said again, "Sir! Give me my six dirhams back." The shopkeeper said, "Take these six dirhams and get out of my sight!" Then he whispered, "You are ruining our work." The man took the money and went off. Then Bohlool said, "The thing is the moment I started counting the coins, I woke up. See! It was just a dream."

In real life situations, time and again we lose wealth (six dirhams) while wide awake, in the hope of getting an imaginary treasure. Hafiz says,

"Give contentment to that given; unloose the frown from thy forehead:
"For, the door of choice is not open to me and thee."

Hafiz does not mean to say that we are not empowered to do what we do, that we do things involuntarily. What he wants to say is there are sufferings, misfortunes and painful events in our life that are the result of our destiny. Yet that destiny is rooted in what we have already done voluntarily.

Chapter Tow:
Types of sadness

Sadness is to be sorted out. A type of sadnesss is indorsed by religion. It is considered, in a *Hadith*, as an act of worship. When you are sad, you are in God's good graces. Another type is regarded as the cause of misery and suffering. Pervasive sadness can make you physically sick. It can also precipitate ageing. With this introduction we should know which type is good and which one is bad.

1. Sacred Sadness

It is stated in some *Hadiths* that if somebody feels sad about missing the opportunity of worshiping Allah, for example, attending the congregational prayers, Allah will reward him because of that sorrow. It is even stated that this feeling of sorrow is more meritorious than that act of worship. If you are given a glass of sweet juice, you may gulp it down quickly, but you are reluctant to take a bitter medicine in such a way, although it is better for you than the juice. As it goes in a narrative:

«كَم مِن حَزينٍ وَقَدَ بِه حُزْنُه عَلى سُرور الأَبَد»[1]

"Many a sad person whose sadness has brought him everlasting bliss."

There are a lot of sadnesses which make person happy. Lots of related narrations exist according to innocents.

Amir al-mu'minin, peace be upon him, said:

«مَرَارَةُ الدُّنْيَا حَلَاوَةُ الْآخِرَةَ، وَ حَلَاوَةُ الدُّنْيَا مَرَارَةُ الْآخِرَةَ»[2]

"The sourness of this world is the sweetness of the next world while the sweetness of this world is the sourness of the next one."

Saadi, the famous Iranian poet, says:

---

[1] Ghurar al-Hikam, page 321
[2] Nahjul Balagha, wise Saying 251

اَلا لا يجارن اَخُ البَلِيَّةً

فَلِلرَّحمنِ اَلطافٌ خَفِيَّةً

Don't let grief overwhelm you my brother, for God has hidden blessings.

We don't understand suffering, only we understand its bitterness.

Imam Ali (AS) has also said:

«إِنَّ مِنْ أَحَبِّ عِبَادَ اللهِ إِلَيْهِ عَبْداً أَعَانَهُ اللهُ عَلَى نَفْسِه، فَاسْتَشْعَرَ الْحُزْنَ، وَتَجَلْبَبَ الْخَوْفَ، فَزَهَرَ مِصْبَاحُ الْهُدَى فِى قَلْبِه، وَأَعَدَّ الْقِرَى لِيَوْمِه النَّازِل بِه»[1]

"The most beloved of Allah is he whom Allah has given power (to act) against his passions, so that his inner side is (submerged in) grief and the outer side is covered with fear. The lamp of guidance is burning in his heart. He has provided entertainment for the day that is to befall him."

Verily the most honored of the servants of God is he whom God has helped to feel sad and stand in awe of Him, and thereby the light of guidance gets brighter and brighter within him.

Prophet Mohammad (pbuh) said in a *Hadith*:

«اذَا أَحَبَّ اللهُ تَعَالَى عَبْداً نَصَبَ فِى قَلبه نَائِحَةً مِنَ الحُزْنِ»[2]

"When God loves a servant, he puts a wailing of sorrow and grief into his heart."

God makes his heart sad (later on it will be explained that although there are cases of sorrow for which there seems to be no rhyme or reason, they touch us for different reasons.) Then the Prophet (pbuh) goes on to say:

«فَإِنَّ اللهَ تَعالى يُحبُّ كُلَّ قَلبٍ حَزِين»

God Almighty loves grieving hearts.

The heavy heart is the dwelling place of God. The curse (wishing somebody ill will) a believing Muslim puts on someone has proved to be dangerous if he is down. When the heart is in a normal state, he may invoke a hundred curses to wish somebody ill will in vain. However, if he

---

[1] Nahjul Balagha, sermon 87
[2] Wasa'il al-Shia, vol. 7, page 76

is heart broken, the curse will be really dangerous. On the positive side, his blessings will be effective too. Then the Prophet (pbuh) continues:

«اغْسِلْ قَلْبَكَ بِماء الحُزْنِ وَ الخَوْفِ»[1]

Give your heart a rinse with the water of grief and fear.

In this *Hadith*, sorrow is likened to water. Yes, the heart can be washed too. Grief and sorrow wash and purify the heart, especially when they make tears flow. Hafiz says:

Arise and fill a golden goblet up
Until the wine of pleasure overflow,
Before into thy skull's pale empty cup
A grimmer Cup-bearer the dust shall throw.
Flow, bitter tears, and wash me clean! For they
Whose feet are set upon the road that lies
'Twixt Earth and Heaven."Thou shalt be pure," they say,
"Before unto the pure thou lift thine eyes."

Rasulullah (pbuh) said:

«يا اباذر ما عُبِدَ اللهُ عَزَّ وَ جَلَّ عَلَى مِثلِ طُولِ الحُزْنِ»[2]

O Abu Dharr, never has Allah been worshiped as a prolonged sadness.

By merely feeling sad, a servant of Allah does nothing. He does not make bow nor does he prostrate, but God regards his sadness as the highest level of worship. If a believing Muslim's heart is filled with sorrow, no act of worship can be compared with it, provided that, the sorrow does not concern mundane and worldly possessions, is not originated from jealousy, greed, avarice, arrogance, and vices that come from the spiritual realm, and provided that, it is related to religious ideas. This sorrow can atone for his sins. It expunges the sins and cleanses his heart and soul for the immense reward. Some sins attack the heart (as there are different kinds of infection like skin infection, bloodstream infection, and inflamation of the bone). The heart may also be affected by some forms of impurity. The Quran says:

«... وَمَن يَكْتُمْهَا فَإِنَّهُ آثِمٌ قَلْبُهُ ...»[3]

---

[1] Nahjul Balagha, sermon 87
[2] Bihar al-Anwar, vol. 74, page 79
[3] Al-Baqara, *Ayah* 283

Conceal not evidence; for whoever conceals it, his heart is tainted with sin.

If your clothes are dirty, you wash them. But how is it possible to wash the heart? God washes the heart by putting sorrow and grief into it. So do not be afraid of these moments of sorrow. Because they come from God they should be welcomed with open arms.

There is a *Hadith* that Imam al-Baqir (AS) quoted from *"the Book of Ali* (AS)[1]" :

«إنَّ المُؤمِنَ يُمسى وَ يُصبِحُ حَزيناً وَ لَا يَصلُحُ لَه اِلّا ذَلك» [2]

The believing Muslim gets sad in the morning; he gets sad at night; he starts his morning while his heart is overwhelmed with grief, and his good is in it; and he can not get reformed but with this same grief.

This is his salvation, and if there was another way to emancipate him, God would lead him towards that. The same *Hadith* has been narrated by Imam al-Sadeq (AS). These *Hadiths* show that devine sorrows and the ones in the way of God is as valuable as worshiping Allah and will purify the heart. Such sad men have the support and grace of God.

Excessive Happiness (Exultation) Brings about God's Wrath.

It is said in the Holy Quran:

---

[1] This book, whose existance is verified by *Ahadith* narrated by Sunnis, was a thick book dictated by Rasulullah (pbuh) to be penned by Amir al-mu'minin (AS). Some great Sunnis have narrated that they were having a meeting with Imam Bagher (AS) when someone came in and asked a question. The Imam turned to his son and asked him to fetch the Book of Ali. He left and after a while came back with the book and gave it to his father. The Imam (AS) then opened it and answered the question–he already knew the answer; he just wanted to show them the book. They said it was a thick handwritten book. Then the Imam said, "This is a book penned by my ancestor Amir al-mu'minin (AS)–dictated by Rasulullah (pbuh) and written by Amir al-mu'minin (AS). It contains all man's requirements and decrees concerning religion and life of this world even the amount of diyat to be paid for scratching someone's skin. There are too many referrals to this book.

[2] Bihar al-Anwar, vol. 69, page 71

«إِنَّ قَارُونَ كَانَ مِن قَوْمِ مُوسَى فَبَغَى عَلَيْهِمْ وَآتَيْنَاهُ مِنَ الْكُنُوزِ مَا إِنَّ مَفَاتِحَهُ لَتَنُوءُ

بِالْعُصْبَةِ أُولِي الْقُوَّةِ إِذْ قَالَ لَهُ قَوْمُهُ لَا تَفْرَحْ إِنَّ اللَّهَ لَا يُحِبُّ الْفَرِحِينَ»[1]

Indeed, Qarun was from the people of Moses, but he tyrannized them. And We gave him of treasures whose keys would burden a band of strong men; thereupon his people said to him, "Do not exult. Indeed, Allah does not like the exultant."

This *Ayah* does not mean to say that God doesn't like happiness; what it means to say is He does not like people who are always laughing and keep looking for buffoonery and happiness.

There is nothing wrong with happiness, but excessive happiness or exultation is not what we are enjoined to pursue. How can one be happy in a society full of problems, orphans, oppressed people, full of people who have lost their loved ones, full of poor, hungry and garmentless people alongside with the victims of floods and earthquakes? If there is humanity in an individual, he or she does not make a show of elation in public.

Not from absence of means has my face become pale,

Concern for the starving has made my heart quail.

A person, who does not care about others' grief and sufferings, has nothing to do with being human.

2. Emancipating Sorrow

One of the most sacred and valuable types of sorrow is the one you feel for the sadness of Ahl al-Bayt. Imam al-Sadeq said:

«رَحِمَ اللهُ شِيعَتَنا خُلِقُوا مِن فاضِلِ طِينَتِنا و عُجِنُوا بِماءِ وَلايَتِنا يَحْزَنُونَ لِحُزْنِنا و يَفْرَحُونَ

لِفَرَحِنا»[2]

May Allah bless our Shiites; they are created from the extra clay of

ours which is drenched and mixed with the water of our love; they grieve

for our sorrow, and rejoice for our joy.

---

[1] Al-Qasas, *Ayah* 76

[2] Al-Hakam al-Zahirah, page 468

In another *Hadith* he says, **"Because they are created from the same clay as we are and because in essence and nature we are the same, the same sadness that touches us gets into their hearts too."** [1] In yet another *Hadith* he says, **"The breath of a person who grieves for us is an act of worship, and paradise will be made obligatory on him for this grief."** [2]

Think of this type of sadness as something very valuable. Try to attend the mourning ceremonies held to commemorate Sayyid al-Shuhada's martyrdom once a week or at least once a month. It works wonders in cleansing your heart of impurities and recovering your mind and soul's equilibrium. In the book "Nafasul Mahmoom" [3] there are a lot of *Hadiths* indicating that you may earn reward by just feeling sad about the problems that befell Ahlul-Bayt . Basically, feeling sorry for the righteous can earn reward. It will be rewarded if you feel sorry for an orphan, help and pray for a neighbor who has problems, and offer condolences to the bereaved. According to a *Hadith*, as the reward, they will dress you in heavenly clothing. If you do these things for Awliya Allah (Friends of Allah), the reward will be greater. If they are for an Imam, just God knows how great the reward will be. As Imam prays, **"O Lord, shower your mercy upon the one who wails and cries for us."**

---

[1] Shaykh Tusi, page 299
[2] Ghurar al-Hikam wa Durar al-Kalim, page 851
[3] Compiled by Shaykh Abbas Qomi

3. Feeling Sad for Unknown Reasons

You feel sad without any rhyme or reason every once in a while. You try to find a reason, but apparently there is no visible reason. Normally, there is an outside reason for feeling depressed, like when you lose money. But in some cases the sadness will be left unexplained. One of the reasons, traditions tell us, is some sins. For example, a tradition by the Prophet (pbuh) says:

«انَّ الْعَبْدَ اذا كَثُرَت ذُنُوبُهُ وَ لَمْ يَكُنْ عِنْدَهُ مِنَ الْعَمَلِ ما يُكَفِّرُها ابْتَلاهُ اللهُ بِالْحُزْنِ لِيُكَفِّرُها»[1]

"When a servant (of Allah) commits a sin and has no good deeds in his record to atone for it, Allah will make him sad for his sin."

There is a narrative saying if a believing Muslim who is walking in an alley, tramples some ants deliberately, as a compensation for his sin God puts sorrow in his heart. Ants in the house that bother us, and we have to get rid of them, are a different story. However, hurting an animal without a reason is not right. According to a *Hadith*, this will bring sorrow. So there is a reason for feeling sad although we don't know what it is. For example, you wake up in the morning and find yourself feeling down, but you do not know the reason. One of the reasons is what was stated.

Abu Basir says: I asked Imam al-Sadeq (AS): sometimes I get sad but I don't know the reason. Could you please tell me why? The Imam (AS) replied:

«انَّ ذلكَ الْحُزْنْ وَ الْفَرَحْ يَصِلُ الَيْكُمْ مِنّا»[2]

"(Shias are connected to us) when we feel sorrow or joy, they feel it too."

---

[1] Osoul-e Kaafi, vol. 2, page 444
[2] Ilal al-Sharayi`, vol. 1, page 94

The joy and sorrow you think has no reason, is not reasonless.

«لِاَنّا اذا دَخَلَ عَلَيْنَا الْحُزْنْ اَوْ سُرُورِكانَ ذلکَ داخلاً عَلَيْكُم»

"The joy and sorrow we come to feel, come to you too."
Then the Imam (AS) said:

«لِاَنّا وَ اِيّاكُمْ مِنْ نُورِاللهِ عَزَّوَجَلَّ...»

"The reason is that we and you are from God's light."

Our Shias are moulded into shape from the same clay as we are. Their sadness and ours are the same. When our hearts get sad theirs do too. They feel happy when our hearts become happy. Therefore, since many forms of sadness link us to the Household of the Prophet (pbuh), they are considered sacred and will be rewarded by God. Imam Reaza (AS) was once asked in the *Hadith* related by Jaber Ja'fi[1]:" Why does one get sad with no good reason?" He replied, "If he comes to grief, he should know that his brother is feeling sad." The same goes for when he becomes happy with no good reason. That's a fact. And there are a lot of facts in the world that we are unaware of. A poet[2] says:

When foliage the wind blows off trees,
Shudder hard the crop, the boughs and the leaves.

When a gust of wind blows a leaf down a tree, the entire tree trembles. When you have a toothache, you cannot think well. Your ears may not hear well either, and you will be in a mood as long as the ache keeps bothering you. Moreover, you will lose your appetite because the whole body is involved. If you take the whole society as a body, it is good to be a gentle soul, have no malice, wish no ill-will on anyone, be respectful and mindful of other people's feelings, and be sensitive to the needs of others. A sensitive, concerned person, who can feel pain, will quickly notice the injury if his hand gets injured. If it hits a hot heater, he will pull it back instantly. That is why his body remains intact. A concerned person will notice it quickly if he gets spiritual pain, so his spirit remains intact. Therefore, he enters the hereafter with a healthy soul. Apathetic and cold-hearted people, on the other hand, who

---

[1] Bihar al-Anwar, vol. 71, page 277
[2] Mohammad-Hossein Shahriar

deem that they are happy, are the most miserable people. They will not notice anything now, even if they get stabbed with a dirk or sword in the soul, even if their soul faces depletion. So in the hereafter they will appear incomplete. The Quran says:

$$\text{«...}\ \text{وَنَحْشُرُهُمْ يَوْمَ الْقِيَامَةِ عَلَى وُجُوهِهِمْ عُمْيًا وَبُكْمًا وَصُمًّا ...»}^{١}$$

"...On the Day of Judgment We shall gather them together, prone on their faces, blind, dumb, and deaf..."

These people have ruined their own true characters. Why? Simply because they were apathetic, Because they kept hurting themselves, and destroying their true and immortal characters unknowingly.

4. Lovable Sadness

Abu Basir says: I asked Imam Sadeq (AS)[2]: I sometimes get sad with no good reason. Could you please tell me why? Imam replied, "The sadness you feel is the same sadness that touches us. When we feel happy or sad, you will be quickly affected by those feelings too, because you have inherited our light, and are moulded out of the same clay as ours." Then he went on to say, "God created Shias from His own "light" and our clay, but their clay is not as pure as our clay. If it were, they would never commit sins and they would be held at the same rank as ours. But their clay, alas, is mixed with a little of our enemies' clay."

This is a discussion that must be dealt with separetly. The *Hadiths* on "Tinat" are quite famous. "Tinat" in Arabic language means clay or mud. Its plural form is "Tin", which means the most basic and important part of something; the essence or nature of something. The Imam (AS) said: your essence or nature is taken from us, but because it has been mingled with a bit of our enemies' "clay", you sometimes fall into sin. The sins you commit are from there, they are not from our code of ethics. If your essence were purely taken from us, you would be invulnerable to sin. Abu Basir says: I asked the Imam (AS), "Do you mean to say that just as we were taken from the light of God and your "clay",

---

[1] Al-Isra,verse 97
[2] Ilal al-Sharayi`, vol. 1, page 94

we will ultimately return to what we were originally made of?" The Imam then answers with a question (pointing to the ground), "Is this sunlight connected to the sun or not?" I said, "Sir, they are separate. The sunlight is here, but the sun is over there, up in the sky." After that the Imam asked, "At sunset, would the light not follow the sun?" I said, "Of course it would." He said, "I swear to God that you are from His light and will go back to Him. I swear to God that you will join us in the Day of Judgment. We will intercede for you and He will accept. Our Shias will intercede too and He will accept." This is good news that there will be a reward for our sorrows. May our sorrows be transcendental and worthwhile, Inshallah (God willing).

5. Blessed Sorrows

In the Battle of Uhud some of the Prophet's companions fell martyred, and the Muslims had to endure an enormous amount of suffering. They also had two typs of distress. One because of their loss and second because they had abandoned the Messenger of Allah (pbuh). The latter, which brought disgrace on them, was worse than the first. God says in the Quran, "I put this grief in your heart." This is called the sorrow of faith. Regretting your sins is faith and continence itself. Because if someone sins and does not feel sorry about what he has done, it shows that he is not faithful, he does not care. The Prophet's companions were trying to find a way to show their loyalty in the aftermath of the battle; to show that they were ready to make the ultimate sacrifice for the cause; that their disobedience was just a mistake that passed and would never return again; they were trying to make excuses for their misdeeds. They were awfully bothered. On the one hand they had their wounds and injuries, and on the other hand, they were sad because the Prophet (pbuh) had called them, but they abandoned him."What should we do now?!" The Quran says:

$$\text{... فَأَثَابَكُمْ غَمًّا بِغَمٍّ لِّكَيْلَا تَحْزَنُوا عَلَى مَا فَاتَكُمْ وَلَا مَا أَصَابَكُمْ ...}^{1}$$

---

[1] Aal-e-Imran, *Ayah* 153

"There did Allah give you one distress after another by way of requital, to teach you not to grieve for (the booty) that had escaped you and for (the ill) that had befallen you."

God gave you sorrow in return for that sorrow. What was it? It was the sadness you felt because things happened the way they did and your wish to make up for the misdeeds. Now notice what a strange thing happened. After the victory, Abu Sufyan's armies were so drunk with happiness that they forgot why they had gone there in the first place. God had actually made them forget. That was one of the divine assistance. They had gone there to take control of Medina and to destroy the basis of Islam. The moment that Islam Army was completely routed there was no impediment in their way. There was just a flat plain and then the unprotected Medina. However, God made Abu Sufyan's army forget it. Four thousand people, all of them forgot it. It is very interesting! Everyone forgot. When they were near Mecca, Abu Sufyan asked, "We had gone there to destroy them; why are we coming back?" Then someone said, "Why didn't you say it?" Another one repeated, "Why did you not say it?" Everyone started saying, "Why didn't the commander say anything?" Everyone, surprised and stunned, said, "Now we are returning." The Prophet's spies reported that the Quraish armies were coming back again. The Prophet (pbuh) gave the orders for Jihad. The Muslims said," Now it is time to compensate." Even many of those wounded got out of bed and wore combat garb. Abu Sufyan heard the news about the changes and that if they went there they would not return safe this time. Therefore, they decided to turn back and not to let their victory be spoiled. This battle is known as Hamra al-Asad Battle. In addition, after those verses that taunted Muslims, some other verses were revealed to compliment the believing Muslims.

A Voice that God Loves

If you keep a song canary in captivity and keep feeding it, it will not sing for you. Because its stomach is full, and gradually fat will surround its throat and it cannot sing beautifully any longer. Nevertheless, if you keep it under the pressure of hunger, then it will sing beautifully. However, when a crow makes a "rattle" sound, first we feed it, and then we will say: go away and do not make noise! I do not like to hear you.

By the same token, when a believer faces a hard situation, he may burst out into tears. Then God will say, "This is what I wanted." We may not get to know the root of this matter, but it is often like this. Imam al-Sadeq (AS) says, **"When a believer prays, God says to the angels: I have answered his prayer, but keep it and do not grant it to him; I'd like to hear the voice of this faithful servant. There are servants whom He does not like to hear, so He says: fulfill his wish quickly. I do not like to hear him again."**[1]

Therefore, sorrows are not always bad. There are many types of sorrow which are valuable in our lives. Grieving for the sin you have committed is one of them. Imam Ali (AS) says:

$$ \text{«سَيِّئَةٌ تَسُوءُكَ خَيْرٌ عِنْدَاللهِ مِنْ حَسَنَةٍ تُعْجِبُكَ»}^{٢} $$

"The sin that displeases you is better in the view of Allah than the virtue which makes you proud."

What it means to say is if you, for example, fail to say your Night Prayers and then you feel sorry for missing the opportunity, you are better than one who prayed and became arrogant. Better yet is one who prayed but did not get arrogant. Committing a sin and feeling sorry and humiliated after that is more valuable than doing a good deed and becoming proud. Sorrow for missing prayers will earn a reward for you. Sadness due to a lack of perfection is also worthwhile if, of course, the sadness is followed by some actions that change you for the better. The grief that man endures for the suffering of other people, neighbors, and Awliya Allah will be rewarded too. God loves those who care for others.

6. Good Sorrow, Bad Sorrow

The apathetic that only see themselves and their own families have no value in Islam. Great people are the ones who care about others. Sometimes they worry so much about other people's distress that they forget their own. They get into trouble for the sake of others. There is a great reward for all these sorrows and sufferings. However, being worried about worldly goods and possessions and thinking too much about them is unseemly and

---

[1]   Osoul-e Kaafi, vol. 4, page 245
[2]   Nahjul Balagha, wise Saying 46

unpleasant. Sadness for not having money, house or luxuries is inhibitory and obnoxious. This kind of feeling may act as a check on human perfection. Allah, in a great many of the Quranic verses, has threatened those whose only aim is the world. We should keep this kind of sorrow out of our lives simply because it is an inhibitor.

Unfortunately, when luxury-oriented secularism and worldly life dominate in society, this kind of grief and sorrow will increase, and various diseases and ultimately death will ensue. You hear time and again that a young man of thirty had a stroke, paralysis or something. This is due to an extremely lavish lifestyle which is based on jealousy, greed, and distress. The most common cause of marital strife, conflict, and divorce is financial difficulties, discontent, and luxury. The covetous woman, in many cases, asks for material possessions that are beyond what the husband can afford. However, he breaks his neck to fulfill the inordinate demands of his wife. In the midst of his ignoble strife he suffers a heart attack and ends in the hospital. In some cases their married life will suffer. Islam forbids loving the world. The Holly Quran has explicitly threatened that if someone chooses the world as his target, Allah will reward his good deeds in the world so he will have nothing in the hereafter. This is dangerous!

$$ \text{مَّن كَانَ يُرِيدُ الْعَاجِلَةَ عَجَّلْنَا لَهُ فِيهَا مَا نَشَاءُ لِمَن نُّرِيدُ ثُمَّ جَعَلْنَا لَهُ جَهَنَّمَ يَصْلَاهَا مَذْمُومًا مَّدْحُورًا}^{1} $$

"Whoso desireth that (life) which hasteneth away, We hasten for him therein what We will for whom We please. And afterward We have appointed for him hell; he will endure the heat thereof, condemned, rejected."

God has explicitly promised Hell to the people who are in love with the world. If someone loves something very much, it will be very pleasing for him to obtain it, and it is very sad for him to go without it. The degree of your sadness in losing things depends on the intensity of your love and interest. A milk tooth comes out with two fingers, whereas a permanent tooth comes out only with

---

[1] Al-Isra, *Ayah* 18

tongs, and with too much pain and bleeding. When the worldly love is rooted in the heart, it will be virtually next to impossible to uproot it. If you're informed that one thousand of your gold coins have been stolen, you will sure be very upset; conversely, you will rejoice at the news that one thousand gold coins have been given to you. Why is it the case? You might simply reply, "Because gold is liked by a lot of people." However, if somebody comes up and says to you, "You have been given one thousand lumps of mud," you will not get happy. And if you are told, "You have been robbed of your mud", you will not get upset, because you have no interest in it. The greater the dependency of the heart on the world, the more reluctantly you will part with it. And this is against asceticism.

Imam Ali (AS) says: **hole of whe T** ;[1] «..الْقُرْآن مِنَ كَلِمَتَيْنِ بَيْنَ كُلُّهُ الزُّهْدُ»

asceticism is confined between two expressions of the Quran,

«..كُمۡ آتَا بِمَآ تَفۡرَحُوا وَلَا كُمۡ فَاتَ مَا عَلَى تَأۡسَوۡا لِكَيۡلَا»[2]

In order that you may not despair over matters that pass you by, or exult over favours bestowed upon you.

When will this spirit come about? When the world becomes small in the eyes of man, his soul grows bigger. However, the smaller your personality is, the bigger the world looks in your eyes. Take a little kid for example. Suppose on the way home you find a piece of wood. You pick it up, give it to him and say, "Do not give it to anybody, this is for you." Then send someone to take that piece of wood from him. Can he take it? Never. He starts to shout and cry. But, when the boy grows up, he will never cry over a piece of wood. Why? Because his personality has now grown up, and small things do not have any value for him. If you blow onto a pond of water, a ripple will be formed on the surface that goes to the other side of the pond. Can you do the same thing with the Pacific Ocean too? A great soul is not simply taken away by a wave. It takes a storm. Small people, however, are taken away by a small ripple. They are easily overwhelmed.

****

A man who gets stormy over such unimportant events, his personality is the size of a pond. Man's personality grows big when he does not get upset a bit

---

[1] Nahjul Balagha, wise Saying 439
[2] Al-Hadid, *Ayah* 23

even in the hardest events. One of Imam Khomaini's students said that when the Imam was informed that his son was martyred, all of the people present there started to cry bitterly, but the Imam said, "Try to be patient. Death is right. Indeed we belong to Allah, and indeed to Him we will return." Whoever came in thought that we were the bereaved and Imam Khomaini was there to offer his condolences! While it was the opposite. He was indeed the embodiment of the following *Ayah*

$$ «...\text{لِكَيْلَا تَأْسَوْا عَلَى مَا فَاتَكُمْ وَلَا تَفْرَحُوا بِمَا آتَاكُمْ...}»^{1} $$

In 1357 when he came back from exile to Iran, he was offered the most unprecedented welcome in history. Yet when a reporter asked him, "What is your feeling now?" He simply said, "Nothing!"

If you give a box of chocolate to the children who have lost their fathers, they will forget their fathers' death. By the same token, if a man's soul is great, problems are easily forgotten, simply because he does not belong here.

Ma'mun Ar Rashid wanted to impress Imam Javad (AS) and have him gaped and humiliated in the crowning glory of his palace. Therefore, at the wedding ceremony of his daughter with the Imam he ordered gold belted servants to cover the path with gold coins. All around him things were embellished with utmost beauty, but the Imam's soul was too big to pay any attention to these things.

7. Harmful Sorrows

A series of sorrows are bad and vilified. They keep people away from their purposes and from the Hereafter. There are a lot of *Hadiths* in condemnation of these sorrows. Here are some:

$$ «\text{الْأَحْزَانُ سُقْمُ الْقُلُوبِ}»^{2} $$

"Sorrows sicken the heart."

Unpleasant, worldly, and deterrent sorrows can sicken the heart. A heart void of joy will get sick and is left nothing. Like the body, the heart also becomes sick. There is a narrative indicating that the disease of the heart is more harmful than the body disease. Then sorrow makes the heart sick and harm the body.

---

[1] Al-Hadid, *Ayah* 23
[2] Ghurar al-Hikam wa Durar al-Kalim, page 321

«الْحُزْنُ يَهْدِمُ الْجَسَدَ» ¹

"Sorrow destroys the body."

We have seen and heard people asking,"Why have you become so thin? Have you got any sorrow or greif?" Sorrows will make the body wither away. A woebegone person was once heard to say, "I lost thirty kgs on account of my sorrow!" He had gotten involved in other pains and problems too.

«الْهَمُّ أَحَدُ الْهَرَمَيْنَ» ²

"Grief is one of the two states of aging."

"Haram" means old age. There are two types of old age: one that comes about naturally, and the other one occurs out of grief when life gets tough. Imam Ali (AS) says:

«الْهَمُّ نِصْفُ الْهَرَمِ» ³

"Grief is half of old age."

The other half is biological or physical aging. Now, if someone who is physically old lives happily, he will virtually be the same age as a young man whose heart is sorrowful. In other words, they are equal in age. Another *Hadith* in this regard says:

«لَا تُشْعِرْ قَلْبَكَ الْهَمَّ عَلَى مافاتَ فَيَشْغَلَكَ عن الاستعداد بما هُوَ آت» ⁴

"There is no point brooding over what you have missed, for you will also miss what is on the way."

The sadness that befalls you about the past and thinking too much about missed opportunities will make you lose the good that lies ahead. A *Hadith* in this regard says:

---

¹ same
² same
³ Nahjul Balagha, wise Saying 143
⁴ Ghurar al-Hikam wa Durar al-Kalim, page 766

«اَلْقِنْيَةُ تَجْلِبُ الْحُزْنَ» ١

"Business entails sorrow."

A man involved in business may grieve over paying tax one day, then over the things that are getting cheaper another day, and yet another day over high prices and black market. There will always be a reason for getting sad. Another narrative indicates:

«مَنْ عَرَفَ الدُّنْيا لَمْ يَحْزَنْ على ما أَصابَهُ» ٢

"He who knows the world (recognizes the real value of the world) does not grieve over what befalls him."

It is not upsetting for him to lose something. Man grieves over the loss when the thing is of value to him. If you give a kid a simple toy and then take it back from him, he may well start to cry. However, the same toy will be of little value to the same kid when he grows up. If it is broken or lost, it does not matter to him. Why? Because he understands that it is worth next to nothing. If human soul grows bigger, if he comes to know what the real essence and nature of the world is, he won't be overawed by its ornaments, palaces, and wealthy people, nor will he get upset after losing them.

The fact that we quarrel about worldly goods and grieve over them is because our soul is small, and these little things are great to us. When an ant looks at a cat, it says, "What a huge beast!", but the cat looks quite small in a man's eyes. When we were kids, we thought that alleyways were very large and wide, but now they are small and narrow for us. They have not got narrower. The truth of the matter is that, the more the man grows, the smaller the objects look. When you climb up a mountain, the higher you go, the smaller the objects look. The more your soul grows the smaller and less important the world will get.

---

¹ same, page 369
² same, page 649

As Imam Ali (AS) said:

«مَنْ عَرَفَ الدُّنيا لَم يَحزُنْ للبلوى» ١

"He who knows the world (recognizes the real value of the world) does not grieve over what happens to him."

In another *Hadith* the Imam (AS) says:

«مَنْ رَضِيَ بِما قَسَمَ اللهُ لَه لَمْ يَحْزَنْ عَلَى ما فى يَد غَيْره» ٢

"He who is content with what Allah has had in store for him will neither grieve nor long for others' gains."

Fate

Fate, by itself, is an important topic for discussion. Is fate right? Do things happen according to our fate? Are achievements our own doing? If fate is always involved, then what is the role of our efforts? If our efforts are concerned, then what does the so-called fate mean?

Fate is right, but it has nothing to do with predetermination. Our fate is written according to our deeds. We try for a goal; we study to get a good grade, for example. Is this good grade our fate or is it the result of our efforts? The answer is both, because God has ordained this fate to be written according to our efforts. The outcome of studying is a good grade. If you engage yourself in mining, it will probably be your destiny to dig out and remove something of value like coal, gold, etc. If you drive fast and carelessly, you will be doomed to crash the car. However, fate does not always go hand in hand with deeds.That is why we sometimes see that someone does not study but he succeeds; and someone else studies hard but does not succeed.

God sometimes shows us that the events of the world are based on His Will. That is, between what we do and what happens

---

[1] Exegesis of Nahjul Balagha Ibn Abi al-Hadid, vol. 20, page 271
[2] Ghurar al-Hikam wa Durar al-Kalim, page 649

is an intermediary factor which is called Divine Will and Providence, and which we often fail to notice. When you say "I studied and I passed; what does it have to do with fate?", it shows that you have disregarded Divine Will.You have failed to notice that if it were not your fate, even if you studied, you could not get a good grade. However, as a matter of course, if you work hard, you will get good grades, and Allah will give His consent to it. **He who is content with what Allah has had in store for him will neither grieve nor long for others' gains.** [1]If man comes to know whatever happens is on the basis of fate, and fate is on the basis of his deeds, most of his sadness will come to an end.

Jesus Christ told the apostles: God says:

«يَحْزُنُ عَبْدِىَ الْمُؤمِنُ اَنْ اَصْرِفَ عَنْهُ الدُّنيا و ذلكَ اَحَبُّ ما يَكونُ اِلَىَّ وَ اَقْرَبُ ما يَكونُ مِنّى...» [2]

"My believing servant becomes sad when take back what (of the world) I have given him whilst this kind of deprevation is the most lovable thing to Me and the nearest way to Me."

«... وَ يَفْرَحُ اَنْ اُوَسِّعَ عَلَيْهِ فى الدُّنيا وَ ذلكَ اَبْغَضُ ما يَكونُ اِلَىَّ و اَبْعَدُ ما يَكونُ مِنّى»

"And when I give him something of the world, he rejoices, whilst this is the most hateful thing to Me and the farthest way from Me."

That is to say, when Allah gives His servant some worldly gains, he gets happy, while he is getting away from God, and does not understand it. And when He takes things back, he gets sad while he has gotten nearer to Him, but he does not understand it. Believing in these things can be very effective in balancing our lives and avoiding excessive grief. That is, with these beliefs you can free yourself from a lot of sufferings simply because many sorrows are because of wrong beliefs.

---

[1] Ghurar al-Hikam wa Durar al-Kalim, page 649

[2] Tuhaf al-Uqul, page 513

The Secret of The World Thou Shall Not Learn, Weep No More!

In a Sacred *Hadith* related by Imam Sadeq (A.S.) Allah says:

«يَحْزَنُ عَبْدِيَ الْمُؤْمِنُ اِنْ قَتَّرْتُ عَلَيْهِ وَ ذلِكَ اَقْرَبُ لَهُ مِنّى...»

"My believing servant grieves when I tighten his sustenance, while this tightening gets him closer to Me."

«...وَ يَفْرَحُ عَبْدِيَ الْمؤْمِنْ اِنْ وَسَّعْتُ عَلَيْهِ وَ ذلِكَ اَبَعَدُ لَهُ مِنّى» ¹

"...and gets happy whenever I expand his sustenance, while that expansion gets him farther from Me."

That is, on the broad spectrum of God's pleasure, the wealthy are on the farthest point. It does not mean, of course, that they cannot reach God's pleasure, but the area of wealth, although close to the expansion of the world, is far from God's contentment. The farthest place where God's contentment is supposed to be is wealth. The servant is happy but does not know that this wealth is the travel companion of hardship and ailment.

«فَإِنَّ مَعَ الْعُسْرِ يُسْرًا» ²

"So, verily, with every difficulty, there is relief."

Find the easy ones. He further emphasises:

«إِنَّ مَعَ الْعُسْرِ يُسْرًا» ³

"Verily, with every difficulty there is relief."

Difficulties and hardships make themselves felt so much that ease does not get the chance to emerge. Yet sucessful men see comfort and ease even in sadness.

---

¹ Osoul-e Kaafi, vol.3, page 364
² Al-Inshirah, *Ayah* 5
³ same, verse 6

8. The secret of the difference between endurances in hardships.

What makes people different in dealing with painful, difficult, or upsetting situationins? A friend of mine, who had been a war captive in Iraq, once said that one of his cell mates had been taken captive in a border town. He said that he did not believe in anything and did not used to say his prayers.The prisoners sometimes joked with him about different things. One day one of them said, "It is quite unclear whether we will ever return to Iran or not." As soon as he said this, he started to cry and said, "Does it mean that I cannot drink a cola anymore in this world?!"

He would cry for a soft drink! How small the personality of a man could get! On the other hand, I saw a man who was captured a year and a half before the war in the sedition of Kurdistan, and during the war, he was betrayed to the enemy. The war lasted eight years, but he was in prison. Even two years after the cease-fire, he was still there. In the twelfth year when the captives were set free, he was detained in a room, because when he was in charge of the camp in Iraq, the prisoners had given out some flyers in Karbala. He was held responsible for it and was sentenced to life imprisonment. Seeing this, all the newly freed captives were sad, but he was laughing and cheerful .His faithful face bore no trace of bitterness or anxiety. You would think there was no feeling of sadness at all in him. What type of soul coexists with the body that can uphold it like this? Why can't others confront hardships like him? The problem is inside us. Most of the sufferings are self-made. In other words, it is we that spawn pain for ourselves. Man must stay away from ugly traits and try to eradicate them from his soul. Gradually he will see that sufferings will start to thaw and get away from him.

The Quran says:

$$\text{«...}\,\text{عَلَيْهِمْ}\,\text{كَانَتْ}\,\text{الَّتِى}\,\text{الأَغْلَالَ}\,\text{وَ}\,\text{إِصْرَهُمْ}\,\text{عَنْهُمْ}\,\text{يَضَعُ}\,\text{وَ...}\text{»}^{1}$$

"(The important mission of the Prophet is) to release them from their heavy burdens and from the yokes that are upon them."

One of the important missions of the Messenger of Allah is to lay down heavy burdens and chains from the necks and shoulders of people. That is, the Prophet (peace be upon him) has come to

---

[1] Al-Araf, *Ayah* 157

save people from sufferings, not to create them. Religion has come for the comfort of the people. Do we not say that the Quran is a prescription? What does a presciption do? It is to heal the human being and to relieve the suffering of illness. This is the duty of Rasulullah (pbuh).

UNIT TWO
The Origin of Sufferings

- Human Nature
- Pain-Inducing Actions
- External Factors of Suffering
- Causes of Miseries (Calamities)

The first thing a physician does to treat a patient is to find out the source of pain. If he fails to do so, he cannot cure the illness at all. Therefore, the first step is to run a pathological test in order to diagnose the pain. Even sometimes, doctors form a medical team to recognize the pain. By comparison, getting to know the source of suffering is as important as finding out the source of pain. We must know the cause of suffering so that we can treat it. The first issue is finding the source of sufferings.

In general, the sources of sufferings can be divided into three categories: human nature, personal deeds and external factors. (The description of these three categories will be given in detail in separate chapters in the same unit.)

Chapter One:
Human Nature

One of the origins of sufferings is human nature. The nature of an object is the quality or feature of it. It is said, for example, that water is fluid, although it can be found in gaseous and solid forms too. Iron is hard and tough by nature, but you may melt it down and change it into a liquid. The nature of an object is the feature normally it is like that.

The question now is what is the nature of man? Man's nature is his characters; the way he is in his normal state. Here we will examine some of the human traits that cause him sufferings.

1. Ungratefulness

One of man's characteristics is ungratefulness. Man is naturally ungrateful; we say "naturally", because in a normal state, he lacks gratitude, or at least his ingratitude predominates over other traits. However, he can be trained to get rid of this state and reach a stage where gratitude will become part of his nature. Nevertheless, an animal like dog has one desireable trait: If you do it good, it will never forget it. Even if you do it good just once, it will forget all the harm you have done it and because of that good, it will put its head in the doorway of your home in servitude. Gratitude in dogs is not, of course, the result of a mental process. What it does is based on instinct; it is part of its nature like the nature of water, which is softness and fluidity.

Some people are naturally good tempered and soft; they do not lose their temper easily but some, on the contrary, get angry quickly. If you burn some people, they try to put the fire out. Yet some people are so hot tempered that they change a spark into a sea of fire. The nature of dog is loyality. Of course, it does not mean that the owner of a bad character trait is not to blame. He is, for sure, blameworthy because we have the power to change our nature. If we did not have the power, God would not reprehend us for ungratefulness; God does not reprehend mere involuntary traits.

It is seen that someone shoots his dog, but the dog remains faithful to him to the end. But, what about human being? Suppose you have been kind to someone a thousand times, and after that you did one bad thing; he can treat you in four different ways:

1. He may say, "Since you have always been kind to me, I will readily forgive you for what you did." This type of behavior is called "munificence."

2. Or he may say, "1000 minus 1 is 999, I still owe you 999." This is called "Justice."

3. He can say, "1000 minus 1 is 0. I do not owe you anything now."

4. Or he might say, "1000 minus 1 is minus one. Those 1000 cases of kindness have now come to nothing, and for this one bad deed of yours I will give tit for tat."

Now, if you were supposed to put these four groups in a four-story building, which story, do you think, would be the most crowded? Unfortunately, experience shows that the fourth would be filled up sooner than the others. Ungratefulness is a big problem in human societies.

Ungratefulness is a component of human nature. The cause of a lot of sufferings is this ugly part of human nature that makes man ungrateful and forgetful about the hard work of others, especially parents, teachers, and all who have a rightful claim on us. God says in the Quran, "We held the children of Israel in high esteem, gave them the Scripture and clear signs, showed them the right and straight path, because they were dear to us, and because they were the descendants of Noah's companions. We also esteemed Noah's companions for the sake of Noah (AS). We held Noah (AS) in great esteem too because he was a grateful servant." To sum it all up, one single moral trait, gratitude, gained respect and admiration for not only Noah (AS) but also for his companions and descendants of his companions:

$$ \text{»وَءَاتَيْنَا مُوسَى الْكِتَابَ وَجَعَلْنَاهُ هُدًى لِّبَنِي إِسْرَائِيلَ أَلَّا تَتَّخِذُوا مِن دُونِي وَكِيلًا«} ^1 $$

After that He says,

$$ \text{»ذُرِّيَّةَ مَنْ حَمَلْنَا مَعَ نُوحٍ إِنَّهُ كَانَ عَبْدًا شَكُورًا«} ^2 $$

"O descendants of those We carried [in the ship] with Noah (AS)! Indeed, he was a grateful servant."

---

[1] Al-Isra, *Ayah* 2: "And We gave Moses (AS) the Scripture and made it a guidance for the Children of Israel that you not take other than Me as Disposer of affairs".

[2] same, *Ayah* 3

That is, because the children of Israel were the descendants of the Companions of Noah, they were also benefited. And Noah (AS) was benefited because he was a grateful servant. A graceful trait was in the nature of Noah (AS) that made him deserve all this dignity.

All the wisdom that God has given to Loghman and all the praise he is entitled to in the Holy Quran are summed up in one word:

$$\text{«...وَلَقَدْ آتَيْنَا لُقْمَانَ الْحِكْمَةَ أَنِ اشْكُرْ لِلَّهِ و»}^{1}$$

"And We had certainly given Luqman wisdom [and said], 'Be grateful to Allah.'"

It is said in a narrative "There is no trait rarer in the world than gratefulness." The Quran says the same thing:

$$\text{«...وَقَلِيلٌ مِّنْ عِبَادِيَ الشَّكُورُ»}^{2}$$

"...And few of My servants are grateful."

Ungratefulness is one of the esoteric knaveries that makes human being ill-fated in the world. It could have serious consequences. Many sufferings and discomforts arise from this trait. It keeps the doors of benfaction shut. Due to ingratitude, those of giving hands decide to be tight-fisted. Trust will die, charity will suffer, Kindness will come to an end, and nobody will be given a helping hand. You might have seen a giving young person who forgives, helps, lends, and accompanies; gradually and frequently, however, his head is hit with stones of ungratefulness. Then, when he is forty or fifty years old, he becomes callous and indifferent even to his neighbor's death. Why does the society become indifferent? One of the important reasons is, sure, this bad character trait. Show ingratitude just a couple of times, and you will become notorious for this trait. Apart from bad spiritual consequences, you will be badly affected by the

---

[1] Luqman, *Ayah* 12
[2] Saba, *Ayah* 13

worldly consequeces of ingratitude too: people around you will become indifferent to your troubles, and you will have to face a host of other problems.

2. Haste

Man is hotheaded. He does things too quickly without thinking. He is hasty in his judgements. He judges people before hearing them out. If you ask him, "How much do you know about this person whom you are judging?" He will say, "I don't know!" "What is his education?" He says, "I don't know!" "What is his scientific capacity? Have you read his book? Have you discussed with him? Do you know his viewpoints?" He says, "No!"

Then, why do you judge? Why do you abuse people? In general, man judges without hearing the words of the other side. For example, a woman moans, "I'm tired of my husband, God damn him." And you make a judgement about him without hearing the words of the husband. Why? Unfortunately we make haste in judgment, in rebuke, in praise, in punishment, in everything.

The opposite of haste is forbearance. Forbearance is a worthy character trait. The reason for angry discussions among some people is that one does not have enough patience to sit down and listen to the other party, and keeps interrupting him. This has also happened to me. Once I was speaking at a council meeting. Whenever I wanted to speak, they interrupted me. So I said, "I am not coming to such meetings anymore." They asked the reason. I said, "Because I couldn't get to the end of my speech in this session and a few sessions before. No one here allows me to express my opinion. Some keep commenting in the midst of my speech before hearing me out and say something against my opinion before getting to know what it is. Hearing this, they all looked apologetically at me and admitted to their misbehavior. This kind of behaviour, I think, is especially unacceptable from people considering themselves erudite.

May God bless late Mr Aboutorabi[1]. One of his wonderful ethical qualities, which he never, even once, violated, was that if you were talking,

---

[1] Seyyed Ali Akbar Aboutorabi Fard was a clerical scholar who devoted himself to the pursuit of interweaving knowledge with good deeds. He could manage, through elevated aspirations and unparalled efforts, to strip his soul of its impurity and to purge his behaviour. He was so full of loving care that whoever saw him would like him more than his own father. Once his sudden appearance in the camp made a prisoner of war lose consciousness out of happiness! Suffice to say, on his grand code of ethics, that Michael, the head of

questioning, protesting, condemning, or approving him, he would just hear you out. Sometimes he kept quiet for so long, that you would feel he had no answer. Then, in a few words he would say something that was like oil poured on troubled waters, and settled everything. I never saw him interrupt anyone and say, "I know what you want to say."

It is said that Allameh Tabatabai enjoyed the same ethical standard. If a cleric in his freshman year in his philosophy class asked him a question, he would never say, "I know what you want to ask. Here is the answer." He used to wait till the student brought the question to an end. However, not everybody is like him. Man is hasty. This is another ugly trait in human. The Holy Quran says:

$$ \text{«...وَكَانَ الإِنْسَانُ عَجُولاً}^{1} \text{»} $$

"Man is ever hasty."

As a matter of fact, too much suffering may follow this trait: prejudice, prejudgments, doing things in a hurry, etc.

A young man goes to a girl's house to ask the girl to marry him. Since the girl's family knows very little about him and his family, they decide to submit the affair to the Holy Quran. But the boy's family insists that it's quite unnecessary. "Let's finish it soon." They say. The girl's family gets

---

the International Committee of the Red Cross in 1980s, lamented, after meeting with him for an hour or so, "I wish there were only six people like Mr Aboutorabi in the entire Europe to salve the spiritual wounds of humanity!" Elsewhere he had said, "Whenever 1 go to church and call the Messiah to my mind, I unconsciously remember Mr Aboutorabi's face!" He loved Allah's servants whole-heartedly simply because he loved Him from the bottom of his heart and considered people as His best-loved creatures. When Zulfiqar, an inmate whose fuss, obsession and maladjustment had given the prisoners a great deal of harm, passed away, everone rejoiced at his death for some reason best known to themselves. However, Mr Aboutorabi took it upon himself to bathe his body. He, then, placed his head upon his chest and cried for so long (as if he had been his own son) that everybody present (Irani and Iraqi) started to cry! And... . He was beyond words. You should only have seen him to be completely infatuated with his kindness. The vexation I once felt due to his untimely death is still a burden on my chest. I have a photo of his at home to apply myself and talk to when I am assailed by grief. I'm of the opinion that if he had lived before the great Prophet of Islam (pbuh), he would have been granted prophethood. In a word, I found in him whatever I have heard so far of the prophets' conducts.

[1] Al-Isra, *Ayah* 11

embaressed and consent to their marriage in haste. Soon after that it dawns on them that the boy is unemployed and addicted. Moreover, he has a bad reputation as a rascal. Why doing things in haste! Saying or doing things without thinking may bring about thousands of problems. Man, even if he reaches the position of Moses (AS), this trait of haste will sometimes bother him. Moses (AS), too, rushed into prejudgement when he was Khidr's travel companion. He repeatedly objected to Khidr's work, and his rash behavior prevented him from continuing his companionship.

3. Avarice

Avarice, an inordinate or insatiable longing for material gain, is a despicable side of human nature.

$$\text{إِنَّ الْإِنْسَانَ خُلِقَ هَلُوعًا}^{1}$$

"Indeed human was created greedy."

He needs a loaf of bread, stores a hundred. One million is enough for passing his life while; he has accumulated a hundred billion in cash. Yet he wants another billion out of pure greed. Avarice or greed is an evil side of man.

4. Fret

$$\text{إِنَّ الْإِنْسَانَ خُلِقَ هَلُوعًا * إِذَا مَسَّهُ الشَّرُّ جَزُوعًا}^{2}$$

"Indeed human was created greedy, Fretful when evil befalleth him."

The Arabic word 'Jaza' means impatient and fret. He who is afflicted by it has a low tolerance threshold. He moans, complains and makes his pains and sufferings seem greater than what they really are.

****

---

[1] Al-Maarij, *Ayah* 19
[2] same, *Ayah*s 19-20

5. Niggardliness

«إِذَا مَسَّهُ الشَّرُّ جَزُوعًا * وَإِذَا مَسَّهُ الْخَيْرُ مَنُوعًا»[1]

"Fretful when evil touches him, and niggardly when good reaches him."

If he is blessed with something good, he hides it. If he has some money, he hides it lest his brother asks him to lend him some. He has enough money to buy a car of the latest model but drives a banger so that others should not know that he is wealthy.

We have a narration from Imam Hadi (AS):

«اذا أَنعَمَ على عَبد نِعمَةً أَحَبَّ أَن يَرى عليه أَثَرَها»[2]

"God loves to see the great effect of the bounties that He has given to his servants."

When God blesses you with some bounty, he wants to see the effect of it in your life. It's a mistake to say, "Hide what you have so people won't give you the evil eye." Incidentally, the narration declares the opposite. This is one of our most painful mistakes. When we keep repeating that we do not have, it really gives us the feeling of empty-handedness, because our emotion is the result of how we interpret reality, not reality itself.

«مَن تَفاقَرَ افتَقَر»[3]

"One who fakes poverty will be made poor."

«تَنزِلُ المَعُونَة عَلَى قَدر المَوونه»[4]

"God's help amounts to our need"

---

[1] same, *Ayah*s 20-21
[2] Shaykh Tusi, page 275, *Hadith* 526
[3] Tuhaf Al-Uqul, page 42
[4] Nahjul Balagha, wise Saying 139

The more you spend (wisely), the more God will give. If you do not spend, God will cut it off. Of course man should not be wasteful. Waste and luxuryism are not desirable. However, the narrative says that God loves to see the effect of His bounty. Do not wear torn and cast off clothes when you have the money. When you can drive a decent car, do not drive a bad one. When you can have a good enough house that accords with your dignity, why living in ruins? If you do, you will be among the people of whom, it is said in the narrative, God will make them poor.

Do not feign poverty. If a wealthy person says, "I have no money," he feels poor. On the other hand, if someone with an average income says, "I have enough of it," he feels the sense of a rich man. Fear of imaginary poverty, which is not there, may make you choose real poverty with your own hand, like someone who takes poison to become immune to diseases, but he will end up dead.

6. Stinginess
The Holy Quran says:

$$\text{«...وَكَانَ الإِنْسَانُ قَتُورًا»}^{1}$$

"Man is (ever) stingy."

Varily, man is stingy by nature unless he is trained. And it is only through divine training that he can get rid of niggardliness and stinginess, otherwise too much suffering will ensue.

Somebody was robbed of all his possessions. When he found out, he got overwhelmingly sad and lost consciousness. Every time neighbors and relatives helped him regain his consciousness, he would remember he had been robbed and hit himself hard on the forehead and fainted. If man is not so stingy and fond of wealth he will not suffer so much. A milk tooth will come out with a bit of effort and a little bit of blood, but the tooth that is firmly rooted may cause bleeding for a few days, because it is rooted and connected to one's life. If the love of the world is rooted as firmly, even a little bit of it won't be extracted without pain and suffering; it is bound to one's life.

Stinginess is a chief agent for sufferings and hardships.

One of these businessmen of old goes to work in the morning and notices that his friend is down. He discovers that his friend is not the same gregarious and talkative person who always joked and laughed. He asks for the cause. He says: (It was the time when sugar and sugar cubes were expensive),

---

[1] Al-Isra, *Ayah* 100

"When I wanted to drink tea in the morning, a sugar cube dropped into my cup of tea." He puts up a serious face and says, "It really is a great calamity. How is it that you did not have a stroke? If I had been in your shoes, I would have died!"

The Holy Quran considers stinginess as the root of all human failures. Of course, it is much more than economic stinginess and includes a wide variety of meanings. Some people are not stingy with their money, but if they are supposed to spend some of their dignity and credit on people, they will flinch away. They are very stingy but think stinginess is only limited to material and financial gains. If our soldiers had not been generous with their lives, today Iraqi soldiers were standing in the squers of our cities. But they were not stingy with their lives. Stinginess, in general, goes beyond financial issues. The root of other evil qualities like cowardice, jealousy, etc is inevitably in stinginess.

Some people say, "Praise be to Allah! We are not stingy." But most of them are while they don't know. If there is no trace of stinginess in a person, he will be prosperous. The Holy Quran says:

$$\text{«...وَمَن يُوقَ شُحَّ نَفْسِهِ فَأُوْلَئِكَ هُمُ الْمُفْلِحُونَ»}^{1}$$

"And those saved from the covetousness of their own souls, they are the ones that achieve prosperity."

$$\text{«فَمِنكُم مَّن يَبْخَلُ وَمَن يَبْخَلْ فَإِنَّمَا يَبْخَلُ عَن نَّفْسِهِ...»}^{2}$$

"But among you are some that are niggardly. But any who are niggardly are so at the expense of their own souls."

Amir al-mu'minin (AS) says:

$$\text{«اَلْبُخْلُ جَامِعٌ لِمَساوِئِ الْعُيُوبِ»}^{3}$$

"Stinginess involves all vices."

All the vices are collected in stinginess. Then the root of every inner vices is stinginess.

7. Weakness

Another natural trait of man is weakness.

---

1   Al-hashr, *Ayah* 9; At-Taghabun, *Ayah* 16
2   Muhammad, *Ayah* 38
3   Nahjul Balagha, wise Saying 378

$$\text{«...وَخُلِقَ الْإِنْسَانُ ضَعِيفًا}^{1}\text{»}$$

"Man was created weak (in resolution)."

Those who have cleared their souls of weakness have done incredible things. When we hear that Sheikh Mofid, because his students Sayyid Razi and Sayyid Mortaza were good-looking, did not look at their faces even once before they reached the young age, we do not believe it. When we hear a mystic was bowing in submission for two hours in the snow on the roof of the Imam Reza holy shrine, while his back was thickly covered with snow, we do not believe it. These people have passed the initial stages and have attained strong and steadfast willpower.

8. Superiority and Supremacy

One of the evil qualities of human being is the sense of superiority. This sense causes trouble. Here a low-scale social example and a high one to elaborate the argument are cited. For example, someone who has gone to his friend's house immediately notices that he has changed the carpets and furniture, bought a new car, and now he is a few rungs above him on the social ladder. "Nobody should be above me," he thinks. It is said of the leopard that if you move lower than him in the mountains, he doesn't mind and you are safe. But if you move above him, he will attack you. We usually say of a person with this quality that he is snotty-nosed like a leopard. This person cannot see anyone above him. This is an internal vice. In order to maintain superiority, the man in the example must now sell his furniture one third of its real price, take a loan, and get himself into a heavy debt to buy a better car in order to prove to his friend that he is above him. And this fierce rivalry goes on and on till he cannot afford his household expenses anymore. He has to face a lot of problems like taking bribes, stealing, and borrowing from others. Where do you think all these thefts and embezzlement

---

[1] An-Nisa, *Ayah* 28

come from? During this nasty rat race, the needy and poor relatives will be forgotten, and the obligatory financial rights are ignored. In short, every value will be trampled underfoot, and no one is able to clean up the mess he has made. In the process he himself suffers most. As you can see, an important cause of suffering comes from wrong attitudes. After all, if you have enough money, so much the better, use it; affluence brings about dignity. The problem arises when you go to extremes, and exceed the limits.

And now the other example: In a larger scale you can cite arrogant powers. In order to establish their supremacy over the world, they resort to arms races. The result is that most of the world's wealth is spent on financing weaponry, and in order to pay for these costs, they have to use the resources of others, fight, plunder, and launch wars to sell their weapons. As a result, the world population will have to face a lot of miseries and problems, like mass starvation. All these sufferings come from the fact that some people want to say that they are higher and superior to others.

Now an important question must be thought about: which one must be eradicated, the roots of this trait or the external events which are the resault of this trait? If those, who after the death of the Messenger of Allah,–forced off the scene the man who threatend their interests–had not felt superior and said, "Our place is that of followers, not that of Imamat. We should follow, we cannot take the place of Imamat," there would have been no suffering, and no problem would have been made. Why did the society have to face all those problems? Simply because a couple of people wanted to say, "We are the most superior of all." They wanted to be at the forefront at any cost. God says in the Holy Quran:

«تِلْكَ الدَّارُ الْآخِرَةُ نَجْعَلُهَا لِلَّذِينَ لَا يُرِيدُونَ عُلُوًّا فِي الْأَرْضِ وَلَا فَسَادًا وَالْعَاقِبَةُ لِلْمُتَّقِينَ.»

"That home of the Hereafter We assign to those who intend not high-handedness or mischief on earth. And the (best) outcome is for the righteous."

The Holy Quran explicitly states that those who seek superiority won't go to paradise. In the above-mentioned Ayah the word "mischief" comes after "high-handedness". It seems that "mischief" is the result of "high-handedness". Depravity and mischief begin when we desire to sit somewhere where we do not belong to and are not entitled to. Like an employee who decides to become the boss, by hook or by crook. Or someone who resorts to anything it takes in order to become a representative in the council or a member of parliament. All these things cause sufferings. It is a vicious trait that afflicts both the individual and the public at large. Therefore, instead of amending the external factors, we must first address this internal trait and put it to rights.

Although Pharaoh knew that Moses was right (actually he was "sure"– the Holy Quran uses the word "sure"), he thought to himself if he admitted the truth, he would have to abide by a lot more. He did not want to show humility toward Moses and confess the truth, because his pride did not allow him to do so. That's why he trampled the truth underfoot and said that the miracles of Moses were but magic." The Quran says:

«وَجَحَدُوا بِهَا وَاسْتَيْقَنَتْهَا أَنْفُسُهُمْ ظُلْمًا وَعُلُوًّا...»

"And they rejected them, while their [inner] selves were convinced thereof, out of injustice and haughtiness."

---

[1] Al-Qasas, *Ayah* 83
[2] An-Naml, *Ayah* 14

Their denial was due to oppression and supremacy. God addresses the Children of Israel at the beginning of the *Surah* Isra:

$$\text{وَقَضَيْنَا إِلَى بَنِي إِسْرَائِيلَ فِي الْكِتَابِ لَتُفْسِدُنَّ فِي الأَرْضِ مَرَّتَيْنِ وَلَتَعْلُنَّ عُلُوًّا كَبِيرًا}^{1}$$

"**And we decreed for the Children of Israel in the Book, that twice would they do mischief on the earth and be elated with mighty arrogance!**"

This is the result of these inner traits and internal vices:

$$\text{فَإِذَا جَاءَ وَعْدُ أُولَاهُمَا بَعَثْنَا عَلَيْكُمْ عِبَادًا لَنَا أُولِي بَأْسٍ شَدِيدٍ فَجَاسُوا خِلَالَ الدِّيَارِ وَكَانَ وَعْدًا مَفْعُولًا}^{2}$$

"**When the first of the warnings came to pass, We sent against you Our servants given to terrible warfare: they entered the very inmost parts of your homes; and it was a warning (completely) fulfilled.**"

Twice you'll seek superiority on the land, and both times God will punish you and pour out His wrath on you through a war-like tribe that ravage your land. The Holy Quran suggests that the reason lies in the fact that you have a sense of superiority within you.

A minor case is when everyone tries to keep up with the Joneses, and to take the lead in consumerism, wastefulness, extravagance, and luxurism. All this happens because they want to say that they are superior. To maintain superiority, they tend to reach out a ravaging hand toward the public purses and things that do not legally belong to them.

---

[1] Al-Isra, *Ayah* 4
[2] same, *Ayah* 5

The Fact That Ahlul Bayt (the Prophet's Houshold) Were Victims of Oppression Was Due to Some People's Sense of Superiority.

Hadhrat Ali (AS), who was Hojat-e Khoda (the leader of people from Allah) and Imam-e bar Haqq (rightly-appointed Imam)—and according to an orientalist, "Ali's sword was one of the causes of the triumph of Islam," fell victim to the sense of superiority of a few companions of Hadhrat Mohammad (pbuh).

Obviously, misplaced superiority disrupts the livelihood system of mankind and destroys the path of sovereignty and prosperity of him.

9. Love of the World

Seeing the world very big, giving it top priority and considering it the ultimate objective of existence is dangerous. This outlook embitters both the life of the Present and that of the Hereafter because when you are particular about something, then you are always worried you may lose it. Take gold for example. If you have not bought any, you are just eating your heart that it may get expensive, and after you buy some, you get anxious about a drop in price. The same is for dollor.

Whatever Islam has said will provide comfort even in this world. Love of the world, however, spoils even the life of the Present. If you are not infatuated with the world, your grief and sufferings are not supposed to be more, but less. When you do not like something you won't grieve for losing it, you will just say, "It doesn't matter. Let it be gone."

I used to work with a friend of mine who was a reciter—He knew the Quran by heart—from Dezfool. One day, when he was reciting the Holy Quran, he stopped reciting for a moment, took me into his cofidence and whispered in my ear, "Somebody has brought news that a rocket has hit our home and some of my family members have fallen martyred; ....oh sorry, which *Ayah* were we reading?"–No, no; make no mistake; he was very kind-hearted! Is it truly possible for a man to be like this, unflappeble in overwhelming calamities? Experience gives the nod.

The child of the revered Prophet of Islam (pbuh) had passed away. Tears were coursing down his cheeks. Someone said, "O prophet, are you crying!?" He said, "My cry is due to human sentiments, I am not ungreatful (to God)." [1]

The Quran says to the believers:

$$...\text{إِن تَكُونُوا تَأْلَمُونَ فَإِنَّهُمْ يَأْلَمُونَ كَمَا تَأْلَمُونَ وَتَرْجُونَ مِنَ اللهِ مَا لَا يَرْجُونَ وَكَانَ اللهُ عَلِيمًا حَكِيمًا}$$ [2]

"If you are suffering hardships, they (thoes without faith) are suffering similar hardships: but you hope from Allah, what they have not. And Allah is full of knowledge and wisdom."

You suffer casuslities, and they do too. You starve, and so do they. There is only one difference. They have no hope for divine reward, but you do. If the path of human life is in the direction of God, then there will no longer be a problem. If someone comes up and says, "Your car is under full warranty of our company and is fully insured. We will give you all mission rights. If an aaccident happens, just leave the car there. We will take it upon ourselves to settle the problem and have it repaired. Your monthly pay will be high enough." Then will you ever get worried and say, "What if I had an accident?" Moreover, in case of an accident your old car will be replaced with a new one. Then you will most probably pray, "May God send a car to hit mine."

Someone told me that once a man who was driving a Paykan on the autobahn to Tehran had hit a high model car. In his

---

[1] Wasa'il al-Shia, vol.3, page 282
[2] An-Nisa, *Ayah* 104

agitation he was wondering how to pay for the damage he had caused. "If I had and sold two other Paykans like this, I wouldn't be able to compensate." He was just standing there deep in thought when the other driver calls his father. After a while, his dad, a well groomed man, gets to the scene of the accident. "Gosh, what are they going to do with me?" He thinks, butterfly in his stomach. The man turns his eyes from the cars to his son," Call a tow truck and have it taken." Then the dad addresses the man, "Why do you drive a car like this?" "I can't afford any better. As you can see, this one is gone, too." Upon hearing this, he reaches inside his pocket for his checkbook, makes out a check and says, "Take this, buy a new car and throw this one away!" Then he gets into his car and drives away

If one really understands that these losses, which we face in the path of God will be rewarded, we should not be sad. The Holy Quran says:

$$\text{«...ذَلِكَ بِأَنَّهُمْ لَا يُصِيبُهُمْ ظَمَأٌ وَلَا نَصَبٌ وَلَا مَخْمَصَةٌ فِي سَبِيلِ اللهِ وَلَا يَطَؤُونَ مَوْطِئًا}$$

$$\text{يَغِيظُ الْكُفَّارَ وَلَا يَنَالُونَ مِنْ عَدُوٍّ نَيْلًا إِلَّا كُتِبَ لَهُمْ بِهِ عَمَلٌ صَالِحٌ إِنَّ اللهَ لَا يُضِيعُ}$$

$$\text{أَجْرَ الْمُحْسِنِينَ»}$$

"Nothing could they suffer or do, but was reckoned to their credit as a deed of righteousness, –whether they suffered thirst, or fatigue, or hunger, in the cause of Allah– or trod paths to raise the ire of the unbelievers, or gain any gain from an enemy: for Allah suffereth not the reward to be lost of those who do good."

If you look from this perspective, then suffering does not make sense. Believers and devoutees who are connected to the source are like small ponds connected to the ocean. However much water you draw from them, they don't dry out. Each looks to be a small pond, but actually it is an ocean.

Ne'er sustains a loss the immense soul of the pious,
'Tis a vast sea where no tempest e'er lashes.

---

[1] At-Taubah, *Ayah* 120

However, if the pond is large, yet it is not connected to the ocean, some of its water goes to the earth, some evaporates, some of it is drawn, and the rest becomes mud, then it will go dry for good. Amir al-Mu'minin, peace be upon him said:

مَنْ اَيْقَنَ بِالْخَلَفِ جادَ بِالْعَطِيَّهِ» [1]

"He who is sure of a good return is generous in giving."

Do you ever scatter a handful of flour over the ground?! But a farmer readily throws grains of wheat onto his farm. Why? Because he knows the land will yield much more. A believer who invests, will never say, "I threw it (money, energy, effort, etc) on the ground." He will say instead, "The result will come back to me."

Our outlook towards the world should be like this. Therefore, one of the vilified sorrows is the sorrow over the world, the root of which is in the affection for the world. If you want to be profitted by the world, you should not like it, and if you want to be profitted by the Hereafter, again you should not like the world.

The only way to get rid of the world and its sorrows is to wrench yourself free of its love. There is not other way. Have you ever seen a handsome person fall in love with an ugly and ill-favoured woman? How unbecoming! Especially when the woman fakes coyness and escapes, and the man has to chase after her all the time. Hafiz says,

O wise heart! Grief for a mean world, how long?
Alas it is that with beauteousness, it became the lover of hideousness!

When you are in love with the world, you will get sad if it makes its escape, as it goes true with a lover whose beloved leaves him. However, when you are interested in motives purer and nobler than the love of the world, sadness cannot find a way into your heart.

Start Edification from Yourself

The basis of all sufferings is man himself. The easiest way to curb them also comes from him. A scientist says, "I felt duty bound, at first, to put my country to rights, so I started to work. Soon I found, the bite was more than I could chew. Then I thought I had to start from my fellow citizens, so I took action immediately. Again it was too heavy a weight to lift. Gradually, however, I came to realise that I had to start from myself."

God says in the Holy Quran:

---

[1] Nahjul Balagha, wise Saying 138

$$\text{«يَاأَيُّهَاالَّذِينَ آمَنُوا عَلَيْكُمْ أَنفُسَكُمْ...»}^{'}$$

"O ye who believe! Guard your own souls..."

$$\text{«...لَا يَضُرُّكُم مَّن ضَلَّ إِذَا اهْتَدَيْتُمْ...»}^{'}$$

"If ye follow (right) guidance no hurt can come to you from those who stray."

If you are guided, then external factors cannot harm you. The fact that the Quran says:

$$\text{«إِنْ أَحْسَنتُمْ أَحْسَنتُمْ لِأَنفُسِكُمْ...»}^{3}$$

"If ye did well, ye did well for yourselves." and

$$\text{«وَكُلَّ انسان أَلْزَمْنَاهُ طَائِرَهُ فِي عُنُقِهِ...»}^{٤}$$

"Every man's fate We have fastened on his own neck", confirms this same point. Therefore, the origin of all the pain and problems we get into, come from ourselves.

From us is our agony and remedy withal;
From us is our anguish and repose withal.

People of old used to say, the apple worm is from the apple itself.

Imam Sadeq (AS) says:

$$\text{«مَن سَاءَ خُلُقُه عَذَّبَ نفسُه»}^{٥}$$

"Whoever gets ill-tempered (ill-natured) only does that to his own agony."

And sometimes this agony is transferred to others. There is no other way except to reform the inside, why? The reason is that the main evil and calamity is from here. You may say, "Do you deny that others cause suffering to us?" We answer, "No, we do not

---

[1] Al-Maeda, *Ayah* 105
[2] same
[3] Al-Isra *Ayah* 7
[4] same, *Ayah* 13
[5] Osoul-e Kaafi, vol.2, page 321

deny it." "So why do you say: whatever suffering there is comes from ourselves and nothing comes to us from outside?" you ask.

We say, "It does not mean to negate external factors." Let me make a philosophical point in plain language to clarify the subject:

We have a common cause and a fragmentary cause. The fragmntary cause, as the name suggests, cannot produce the effect by itself, but its absence can nullify the effect. For instance, to make a fire, three factors need to be at work: 1.a combustible object, 2.air, 3.heat. Each of these is a fragmentary cause and all of them together are the common cause. If any of these three factors are removed, the fire will be extinguished. However, none of them by itself is the cause of combustion. We always remove that factor which is the easiest to remove: it is almost impossible to remove the air; removing the combustible object is hard too, but it's easier to remove the heat. We do not believe that none of the suffering that comes to us is not from outside: human sufferings can be the result of external factors too. But which of these three factors, the people (who are beyond our control), unwanted events (over which we have no control either), and our own self is more controllable? Certainly, it is easier to harness our own self.

Man cannot force people to behave according to his wish. This is impossible– even the most tyrannical rulers, history has shown, cannot do that. We cannot change incidents according to our desire either. So the best way is to correct ourselves. If we can control ourselves (the internal agent), all events will change, and there will be no sufferings. The cause of sufferings is the triangle that was mentioned. That is why both the Quran and *Ahadith* emphasize that you should shape yourself up.

Great men of wisdom have said on the same basis, "Nothing comes to us from outside." The Holy Quran also says:

«ذَلِكَ بِمَا قَدَّمَتْ أَيْدِيكُم...»¹

You yourself are the agent. For example, to turn a light on, too many factors are involved: the main power plant, smaller power plants on the way, all the power lines, etc. The electrical connections and wiring of the building are also involved. Moreover, the light and its electric switch must be there too. Now, what is the most convenient option if you want to turn off the light? You may say, "We unscrew the light bulb," but it needs a ladder. Or you may say, "Let's go to the power plant and destroy it with a bomb, then the light will be off." But is it really the right thing to do? Perhaps you say, "We will cut off the high-voltage power lines in the desert." Well, with this, the light will shut down, but the easiest thing to do is to switch the light off. Wisdom says, "From this set of causes, eliminate just a small cause, and the light will be turned off." This is the easiest thing to do. A narrative says:

«وَ معلّم نَفسه وَ مُؤَدِّبها أَحَقُّ بالاجلال من معلّم النَّاس وَ مُؤَدِّبهم»²

"The person who teaches and instructs his own self is more entitled to esteem than he who teaches and instructs others."

If a person can hinder his own self, the problem will be solved, yet we are used to blaming external agents. If you want to get married, you will consult some people: some of them will give their opinions, some of them wil insist, and some will roll their eyes. After the marrige, if things are okey, so much the better, but if things go wrong, the very first thought that strikes you is to put the blame on somebody. We never think who the main culprit was! **Every man's bad omen is fastened on his own neck.**

---

¹ Aal-e-Imran, *Ayah* 182: "This is because of the (unrighteous deeds) which your hands sent on before ye."

² Nahjul Balagha, wise Saying 73

The Problem Is Within Us

To see the cause of your misdeeds and their results, you need to turn your eyes toward yourself rather than pointing the finger of blame at others. Moulavi has a poem to this effect: why do you grab Zeid or Amr by the collar? You ought to grab yours. About thirty years ago, when I was in a commemoration gathering, I sat next to someone. He smelled bad like an apothecary who had worked from morning till night producing medicines out of bad smelling herbs. I felt bad. I got up from his side and sat next to another person. He had the same smell. I changed my place again, but still the same smell disgusted me. I rose and left the service. Then I thought that the smell must be from me. I was wondering where the pungent odor was coming from when one of my relatives came up and said, "What is this on your shoulder?" It was one of these foul-smelling green beetles.

The Holy Quran says:

$$\text{«وَكُلَّ إِنسَانٍ أَلْزَمْنَاهُ طَائِرَهُ فِي عُنُقِهِ...» }^{1}$$

"Every man's fate We have fastened on his own neck."

People used to say to the prophets (pbut), "Since you have come here our economic conditions have become bad, our living conditions are upset, tribal and family discord among us have surfaced." The Holy Quran says:

$$\text{«قَالُوا إِنَّا تَطَيَّرْنَا بِكُم...» }^{2}$$

"They said: "For us, we augur an evil omen from you.""

God in return says to the prophets: say to these people: these are your own deeds, do not blame others. The bad smell is not from outside, but man's misery is that he never smells his own bad smell. All people can smell the odor of garlic, from a person who has eaten some, from a distance of two or three meters, but they themselves do not feel its smell at all. Have you ever heard

---

[1] Al-Isra, *Ayah* 13
[2] Ya Seen, *Ayah* 18

any smoker say that he or she quit smoking because of the bad smell of cigarettes?

A good many *Ayahs* and *Hadiths* try to convey this very difficult fact to people. It is said in physics, for example, that energy cannot be created or destroyed, neither can matter. But a layman does not understand this. Such a person might say, "The sun shone brightly last year, so where's its energy?" Nevertheless, a highly educated person can easily get the point. Someone else may show you a dry stick and say, "With this stick I will prove your theory is invalid." Then he throws it in a fire and after the wood is turned into ash, he says: "Where is the wood now?" You will say, "The wood is disintegrated, not destroyed. Some of it was turned into ash, some of it into gas, some to smoke and some is changed to heat. If there were some power that could return these, it would change them back into wood."

Galileo used to address people, "Let's make no mistake! Let's not be misled by seeing the sun rise on this side and set on the other side, and thinking the sun is revolving. This is merely an optical illusion. In fact it's the earth that revolves around the sun, not the other way round." But the people would not accept. They used to say that they were seeing with their own eyes the opposite of what he was claiming, and nobody was able to open their eyes to the fact. Now, imagine that someone decided to take it upon himself to get Galileo's contemporaries to accept the fact that the earth would revolve around the sun, how would he undertake this extremely difficult task and make them reevaluate their opinions?

The Main Factor

The Quran wants to prove to people that the main cause of their problems is their own deeds, but people do not accept. Why? Because the appearance is the opposite of reality.

«وَكُلَّ إِنْسَانٍ أَلْزَمْنَاهُ طَآئِرَهُ فِي عُنُقِهِ...»[1]

Getting the people to know this truth is very difficult. Yet, if one gets to know this, he will prosper. In short, there is an important fact: the root and the most controllable factor of the sufferings and miseries that come to us are internal rather than external. The big mistake of people is that they leave the inner factors and seek to find the cause among external factors. Just like the one who wants to turn off the light, instead of switching it off, he goes and cuts off the wires in the alley!

Someone once said: I wanted to go into a building for some construction work. I reached into my pocket for the key, but it wasn't there. I asked one of the workers to climb up the wall, jump in, and open the door. In the afternoon, when we wanted to leave the place, the worker closed the door, climbed up the wall and jumped down into the street next to where I was standing. I asked, "Why did you do that?" He said, "There was no key!"–not the brightest bulb in the pack! I said, "Well, you could have got out through the door and close it. He sighed and said, "It didn't cross my mind."

Most often what we do is like this. We make mistakes. We understand the problem well, but we choose the harder solution. For example, the alarm clock goes off, and not knowing how to stop it, we hit it with a hammer. Facing a problem, we cut relationship with people, thinking the problem will be solved; but we never think about the consequences. These are not viable solutions to problems. In our quest to find the enemy, we overlook the fact that the main enemy is within us. The mother of idols is the idol of self! The Prophet (pbuh) said in a *Hadith*:

«أَعدَى عَدُوّكَ نَفسكَ الَّتى بَينَ جَنبيكَ»[2]

"Your archenemy lodged between your two flanks is your self."

The fact that in religious teachings so much emphasis is put on self-edification, is due to this reality that one end of all problems is the evil side of self whose anihilation will turn down the heat of sufferings. Among all the solutions, this one is the easiest. Yet, this easy solution, ironicaly, turns out to be very hard because holding the slippery self under grip involves too much dedication and hard work.

Wherever the word "Insan"–meaning Human Being–is used in the Quran, it is used with severest form of reproach. "Insan" in the Quran is the

---

[1] Al-Isra, *Ayah* 13
[2] Bihar al-Anwar, vol.67, page 64

symbol of the ugliest natural traits. "Bani Adam"–meaning Children of Adam–is used with a different connotation, and the word "Bashar"–which means Man– in the Quran is used to refer to animalistic aspects of Man. It is only "Insan" who is reproached and criticized. "Bani Adam" symbolizes temperament, "Bashar" symbolizes instinct, and "Insan" is taken symbolically to reffer to nature. Human nature, if left untrained, is despicable. That is,

-it is intermingled with niggardliness, **man is for**; «...وَ كَانَ الْإِنْسَانُ قَتُوراً»[1] **ever niggardly.**

-It is mixed with greed, «إِنَّ الْإِنسَانَ خُلِقَ هَلُوعًا»[2]; **verily, man is born with a restless disposition.**

-When facing calamities, he is fretful and impatient, «إِذَا مَسَّهُ الشَّرُّ جَزُوعًا»[3]; **fretful when evil befalleth him.**

-He is feeble and weak, «...وَ خُلِقَ الْإِنسَانُ ضَعِيفًا»[4]; **for man was created weak.**

-He is ungrateful, «قُتِلَ الْإِنسَانُ مَا أَكْفَرَهُ»[5]; **Cursed be man! How ungrateful he is.**

Therefore, these are human traits in the normal state. Usually every animal has an admirable characteristic. For example, cocks, dogs and many other animals enjoy one. However, if man does not correct himself, none of his charesteristics is beautiful. For example, dog is naturally loyal. If you give it a bite of bread, (even if you beat it a hundred times on the head,) it will never forget that morsel. But none of the traits of man, deprived of divine training, is beautiful in itself. The Holy Quran says, "Man is infidel and ungrateful, stingy, weak and very impatient, etc.

$$«...إِنَّهُ كَانَ ظَلُومًا جَهُولًا»[6]$$

---

[1] Al-Isra, *Ayah* 100
[2] Al-Maarij, *Ayah* 19
[3] same, *Ayah* 20
[4] An-Nisa, *Ayah* 28
[5] Abasa, *Ayah* 17
[6] Al-Ahzab, *Ayah* 72

He is cruel and ignorant. That is, if man is not under divine education, he is worse than any quadruped. God says in the Quran:

$$\text{اِنَّ شَرَّ الدَّوَابِّ عِنْدَ اللهِ الصُّمُّ الْبُكْمُ الَّذِينَ لَا يَعْقِلُونَ}^{١}$$

"For the worst of beasts in the sight of Allah are the deaf and the dumb,–those who understand not."

This is a plunge into the lowest of the low. You may say there is an *Ayah* in the Quran in which man has been admired:

$$\text{لَقَدْ خَلَقْنَا الْإِنْسَانَ فِي أَحْسَنِ تَقْوِيمٍ * ثُمَّ رَدَدْنَاهُ أَسْفَلَ سَافِلِينَ}^{٢}$$

"We have indeed created man in the best of moulds, then do we abase him (to be) the lowest of the low." We say in response: It has nothing to do with the admiration of man, because firstly, here what is praised is God's deed "We created". Secondly, this is something against man, as a father says to his son, "I provided the best educational conditions for you. What did you do in return? Is this the result?" There is nothing wrong with the creation of God.

Hafiz says:

Thou who ne'er hast issued from the shrine of sense,

How to Truth's high pathway canst thou journey hence?

"The shrine of sense" is the ugly side of human nature that lurks within us. We, regretablly, pay not much attention to it and never think of harnessing it. Nevertheless, all the pains, problems, and sufferings of both this World and the World to come are in this "shrine of sense".

Moulavi, the poet, narrates the story of a man who had a plot of land but did not have time to build a house on it during day time, so he did it at night. One day after the house was completed, he went into it, but he saw someone standing there. The man asked him: "You built a house here?" He said, "Yes." The man said, "But it is my land." He said, "Oh, what a terrible mistake! But...isn't it

---

[1] Al-Anfal, *Ayah* 22

[2] At-Tin, *Ayah*s 4-5

possible now to change our lands?" He said, "No, and here are my deeds and document. You see you have built a house on my land." Then Moulavi says:

Do not make your home in other men's land:

Do your own work; don't do the work of a stranger.

Who is the stranger? Your earthen body,

For the sake of which is (all) your sorrow.

Sometimes what we do is like this. We put all our efforts on others' land and we are unaware that our deed is in vain.

The Quran says:

$$\text{«قُلْ هَلْ نُنَبِّئُكُم بِالْأَخْسَرِينَ أَعْمَالًا * الَّذِينَ ضَلَّ سَعْيُهُمْ فِي الْحَيَاةِ الدُّنْيَا وَهُمْ يَحْسَبُونَ أَنَّهُمْ يُحْسِنُونَ صُنْعًا»}^{1}$$

"Say: "Shall we tell you of those who lose most in respect of their deeds? –those whose efforts have been wasted in this life while; they thought that they were acquiring good by their works?"" [1]

It is a big mistake to get pleased when we are admired, and it is also wrong to take censure as bitter as poison. The former is not to our benefit but in the latter is our well-being. If somebody disapproves us, we get irritated, and thinking he mistrusts us, we cut our relation with him. In order to find out true qualities of the people around you, you can put them to the test. Admire one of them with a hundred lies. He does not get upset. He won't ever say all the statements are but falshoods. However, if you critizise him with one single fact which is true about him, he will get irritated. Such a person, regretablly, cannot correct himself.

If we were able to control our inner nature, then we would end up in a condition which is called "immaterialism." Immaterialism is the state in which the material veils of this earthly world are drawn back. Then we would see the reality of the universe; we would reach the point where we are even able to see the angels and contact the dead. We could feel many of the facts that the humans, hemmed in all sides with this material world, are not able to understand. You can prove with reason and knowledge that things can exist

---

[1] Al-Kahf, *Ayah*s 103-104

outside time. For example, God is not limited by time, but can you also imagine and touch this fact? Once a man is immaterial, he can understand these heavy concepts, touch and feel these facts, and even see them. This situation is called "intuition."

When a baby is born, he or she is said to be pure and clean. It is true that the baby is innocent and is not called to answer, but he or she has evil traits that lie dormant within him or her: stinginess and envy are in him or her; those traits of the ugly nature, the veils, which are mentioned in the Quran are with him or her. If they weren't, the baby could see the angels. Why do you think the baby who has no guilt must not be able to open his or her eyes to the unseen world? It is true that he or she is guiltless, but there are obstacles. A man, who is able to get away from the ugly sides of his nature is even purer than the baby, because the baby, though free from sin, he or she is infected by impurities of nature, but this pure man is free from both.

As you may know, there are two kinds of obstacles. The first one is made by our actions and deeds. The other one, which we have in common with children, is innate. Upon reaching puberty, a child may break through this second obstacle by exerting himself. If he does, his actions will also be corrected. Then gradually he becomes immaterial, and as Hafiz says, "Pure and immaterial he rises to mastery and kingdom of heaven." He breaks this carnal mould and "sees the unseen," and achieves emancipation from all deterrent sufferings. The Holy Quran says:

$$
\text{«وَمَن يُهَاجِرْ فِي سَبِيلِ اللهِ يَجِدْ فِي الأَرْضِ مُرَاغَمًا كَثِيرًا وَسَعَةً وَمَن يَخْرُجْ مِن بَيْتِهِ}
$$
$$
\text{مُهَاجِرًا إِلَى اللهِ وَرَسُولِهِ ثُمَّ يُدْرِكْهُ المَوْتُ فَقَدْ وَقَعَ أَجْرُهُ عَلَى اللهِ...»}^{1}
$$

"He who forsakes his home in the cause of Allah, finds in the earth many a refuge. And abundance should he die as a refugee from home for Allah and His messenger, his reward becomes due and sure with Allah: and Allah is Oft-forgiving Most Merciful."

The literal meaning of the *Ayah* is there. But there is a mystical interpretation of it: since the ultimate destination of this migration is Allah and His Messenger (pbuh), and because Allah and His Messenger (pbuh) are not places to go to, it's quite clear that this migration has nothing to do with locality. By the same token, "death" is not that of the body, nor is "home" a material home. "Home" here means the ugly aspects of human nature in

---

[1] Al-Isra, *Ayah* 100

which "the self" is taken captive, and forsaking it is leaving behind these aspects as he approaches death. Then Allah's reward is his due, and Allah knows well enough how to reward. Freedom from all pain and suffering is but a small part of the reward that ensues.

Chapter Two:
Painful Deeds

Among all the sins, there are a number of them that lead to man's hard downfall, make his life miserable, and cause him great sufferings; then his prayers won't be answered, no matter how much he prays to God for an end to his sufferings. Now, we are going to address ourselves to some of these sins that cause great sufferings and have special features.

1. Heart-Breaking

One of these sins is breaking somebody's heart. Of course, I sould say at first that breaking someone's heart will have evil consequences only if it is unjustified. Let me get the point across with an example: a judge has to issue a death sentence for a person who has committed a deliberate act of murder, and the aggrieved party consent to nothing except retaliation. For sure, the hearts of the killer's children will break, but the judge cannot say, "I am afraid hearts will break here, so I don't want to give the sentence of execution." This is a just verdict. The effects of breaking the heart are for a time when it is unjustified. In that case, it has devastating effects on human life, eliminates human comfort and causes unbearable sufferings in life. It has even been experienced that if you make amends and satisfy the other side, it is still unclear whether or not the problem is completely solved. We must be very careful not to break any hearts, especially the heart of minors and pure, believing people.

A blazing sigh may wreak havoc on a household.
An army's back may break by a groan ice-cold.[1]

It is said that sometimes a moan breaks the back of a corps. We must be quite careful not to break anybody's heart unjustly. Sometimes a single word is all it takes to break a heart. Sometimes an ostentatious display of wealth, knowledge or skill can do the job. Sometimes our actions and behavior can do it. If it is said that wealthy people should take the middle course in their standard of living, is not just for becoming immune to evil eyes, but mostly

---

[1]   Moeini Kermanshahi

because hearts won't break if they do. Someone who has amassed a fortune and luxuries while his neighbors are poor and have to grapple with a number of financial problems, wondering how to make ends meet and how to open the tight knots of their lives, and he flaunts his facilities, car, and luxuries, then one of these people in need may emit a sigh of envy threatening to topple, at any moment, whatever this rich man has towered shakily. We should beware of saying anything that might leave a scar on somebody's heart because a moment's inattention might well make us lose the straight path.

Malice: A Deadly Characteristic

A man who is purified in mind will rejoice to see people live in comfort; the sign of evil and impure conscience is to enjoy the suffering of others. Neither prayers nor fasting nor any other good deeds from such a person will be accepted and he will ultimately be a Hell dweller. Why should the happiness of a person make me upset? Why should I suffer because others are happy? Why should I put a spoke in other people's wheel? This is one of the deadliest sins. If I cannot cheer a heart up, why not at least praying to God for the happiness of the believing Muslims? Such a prayer itself will bring about joy.

«مَنْ ساءَ خُلْقُهُ عَذَّبَ نَفْسَه» [1]

One who is bad-tempered will plunge in agony (both in this World and in the Next.)

The Heart of The Faithful is More Sacred than the Mosque

If someone treats a mosque without respect, say by throwing sweepings in it, God does not let him get away with it. If someone destroys a mosque with a pickaxe, this is a massive crime (ruining mosques has various kinds, one of which is the physical destruction). The Quran says:

«وَمَنْ أَظْلَمُ مِمَّنْ مَّنَعَ مَسَاجِدَاللهِ أَن يُذْكَرَ فِيهَا اسْمُهُ وَسَعَى فِي خَرَابِهَا...» [2]

"And who is more unjust than he who forbids that in places for the worship of Allah, His name should be celebrated?–whose zeal is (in fact) to ruin them?"

---

[1] Osoul-e Kaafi, vol.2, page 321
[2] Al-Baqara, *Ayah* 114

He is the most ruthless person. Why are mosques consecrated? Because they are places where God's name is recited, why is the Quran Holy? Because it is a reminder of God. Why are the prophets and messengers Holy? Because they remind us of God. Anything, to the extent that reminds man of God, is sacred. A heart in which God is constantly mentioned is a Holy heart; that heart is like the mosque, but even more valuable than the mosque. According to Maulavi:

> The only true mosque is that in the hearts of saints.
> The mosque that is built in the hearts of the saints
> Is the palce of worship of all, for God dwells there.

Maulavi is right to say that the heart of Saints of God is a mosque.

$$\text{«...فِي بُيُوتٍ أَذِنَ اللهُ أَن تُرْفَعَ وَيُذْكَرَ فِيهَا اسْمُهُ...»}^{1}$$

"Houses" is interpreted as the bodies of infallible Imams (AS) in which their pure souls are lodged. It says Allah has permitted His name to be celebrated in such hearts. Ghotadeh, a Sunnite interpreter from Kufa, says, "Once I was in the presence of the Imam (AS). He turned to me and complained, 'Why do you interpret the Holy Quran according to your own taste? Beware! You are sitting before one of the houses of Allah.'" Ghotameh goes on, "I was overawed by the Imam's presence."[2]

So how horrible is the crime of a person daring to desecrate a mosque? If the believers' hearts, which are as sacred as mosques, are treated without respect, if they are demolished with the pickaxe of tongue and misdeeds, it will leave unwholsome effects on life. A *Hadith* from Imam Sadeq (AS) says:

$$\text{«القَلْبُ حَرَمُ اللهِ فَلَا تُسْكِنْ حَرَمَ اللهِ غَيْرَاللهِ»}^{3}$$

"The heart is Allah's sanctuary. Do not let anybody except Him get into it."

Is there no punishment for someone who throws sweepings in this shrine of Allah? Even tarnishing the believer's heart with dust of sorrow has a great punishment. Sometimes it topples a family life. Sometimes slips like this, create a lot of trouble and pains in life, and sometimes it becomes a headache

---

[1] An-Noor, *Ayah* 36: "(Lit is such a Light) in houses, which Allah has permitted to be raised to honour; for the celebration, in them, of His name."

[2] Osoul-e Kaafi, vol. 6, page 256

[3] Bihar al-Anwar, vol. 67, page 25

that will not go away by any prayer unless you find the person and get on your knees begging pardon. Even in that case you cannot efface the scar. Moreover, by breaking somebody's heart, two rights are violated: the right of that person and the right of God. Because as it was said the heart is Allah's sanctuary, so He takes it upon Himself to punish. Therefore, we should take heed not to break any heart nor to throw it into the trap of despondency. The opposite is also true: sometimes enlivening a heart will solve a problem. Amir al-Mu'minin (AS) said: **"If ever someone pleases another's heart, Allah will create a special thing out of this pleasing so that whenever any hardship befalls him it will come running like flowing water and drive away the hardship as stranger camels are driven away."**[1] (All the camels that live and feed together know each other and refuse to accept a strange camel out of habit and push him out.)

2. Tongue

Another sin, which creates problems and sufferings, is that caused by the tongue. Many people do not know what bad effects the tongue has in life. Unfortunaely, not much has been said about the tongue, and *Hadiths* in this regard are not sufficiently recited to people. At first some narratives are given:

«مَنْ صَمَتَ نَجا»[2]

"Silence brings about salvation."

Sometimes checking the tongue and keeping quiet will save us. In *Ahadith* and the Quran we are enjoined not to say anything unnecessary and without any good reason. The Holy Quran says:

«قَدْ أَفْلَحَ الْمُؤْمِنُونَ *... * وَالَّذِينَ هُمْ عَنِ اللَّغْوِ مُعْرِضُونَ»[3]

"Successful indeed are the Believers...who avoid vain talk."

"Vain" means useless and futile words and deeds. The *Ayah* does not say sinful words and deeds, but rather those uttered and done in vain. They are not morally wrong or wicked, but they are not useful either.

---

[1] Nahjul Balagha, wise Saying 257:

«مَا مِنْ أَحَدٍ أَوْدَعَ قَلْباً سُرُوراً، إِلَّا وَ خَلَقَ اللهُ لَهُ مِنْ ذلِكَ السُّرُورِ لُطْفاً، فَإِذَا نَزَلَتْ بِهِ نَائِبَةٌ جَرَى إِلَيْهَا كَالْمَاءِ فِى انحِدارِهِ، حَتَّى يَطْرُدَهَا عَنْهُ كَمَا تُطْرَدُ غَرِيبَةُ الابِلِ.»

[2] Wasa'il al-Shia, vol. 12, page 251

[3] Al-Mumenoon, *Ayah*s 1 & 3

In order to find out what portion of a day is spent talking, record what you say during the day. Then multiply it by thirty, then by twelve, and then by your age. You will see how much time of your life is used in talking. Then calculate what percent of it had been useful.

Imam Sadeq (AS) asked one of the companions with surprise: **Do you practice speech? In previous nations great men of God would practice how to remain silent.** After that Imam said: **They used to put pebbles in their mouths in order not to speak without necessity.**[1]

When the corpse of the late Ayatullah Sayyid Ali Ghazi (Allameh Tabatabai was his disciple and proud of his discipleship. In the world of mysticism he is unequalled or rare) was in the mortuary, and the undertaker was washing his body, he noticed some callus under his tongue! He told the Ayatullah's son, "Till now I have not seen someone having a callus under the tongue!" He answered with tears coursing down his cheeks, "He used to put pebbles under his tongue so as not to say undue words." At first glance this habit of his might seem to be sanctimoniousness and going to extremes. But wait; it is premature to make a judgement now. When you read the following *Hadith*, you will understand that this is not extremity. You will also know how much we are in danger just because of our tongue.

Imam Ali (AS) says, **"Well-being (*Afiah*) consists of ten parts: nine parts are in keeping one's quiet and one part in keeping away from those who are in want of intelligence."**[2]

Now, what does "*Afiah*" mean? Some people think "*Afiah*" means enjoying good health, whereas it has a much wider meaning including good health. "*Afiah*", as an umbrella term, means to be away from any source of suffering: illness, sadness, bad friends, a bad spouse, bad relatives, financial and social problems, and so on. A person having "*Afiah*" has no sufferings of any kind. What I mean here, of course, is uncalled for sufferings, not those we take upon ourselves voluntarily, like when we fast and say prayers because we choose to fast and pray but we never choose social problems on our own accord.

The Prophet (pbuh) was once asked: **What is good to ask for in the "Qadr Night?" He answered, "*Afiah*."**[1] The Infallible Imams (AS) have

---

[1] Mustadrak al-Wasa'il, vol. 9, page 21

[2] Bihar al-Anwar, vol. 47, page 732: «العافِيَةُ عَشَرَةُ اجزاءٍ تِسْعَةٌ مِنْها فِى الصَّمْتِ الَّا بِذِكْرِ اللهِ وَ واحِدٌ فِى تَرْكِ مُجالَسَةِ السُّفَهاءِ»

also recomended us to ask for "*Afiah.*" The fact that we are advised not to consort with the silly–according to Imam Ali (AS)–indicates that socializing with them entails punishment. It is also a divine decree to stay clear of those who, for want of wisdom, stop at no foolhardy act or word. The Holy Prophet (pbuh) says:

«نجاةُ المُؤمن فى حفظ لسانه»٢

"The salvation of the believer is in keeping his tongue," because we do not know whether or not many of the words which we utter are sinful. The Holy Quran says:

«يَاأَيُّهَا الَّذِينَ آمَنُوا اتَّقُوا الله وَقُولُوا قَوْلًا سَدِيدًا»٣

"O you who believe, fear Allah and make your utterance straight forward."

The word "*Sadeed*" in the Quranic terminology is used for a statement which is not uttered in vain; moreover, it is not sinful. The reward of such a statement is twofold:

1- «... يُصْلِحْ لَكُمْ أَعْمَالَكُمْ»٤; **He may make your conduct whole and sound.** God will solve all your problems in life.

2- «... وَيَغْفِرْ لَكُمْ ذُنُوبَكُمْ»; **Allah will forgive you your sins.** Those sins which were the cause of complications in life will be removed due to "*Sadeed*" remarks. God does not want us to be silent but orders for honest and open words. He promises if someone speaks such words, He will level the ups and downs of his life and forgive his sins and then says in *Ayah* 71 of *Surah* Al-Ahzab: «و...

«مَن يُطِعِ اللهَ وَ رَسُولَهُ فَقَدْ فَازَ فَوْزًا عَظِيمًا»; **He that obeys Allah and His**

---

1 Mustadrak al-Wasa'il, vol. 7, page 458: «قيل لرسول الله (ص): إن أنا أدركتُ ليلةَ القدر فَما أسال ربّى؟ قال(ص):«العافيهَ».»

2 Osoul-e Kaafi, vol. 2, page 411

3 Al-Ahzab, *Ayah* 70

4 same, *Ayah* 71

messenger, has already attained the great victory. It is said that the Prophet (pbuh) was so interested in this *Ayah* that whenever he ascended the pulpit of his mosque he recited it. It is interesting to note that this *Ayah* is written on the entrance to the Masjid-al-Nabi (Bab al-Jabra'il):

يَاأَيُّهَا الَّذِينَ آمَنُوا اتَّقُوا اللهَ وَقُولُوا قَوْلًا سَدِيدًا ۝ يُصْلِحْ لَكُمْ أَعْمَالَكُمْ وَيَغْفِرْ
لَكُمْ ذُنُوبَكُمْ وَمَن يُطِعِ اللهَ وَرَسُولَهُ فَقَدْ فَازَ فَوْزًا عَظِيمًا

"O ye who believe! Fear Allah, and make your utterance straight forward: that He may make your conduct whole and sound and forgive you your sins: he that obeys Allah and His Messenger, has already attained the great victory."

All the things that must be said about straightforwardness cannot be stated at the same time. They should be said one at a time and step by step. Suppose a person has done something wrong and deserves to get sick. I come, for example, and start backbiting him. (As it is said in a *Hadith* that if you backbite somebody, his sins will be taken and transfered to your account.) The sin for which he was going to be punished and suffer the disease will come to me and I fall sick instead. Then I will complain accusingly, "What did I do to get such rough treatment?" See! I suffer for just a few (malicious) words!

Amir al-mu'minin, peace be upon him, said:

«الْكَلَامُ فِى وَثَاقِكَ مَا لَمْ تَتَكَلَّمْ بِهِ، فَإِذَا تَكَلَّمْتَ بِهِ صِرْتَ فِى وَثَاقِهِ، فَاخْزُنْ لِسَانَكَ كَمَا
تَخْزُنُ ذَهَبَكَ وَوَرَقَكَ فَرُبَّ كَلِمَةٍ سَلَبَتْ نِعْمَةً وَ جَلَبَتْ نِقْمَةً»[1]

"Words are in your control until you have not uttered them; but when you have spoken them out you are under their control. Therefore, guard your tongue as you guard your gold and silver, for often one expression snatches away a blessing and invites punishment." As you know, words are loaded with meaning. Do we ever stop and wonder about the significance and accountability of the words we use? Do we ever think that the dignity of a person might be in danger due to our words? Somebody's prestige could be soiled? Someone's heart may break? We do

---

[1] Nahjul Balagha, wise Saying 381

all these things, but then, when things get complicated in our lives, we ask ourselves, "Why should this have happened to us?" I have an idea. Let's write what we say in one day, and see how problematic they could have been.

The world of speaking is a strange world. As speaking has many good effects, it also has many bad ones. Someone met Imam Sadeq (AS) and said: A person came up to me and said that he wanted to go on a pilgrimage to Mecca and that he had a few marrigeable daughters. Then he went on to ask, "Am I supposed to spend this money on providing my daughters with *dowry* or on the journey to Mecca?" I replied, "Your 'Mecca' is your daughters." So he gave up going to Mecca, and the caravan moved off without him. Now I want to know whether or not my answer was right?

Hearing this, the Imam became upset and said: why did you do that? Why did you prevent him from carrying out his mandatory Hajj? Didn't you know that he was physically and financially capable of undertaking the Journey? Why did you say something you did not know? Then the Imam (AS) said, "Do you know what punishment God will inflict upon you? You will be sick for one year."[1]

The illness of that man began some days later and lasted a lunar year. Whatever treatment he received, his body didn't respond well to till the end of the year. When the will of God is not there medication will be rendered ineffective. Sometimes the doctor is not to blame: God does not allow him to diagnose the disease. Sometimes the disease is misdiagnosed, sometimes there is a mistake in prescribing the medicine, and sometimes there is no medication for the pain at all.

Tongue is Called to Account Minutely

Sometimes we get into trouble for words that are not sinful to say. For all this, there is a proof both in the Quran and in the *Hadith*. Imam Javad (AS) said:

$$\text{«اِظهارُ الشَّىءِ قَبلَ اَن يُستَحكَمَ مَفسَدَةٌ لَه»}\,^{٢}$$

"If you say you are going to do something prior to actually doing it, it will be spoiled."

That is to say, you are bound to face problems, and you fail to do it. Why? What kind of relationship exists between saying to do and inability to do? For now, I'd rather let it rest. I can just say that some sort of relation does exist between the two. First do a thing, and then say you have done it.

---

[1] Osoul-e Kaafi, vol. 4, page 271
[2] Tuhaf al-Uqul, page 457

Is it really sinful to say that you are going to do something tomorrow? Not at all, but it leaves a bad effect. As you can see, things related to the tongue are so intricately iterconnected. The Holy Quran instructs the Prophet (pbuh): «وَلَا تَقُولَنَّ لِشَيْءٍ إِنِّي فَاعِلٌ ذَلِكَ غَدًا»; [1]**nor say of anything, "I shall be sure to do so and so tomorrow"**, «...إِلَّا أَن يَشَاءَ اللهُ»; [2]**except "If Allah so wills."**

Sometimes we are forced to speak about our plans, so by saying, "If Allah so wills," we make an exception. Allah said in *Ayah* 17 of *Surah* Al-Qalam: The owners of a garden vowed that they would pluck its fruit next morning, (and give nothing to the needy)–, «وَلَا يَسْتَثْنُونَ»; [3]and made no exception (for the will of Allah). The next day, they went to the garden, only to find it burnt. God enjoins the Prophet of Islam (pbuh) to avoid saying what he will do the next day unless he says, "If Allah so wills."

Some disbelievers went up to the Prophet (pbuh) and said: If you answer these three very important questions, it will turn out that you are indeed a prophet. 1- Who was Zul Qarnein? 2- What is the soul? 3- Who were the Companions of the Cave? The Holy Prophet (pbuh) said: I will answer tomorrow. (He did not say "If Allah so wills.") The Prophet couldn't wait to receive a revelation, but he got no message from Allah. The polytheists were also waiting for the answer, but because they got none, they started teasing him. Teasing, mocking, and upsetting the Prophet (pbuh) went on for forty days. They were very happy and thanked the Jews for suggesting those questions that the Prophet (pbuh) failed to answer. After forty days when Gabriel descended, the Prophet (pbuh) asked him: Why did you forsake me? Why did Allah not send you? Gabriel replied: O Messenger of Allah, when you said, "I will answer tomorrow," You did not say, "If Allah so wills." Then the Prophet (pbuh) said, "If Allah so wills." on the the spot.– Commentators, in this regard, say, "If you intend to do something, and forget to say 'If Allah so wills', as soon as you remember, say it even if there is a lapse of forty days. Anyway, afterward *Ayah* 64 of *Surah* Maryam was revealed:

---

[1] Al-Kahf, *Ayah* 23
[2] same, *Ayah* 24
[3] Al-Qalam, *Ayah* 18

«وَمَا نَتَنَزَّلُ إِلَّا بِأَمْرِ رَبِّكَ لَهُ مَا بَيْنَ أَيْدِينَا وَمَا خَلْفَنَا وَمَا بَيْنَ ذَلِكَ وَمَا كَانَ رَبُّكَ نَسِيًّا»

"[Gabriel said], "And we (angels) descend not but by command of thy Lord: To Him belongeth what is before us and what is behind us, and what is in between: And thy Lord never doth forget.""

The answers to those questions were given, and polytheists were bound to close their mouths. This incident in which the prophet, after a lapse of forty days, received the revelation again became known as Disruption of Revelation.

Did the Prophet commit a sin by not saying, "If Allah so wills?" Is it mandetory to say it? Is it a sin to skip it? No, none of them. But, as you see, it can cause trouble, and extreme care is needed in handling the tongue. That is, sometimes not expressing a few simple words, whose lack of utterance does not entail a sin, may cause sufferings. On the other hand, there are a number of narratives asserting, **"If you keep quiet for three days about the trouble you have got into, God will take it upon Himself to help you out of it."** [1]The narratives, of course, imply complaining to people about the pain or problem, not talking to a doctor, a judge, and the like about it. Let's be careful not to misunderstand the implication. The narratives say, "Do not say anything; do not complain about your pain." Why? Because after three days' reticence, God will remove that pain.

It is said in the Quran, when the children of Jacob asked their Father not to cry so much lest he might get sick or die, he replied, «قَالَ إِنَّمَا أَشْكُو بَثِّي وَحُزْنِي إِلَى اللهِ....» [2] "I only complain of my distraction and anguish to Allah," Then he says

«....وَأَعْلَمُ مِنَ اللهِ مَا لَا تَعْلَمُونَ»

"I know (some wisdom) from Allah that which you know not." The wisdom Jacob knew was hiding the pain from people, because it accelerates treatment. He continues and says:

---

[1] Tuhaf al-Uqul, page 120: «الإمام عليّ (ع): مَن كَتَمَ وَجَعاً أَصَابَهُ ثَلَاثَةَ أَيَّامٍ مِنَ النَّاسِ وَشَكَا إِلَى اللهِ، كَانَ حَقّاً عَلَى اللهِ أَن يُعَافِيَهُ مِنهُ».

[2] Yusuf, *Ayah* 86

$$يَٰبَنِيَّ اذْهَبُوا فَتَحَسَّسُوا مِن يُوسُفَ وَأَخِيهِ وَلَا تَيْأَسُوا مِن رَّوْحِ اللَّهِ إِنَّهُ لَا يَيْأَسُ مِن رَّوْحِ اللَّهِ إِلَّا الْقَوْمُ الْكَافِرُونَ$$ [1]

"**O my sons! Go ye and enquire about Joseph and his brother, and never give up hope of Allah's Soothing Mercy: truely no one despairs of Allah's Soothing Mercy, except those who have no faith.**"

When his son Joseph is found, he says to his sons: "Did I not tell you I know something of God that you do not know?"

Is it a sin if a person gets things off his chest by talking to someone? There is a *Hadith* in this regard saying: Concealing pain is a heavenly treasure. If you do not tell anyone about your pain, this is a treasure. Many of our problems and sufferings are due to our loose tongue. Basically, it is the loose tongue, a tendency to speak indiscreetly, which is the source of most of our failures and sufferings.

Loose Tongue, The Cause of Deprivation

One of the reasons that Imam Mahdi (May God hasten his glad advent), lives in occultation away from the Shias' eyes is that their tongues are not under their control. Because they may make it public that they have seen him. Nevertheless, those of firm tongue can see their Imam Zaman. There are many whom the Imam loves and prays for. [Actually the people whom the Imam prays for, according to Ayatollah Javadi, are more honored than those who are vouchsafed to see him]. But these people suffer a character flaw that makes them unworthy of meeting their Imam Zaman, and that is their loose tongue. Can you imagine how much suffering it can cause?

Maulavi has narrated this issue very beautifully in his story of "The Parrot and the Merchant". A merchant told his parrot: "I'm about to travel to India. What shall I bring back for you?" she complained: I do not want anything. What is a parrot in bondage supposed to want? Just tell the parrots of India to appreciate their freedom, and remember the one imprisoned in a cage."

Praise (be to God) that you are among the grassy meadows, drinking a dawn cup

Bring glad tidings of the beloved to those in strict bondage.

The merchant went to India. One day he was taking a walk in the forest, when he saw a flock of parrots sitting on the top of a tree. He said, "O

---

[1]   same, *Ayah* 87

parrots! One of your friends is in the cage in my house, and asked me to give you a certain message. ...Hearing the message, one parrot let out a screech, trembled greatly, fell, and died. The merchant became sorry about telling such news, and said: "Wow, I killed this animal." When he returned, the parrot said: "Did you deliver my message?" He noded and said: I wish I had not! The merchant then told her the whole story. Suddenly the parrot screamed in the cage, trembled, fell, and became cold. The businessman cried out, "Why did I foolishly bring such a crude message out of ignorance and thoughtlessness?" Maulavi here says:

But you are treasure too, which will endure

As well as pain for which there is no cure;

Finally, he took the parrot and threw her out of the cage. The little parrot flew to a high branch. Then the parrot said, "She gave me advice by her very action:"

Since it's my voice for which I've been confined–

She acted dead to bring this to my mind.

Do you know why you are put you in the cage? For your tongue's sake. If you want to be saved, be quiet and control your tongue as if you are dead. The fact that the narrative says, **"Delivered is one who keeps silent,"** [1]is the expression of this truth.

Some people say that if they do not get everyday issues off their chests, the issues will turn into lumps in their throats. I think this manner of looking at problems is dangerous and counterproductive. The more often you talk about problems, the more firmly they stick in your mind, and the more frequently they fan the flames of your heart. If you manage to take your mind off the problems, you will soon forget them. But if you recycle them all the time–like the memory of an event that you keep telling others–they are bound to stay for life.

You may well say that Allah has advised us to make our UTTERANCES straight forward; why didn't He say, "If you keep your quiet, I will reform your deeds?" The answer is: sometimes silence is sinful. Amir al-mu'minin (pbuh) said: **There is no advantage in keeping quiet about an issue of wisdom, just as there is no good in speaking out an unintelligent thing.** [2]The problem is, where we have to speak we are silent, and where we should

---

[1] Wasa'il al-Shia, vol. 12, page 251

[2] Nahjul Balagha, wise Saying 182: «لَا خَيَرَ فِى الصَّمتِ عَنِ الحُكمِ، كَمَا أَنَّهُ لاخَيَرَ

فِى القَولِ بِالجَهلِ».

be silent we speak (for example, to promote virtue and prevent vice). Sa'di expresses this in a poem:

Blindness of judgment just in two things lies,
To speak unwished, not speak unseasonably.

We should take it upon ourselves to make use of our tongues appropriately such as speaking against any vice or guiding the ignorant. On the other hand, it behooves us to control our tongues if it is not the right time or the right place to talk. Therefore, instead of "If you are silent, God corrects your deeds," the Quran says, "Utter straightforward words," that is speak appropriately, which is far more complete than just saying to be silent. That is because the Quran is an exact book. Then two promises are given after this commandment: God will reform your deeds, and forgive your sins.

Our Word Is Reasonable

As it went so far, sins that entail agonies like breaking people's heart and those committed by the tongue are regretably quite common among people. Regarding the latter type, Allameh Hassanzadeh Amoli relates some of his revelations in his book entitled "Man in Mysticism". Allameh, who is a mystic and one of the *"Abdal"*–in Islamic mysticism, *"Abdal"* refers to a particularly important group of God's saints– in the sixth revelation says:

I saw in a vision that I was imprisoned in a building with no exit. No matter what way I took, I couldn't get out. In great dismay, I swore those around by God imploringly to show me the way out. Then they told me I was there because I was talkative –they didn't say I talked sinfully, rather I talked too much, used more words than needed– Then he goes on: I swore God in the name of His Messanger (pbuh) to help me out. My petition worked; the north wing was rent asunder and I got out.

In the eighteenth revelation, he says: one night I had a certain feeling. The curtains went aside; I saw a group of angels sewing my lips, and I did not have the power to speak. I said by gestures pleadingly, "What sin have I committed?" They said, "You talk too much." I know Allameh Hassanzadeh. He is a reserved man! We should use our tongue in a calculated way. What we say must be to the point. Narrations testify that many of the sufferings of our lives are from the language domain. According to Maulavi:

O tongue, you're like both fire and stacks of hay;
How long will you set them alight this way?

3. Breaking One's Ties of Kith And Kin

Narratives and even the Quran tell us that paying not due attention to our relatives may take its toll on us by making us endure a life of suffering and privation and by facing relentless knotty problems. "Relatives" here are meant to be blood relatives, rather than those by marriage. Classification of relatives in this regard bears a close resembelance to those receiving inheritance. Heirs are pigeon-holed in three different levels: on the first level there are parents and children, the second level is for the siblings and ancestors, and the third is allocated to paternal and maternal uncles and aunts. Relatives are classified in the same way. Closer relatives take priority over the farther ones.

Cutting relation with relatives is tantamount to annoying them, and making them suffer in one way or another. In other words, if you cause them no harm, you haven't broken your relationship with them. Sometimes the suffering you cause them is light; sometimes it is severe and serious. The more serious it is the harsher is the punishment. On the other hand, there are some narratives indicating that the least you can do in giving consideration to kin is "not bothering them". Keeping yourself from worrying or troubling your relatives is the smallest favour God has enjoined you to do.

In order to give consideration to your relatives, you do not have to stop by as some people think they should. Paying all the relatives a visit even for a short while may take you one entire Friday. And it is not quite clear at the end whether or not you would be able to visit all. But you can stay home and call them, especially those living in other cities. It won't take more than an hour to greet them on the phone and know about their health; it works wonders in boosting their and your morale. Unfortunately, we telephone our relatives when we have some work for them to do. In these cases, we usually start with some greetings, and our relatives become happy that we have called to wish them good health and happiness. However, when we go on to make a request for help; they will say to themselves, "So...that's why he called." It should not be like this.

Reward of Respecting Ties of Kith And Kin

According to a *Hadith*: «مَنسَأَةٌ فى الأَجَل»; [1]**keeping a friendly relation with relatives makes "Death" forget you.** In other words, it gives you such a long lifespan that it seems "Death" has forgotten you are still alive. On the other hand, breaking up with relatives will shorten your life. It is seen frequently that people who cut connection with their kin, do not reach an old age. If you see someone who has no relation with his relatives and has reached

---

[1] Nahjul Balagha, sermon 110

an old age, make sure he has done some good deeds, so Allah has given him respite. It is not impossible, it has happened but in the normal course of things such people do not live a long life.

Do Not Make Friends with Them

In a *Hadith* Imam Baqer (AS) [or Imam Sadeq (AS)] gives a directive to his companion: «اِيَّاكَ وَ مُصاحَبَةَ القاطِعِ لِرَحِمِهِ»[1] **Beware of making friends with those who break ties of kith and kin.** Take notice, the Imam (AS) did not say: Beware of breaking your ties of kith and kin. You may warn someone of, let's say, overeating, or getting addicted to a drug, but it is quite a different story to say, "Beware of making friends with a drug addict." The Imam (AS) cautions against making friends with the person who breaks ties of kith and kin. Why? He reasons, **"I found him cursed in the Book of Allah."**[2] Here are some instances of divine curse that befalls such people:

Allah says in *Ayah* 27 of *Surah* Al-Baqara:

$$\text{«...وَيَقْطَعُونَ مَاأَمَرَاللهُ بِهِ أَنْ يُوصَلَ وَيُفْسِدُونَ فِي الأَرْضِ...»}$$

"Who break the covenant of Allah after contracting it and sever that which Allah has ordered to be joined and cause corruption on earth. It is those who are the losers."

$$\text{«يَقْطَعُونَ مَاأَمَرَاللهُ بِهِ أَنْ يُوصَلَ»}$$

"...which Allah has ordered to be joined..." in the *Ayah* is interpreted as: respecting ties of kith and kin.

Allah repeats the above statement in *Ayah* 25 of *Surah* Ar-Ra'd and then says: **"on them is the curse; for them is the terrible Home."** "Them," here means those who cut their relationship with relatives.[3]

Then God says in *Surah* Mohammad:

$$\text{«فَهَلْ عَسَيْتُمْ إِنْ تَوَلَّيْتُمْ أَنْ تُفْسِدُوا فِي الأَرْضِ وَتُقَطِّعُوا أَرْحَامَكُمْ * أُولَئِكَ الَّذِينَ لَعَنَهُمُ اللهُ فَأَصَمَّهُمْ وَأَعْمَى أَبْصَارَهُمْ»}[1]$$

---

[1] Osoul-e Kaafi, vol. 2, page 377
[2] same, page 378: «فَإِنِّي وَجَدْتُهُ مَلعُوناً فِي كِتابِ اللهِ»
[3] Osoul-e Kaafi, vol. 2, page 287

"Then, is it to be expected of you, if you were put in authority, that you will do mischief in the land, and break your ties of kith and kin? Such are the men whom Allah has cursed, for He has made them deaf and blinded their sight."

As you can see, in two or three places in the Holy Quran, Allah has cursed those who cut their relationship with their relatives.

The reverend Prophet of Islam (pbuh) said in a *Hadith*, **"Anyone who breaks his ties of kith and kin will be dominated by a villain who deprives him of his riches."**[2] Once there was a man who had cut his relationship with his relations; a fraud arrived, cheated his way into his life, and tricked him out of his life work. Although the case was reported to the police, he got no result. This is a divine tradition. We need to be careful to find out what portion of our deed has gone wrong. If one of your relatives has given you the cold shoulder, try to forgive and forget; you can think of his maltretment as some expense in maintaining a divine value. In cases like this, you climb down and swallow your pride. It is wrong to say, "Since he started, it is *he* who should finish it. *He* is not in speaking terms with me, why should *I* begin to speak. If he doesn't come over, I won't either." This manner of thinking is unwelcome in Islam. It is actually inflicting blows on us.

Recommended
Another point about maintaining relationships with kith and kin (*Arham*) is that parents have a special place among them. In five different places in the Quran, Allah has invited first to monotheism, and then to benevolence to parents. This means, after monotheism, nothing is more important than kindness to parents. On the other hand, disobidience to parents or "*Aq Walidayn*" entails much severer chastisement than breaking ties with them. A *Hadith* in this connection states: **The fragrance of Paradise is perceived even at a distance of one thousand year's walk, but those who are disobedient to their parents will not be able to smell it (that is to say, they won't go to Paradise). They cannot even get anywhere near it.**[3] **Parents have a huge right.**

---

[1] Muhammad, *Ayah*s 22-23
[2] Wasa'il al-Shia, vol. 11, page 513
[3] Bihar al-Anwar, vol. 74, page 62: «ايّاكم و عقوق الوالدين فانّ ريح الجنّه توجد من

مسيره ألف عام و لايجدها عاق و لا قاطع رحم»

Allameh Tabatabaei says, "The reason that Allah immediately after ordering us to believe in monotheism orders to do good to our parents is to make it clear that no religeous duty, after believing in monotheism, is as important as kindness to our parents. To give it another interpretation, no sin, after polytheism, is greater than *Aq Walidayn*. Abandoning the responsibility which devolves on us in this respect is a great sin with crushing and destructive results."

You may say, "My parents do not have a good conduct, their way of life, ideas and customs are not well-accepted by the society. Their mannerisms are irritating. They have been brought up in a bad environment. They are bad tempered and demanding." Let's suppose you are right. However, what makes you remarkable as a dutiful son or daughter is your skill in dealing with such parents. Treating well- behaved and well-bred parents requiers no skill. It is more meritorious and more rewarding to do good to nagging, fault-finding, ill-tempered, irritating, and rash parents. The harder they are to deal with, the more you reap the reward of holding them in high esteem. Interestingly, nowhere in the Holy Quran can you find an injunction to "*Tawhid*" (to recognize Allah's oneness) which is not accompanied by another injunction to be benevolent to parents.

«وَاعْبُدُوا اللهَ وَلاَ تُشْرِكُوا بِهِ شَيْئًا وَبِالْوَالِدَيْنِ إِحْسَانًا...» ¹

"**Worship Allah and associate nothing with Him, and to parents do good...**"

Modification of Luqman's Advice in the Holy Quran

Allah says in verses 14 and 15 of the *Surah* Luqman, "And (remember) when Luqman said unto his son: O my dear son! Ascribe no partners unto Allah. Lo! To ascribe partner (unto Him) is a tremendous wrong." Here Allah interrupts Luqman and says: «...وَوَصَّيْنَا الْإِنسَانَ بِوَالِدَيْهِ»; **And We have enjoined upon man concerning his parents.** Aftar enjoining man to be kind to his parents (especially to his mother–Although the specific word 'mother' is included in the more general word 'parents', God has deliberately seperated 'her' to stress the unique position of mothers,) He goes back to resume Luqman's advice. Because after the invitation to "*Tawhid*" Luqman fails to advise kindness and consideration to parents, Allah does the job instead!!

What message does Allah want to convey by this? Everybody, especially the youth should take heed to respect and honor the parents because nothing

---

¹ An-Nisa, *Ayah* 36

equals this in man's well-being and driving sufferings out. When we are at loss, we say, "Mom, Dad! Put up a prayer for me." But, do you know when their prayer is the most effective in solving our problem? When it gushes forth on its own from the bottom of their hearts. That is to say you ought to act in a way that your parents pray for you on their own accord, rather than asking them to do so. Luckily, they usually get pleased at the slightest service you do them.

Let me mention this point also that we have two general duties related to parents, which God has stated in *Surah* Al-Isra: 1- Financial assistance: If they are in need and you can afford to meet their needs, they will become eligible to receive alimony. 2- Speaking courteously to them. You might say: I am not in a good financial situation to help them. But can you also say, "I'm used to bad-mouthing?" Elegant language will cost nothing. God has made us speak to them with kindness.

$$\text{«وَإِمَّا تُعْرِضَنَّ عَنْهُمُ ابْتِغَاءَ رَحْمَةٍ مِّن رَّبِّكَ تَرْجُوهَا فَقُل لَّهُمْ قَوْلاً مَّيْسُورًا»}^{1}$$

"And even if thou hast to turn away from them in pursuit of the Mercy from thy Lord which thou dost expect, you speak to them a word of easy kindness." So, you say you do not have the money to help your parents? That's all right. What about a civil tongue in your head? There are some people who staunchly support their parents in monetary affairs, but unfortunately fall short of courteous words and nice behaviour. In other words, their tongue and treatment fail to do justice to their parents.

4. Defaming the Believers

The fourth misdeed that gets people into trouble and damages their credit and reputation is dishonouring the believers. Islam holds in high esteem the personality of any respected individual especially the believers and the punishment for soiling it (especially, if the slandered person is a faithful Muslim) is great.

'Dishonoring' has various forms. By the term 'dishonoring' we mean revealing someone's hidden faults. If there are no faults, that is called 'calumny' or 'false accusation', which is a serious crime. We say, "Don't backbite." He says, "It is his attribute." O, servant of God, if it were not his

---

[1] Al-Isra, *Ayah* 28

attribute, this act of yours would be calumny! If you attribute something to somebody which he hasn't done, you are slandering about him. Backbiting, on the other hand, means that the person has done something or has a defect, and you unveil it.

Allah loves covering people's faults. But one of the cases in which God avoids hiding our faults is when we defame somebody, God stores this misdeed away and defames us somewhere. Actually, God lets all the sins of defamation build up, and then He gets them all together and returns them all at once. As you see, God is sometimes disinclined to cover our faults. The Prophet of Islam said, **"The sin of receiving one Dirham of usury is tantamount to committing incest in Kaaba."** Then he said, **"The most critical usury is dishonoring a Believer."**[1] Let's not defame people. Let's cover their faults. As a matter of fact, covering people's wrong-doings and faults gives rise to forgiveness of sins.

A kind-hearted, considerate teacher brings a school drop-out (He was expelled from his previous school for all the failing grades he had got) to the school where he was working. With his insistence the boy is accepted in the new school. None of the pupils knows the newcomer. He brings him to class and tells the students, "He is elite. Today he has come to your class. The fact that he is your classmate is something to be proud of. You may ask him any questions you have. But nobody has the right to ask a question now, because he has been too busy and tired now. I have asked him not to answer any question for two three weeks, but after that, you may ask whatever you want." The student sees what personality the teacher has given him. For a moment, he tastes the pleasure of being held in high esteem (after all that indifference and dishonor). He starts burning the midnight oil and studying day in, day out for a whole month. Meanwhile, his parents, dreading he might lose his health, urge him to give himself a rest, but their requesr falls on deaf ears, simply because he needs to preserve the precious thing the teacher has bestowed upon him– his new personality. He has all the lessons down pat. After a couple of weeks, the students who cannot wait any longer, direct a barrage of questions at him. Our student, who has now undergone an amazing metamorphosis from a lazy student to a diligent one, answers all their questions. Moreover, in order to safeguard his dignity and to prove to the teacher that his faith in him was not misplaced, he never stops studying until he achieves the top rank in the province.

---

[1] Man La Yahduruhu al-Faqih, vol. 4, page 367

Sometimes saving a believer's face makes for improvement in him. But if you disgrace or disrespect him, he will say, "In for a peny, in for a pound." He will stop at nothing. Then the sin of what he does befalls on the one who has dishonored him. People's honor, especially that of the believers needs to be maintained. Hafiz says:

I asked the Master of the tavern to show me salvation
Asked for a cup, said keeping secrets alone.

Disgraceful Media Behaviour

We are to veil people's faults, not to broadcast them. Betrayal of secrets is a deadly sin. If God decides to reveal someone's secrets and disgrace him, He inclines him toward deriding people and making a plaything of their dignity and fame. Pages of history are full of people who have dishonored innocent ones, especially those who have the pen and the media under control. Nowadays, unfortunately, the media is into scandal-mongering, and have learned it to perfection. Having overcome their moral scruples, they easily pick on a Believer, demonize and disgrace him. They cannot get away with this. Allah will dishonor them both in the life of the Present and in the Hereafter. There is an astonishing number of narrations about saving the believers' face. How much does God know about our misdemeanors? How many of them has He brought to light? If we are supposed to be godly, we should also cover each other's faults.

5. Haggling with People to Please One's Self

In human societies, most of the catastrophes are due to selfishness, aren't they? In arguements, transactions, social intercourses and communications everyone tries to meet the demands of his own heart and sees his success in this, while this is not the case. In group expeditions and campings, in all probability, angry discussions suddenly break out over taking the best place. Why? It goes without saying, because every one wants to enjoy himself more than others. Have you ever heard someone demand to give him the worst room? Never. So, the essence of all fights is self-centeredness.

Take a popular sport like football as an example, and imagine a common scene soon after the game is over. For the winners it was a super-duper match. They are ecstatic and adored by their fans. What about the other team? What troubles them is the assumption that they have reached the end of all hope and feel sad to the back teeth. The winners see their success in getting joy at the cost of defaming the defeated players. Their inner voice, "Let's get pleasure even at the expense of trampling others underfoot."

One of the wrestlers in Yazd, who is still alive, had participated in wrestling competitions. (There were not broadcast on television at that time, and people generally did not have television.) When he came back from the tournament, he was asked how it was. He said: I failed. But later on, it dawned on them that he had made his opponent's back touch the ground. He just pretended he had been defeated to preserve the reputation of his opponent. This is what champion means in every sense of the word. By this comparison, I don't want to question the behaviour of the imagined footballers. Behaviours like this are quite normal in everyday life. What I mean to say is even these normal things can be problematic.

May God bless the late Mr Aboutorabi! He had formed a football team in captivity named the Old Men Team. Some friends, who were his fellow cellmates, once said: Why he, an Imam's (Imam Khomeini) disciple decided to play football at that age was quite beyond us. We thought it was infra dig for him to go and play football. Later on we saw that he wanted to teach us a moral lesson with this. In the first match, the other team won by seven or eight goals to none. His teammates were quite down, but he was as fit as a fiddle. "What's the laugh for after this humiliating crushing defeat?" we objected. He said, "Don't look at the goals, see how pleased the other team is! See how many hearts you have made happy. Moreover, you have suffered no damage."

6. Bad Habits

The cause and the source of other sufferings are unpleasant habits. A *Hadith* by Imam al-Askari (AS) states:

«رِياضَةُ الجَاهِلِ و رَدُّ المُعتادَ عَن عادَتِه كَالمُعْجِزِ»[1]

"Training a person who is unwise (ignorant), and making a person break his bad habits is like a miracle."

It is hard work. If you can make a person get back from the bad habit he has, your work is nothing short of a miracle. So, it turns out that habits are very penetrating. When you learn a foreign language, you need to focus, in order not to spoil speech by misplacing verbs, subjects, and adverbs. In Arabic, for example, you have to pay attention to the subject, predicate, parts of speech, whether to start the sentence with a verb or a noun, and a lot more. And in the end, you keep stumbling over words and make mistakes, which a person familiar with Arabic can easily spot. But when you speak your native language, you do not even notice the subject, the verb, and the noun. Many of

---

[1] Tuhaf al-Uqul, page 489

you may not even know the grammar of your mother tongue, but you use it correctly not only in wakefulness, but also in the state of delirium. That is, if someone listens to you while dreaming; he can make out what you say because every part of the sentence is in its own place. This is what I mean by habit. Take another example; someone who has just learned driving, In spite of the fact that he knows different parts of the car, the steering wheel, the clutch, and the gears, and he can drive well in normal conditions, when he suddenly sees someone ahead, instead of slamming on the brakes, he stepps on the gas pedal by mistake. Why? Because driving has not yet become a habit for him. But professional drivers are not in the least perturbed by things like that. What is more, it is even said that truck drivers have their snooze behind the wheel! To remove my doubt, I made an investigation and found that they were right. They swore they would drive something like a hundred kilometers while they are neither quite asleep nor awake because they have got into the habit of driving. Nothing is difficult once you get the hang of it. They are busy talking on the phone when they see a car is coming their way, for example, and they instantly brake out of force of habit. A narration goes:

$$\text{«فَانَّ الخَيرَ عادةٌ»}^{\,1}$$

"Benevolence is based on habit."

If you desire benevolence to become your second nature, you need to get used to it. Things will become your habit if you keep doing them. If they are bad, doing bad things will become your habit. If they are good, good things will become your habit. Women having a period, according to Islamic Jurisprudence, had better just sit on the prayer rug praising God–rather than saying prayers because in this condition saying prayers is prohibited (*Haram*)–the same amount of time it takes them to say prayers. Shahid Thani, after mentioning this, goes on to say, "Benevolence is based on habit."

Bad Habits Make a Bad Man

One of the causes of suffering is bad habits: bad habits in speaking, cussing, and bad-mouthing. One of the officials in a meeting said he had gone to one of the villages for an opening ceremony. The village headman first went to the stand, introduced him, welcomed him and spoke a few words to the villagers. Then he asked him to go to the stand and said something about the opening; while he was giving the speech, the headman spotted somebody talking in the crowd. In anger, he started to pour out some four-letter words

---

[1] Ghurar al-Hikam wa Durar al-Kalim, page 254

on him. Then he said, let's see what this guy (pointing to the official and cussing him) wants to say.

There are other bad habits you should apply yourself to stay away from, such as irascibility, haste, argument, and bad-mouthing. In good time, I will propose ways how to get rid of them. Of course, it must be accompanied by prayer and trust in God.

7. Flattery

A major cause of suffering which is mentioned a lot in the verses of the Quran as well as the narrations of the infallible Imams (AS) and which is, unfortunately, neglected is praising each other insincerely. One of the relatives came up to me one day and told me with great caution, "You have a certain behaviour which is not very becoming for you." I said, "When did you first see this behaviour in me?" He said, "Two or three years ago." I said in anger, "You made a great mistake that you did not tell me earlier, you should have reminded me before."

Why should we be afraid of each other? If I feel that my friend will not be discomfited when I tell him about his flaw, I will be encouraged to do so. Let's give each other courage to criticize. Once, I decided to install a small box in the doorway, so the people who felt too shy to talk to me face to face would write about me and put it into the box. On the face of it, it seemed a great idea. However, I changed my mind lest some people ridicule me in the future. Yet I was really determined to do it. Do you think there is something wrong with my idea? I don't think so. We need to hear about our mistakes out of the others' mouths.

8. Prayer (Dua')

Prayer (*Dua'*) is a constructive daily pursuit. It will stregthen our relationship with the creator. Cut or lower the relation, and you will suffer a lot. The Quran remarks:

$$\text{«...ادْعُونِي أَسْتَجِبْ لَكُمْ إِنَّ الَّذِينَ يَسْتَكْبِرُونَ عَنْ عِبَادَتِي سَيَدْخُلُونَ جَهَنَّمَ دَاخِرِينَ»}^{1}$$

"Call on Me; I will answer your (prayer): But those who are too arrogant to serve Me will surely enter Hell abased."

---

[1] Ghafir, *Ayah* 60

$$\text{«قُلْ مَا يَعْبَأُ بِكُمْ رَبِّي لَوْلَا دُعَاؤُكُمْ...»}^{1}$$

Say: "My lord would not concern Himself with you but for your call on Him..."

The value of a believer is up to his pray, devotion, and supplication to God. If he doesn't, he may well suffer problems. God sometimes inflict problems upon a believing Muslim to compensate all the shortcomings and defects that he has caused by a failure in praying. A devout person must endeavor to establish a relationship with God through *Dua'* and supplication. Even if this relation is too feeble, it is better than nothing, and cutting it is unwise, although *Dua'* is essentially *Mostahab* (recommended) rather than *Wajib* (indispensable). In the book "*Osoul-e Kaafi*" there is a section named "Book of Prayers" that includes four hundred narrations about prayer. The essence of some of these narrations is that if a misfortune befalls a person and then a desire to pray gets into his heart, this is a sign that the misfortune has come to an end. But if a scourge comes to him and still he has no desire to pray, this is a sign that the scorge is here to stay. Thus, it turns out that abandoning even some of the non-obligatory deeds may give rise to flaws in the self, and God spawns sufferings in order to fix the flaws.

Relation between Traditions and Tranquility

Breaking with good traditions could cause sufferings. You may ask, "Is it obligatory (Wajib) to follow traditions?" I daresay no. The traditions that come in Shia's narratives and scriptures like brushing teeth and clipping nails are the traditions that we are strongly advised to pursue. Abandoning them may plunge us into trouble. A narrative on tooth brushing goes that the companions of the Prophet (pbuh) experienced some hardship in one of the wars. No matter what they did, they couldn't surmount the difficulty and defeat the enemy. They wondered what the root of the problem was that even God turned His back on them. So they consulted. One among them said, "Maybe we have missed out on one of the necessary traditions." They saw that they had not brushed their teeth for a few days. So, they all started doing it.

$$\text{«السِّوَاك مِنْ سُنَنِ الْمُرْسَلِينَ»}^{2}$$

"Brushing teeth is a traddition practiced by prophets."

---

1   Al-Furqan, *Ayah* 77
2   Osoul-e Kaafi, vol. 3, page 23

The enemy, whose eyes were locked on them, saw from afar that they were doing something weird. Thinking that they were whetting their teeth, they were too scared to stay and keep fighting. Thus keeping a simple tradition tilted the balance in favour of the Muslims. Even leaving one tradition may cause suffering.

"Abandoning the Better" Causes Troubles for the Faithful

Our problem is that we think there is nothing wrong with abandoning the recommended *(Mustahabbat)* and doing the abominable *(Makruhat)*; whereas this is not actually the case. Even] doing well but abandoning the better *(Tark al-Awla)* can get not only the prophets (pbut) but also the believers into trouble. You want to say your prayers, for example. You can do it either at home or at a mosque. Which one is better? Of course at a mosque. If you say your prayers at home, you have done *Tark al-Awla*, which is a demerit for devout Muslims. It is said in a narrative that the prayers of those who live in the vicinity of a mosque but say their prayers at home are imperfect unless they are sick or in trouble. Imam Baqer (AS) said:

«لاصَلاةَ لِمَنْ لاَيَشْهَدُ الصَّلاةَ مِنْ جِيرَانِ الْمَسْجِد إِلَّا مَرِيضٌ أَوْ مَشْغُولٌ» [1]

Let's not assume that *Tark al-Awla* was only for the prophets (pbut). No! It has an adverse effect on devout Muslims too.

There are some people who do not say their prayers in the mosque even once in a season. Look around you, and you will see even practising Muslims who have a very poor attendance in the mosque except in the Holy month of Ramadan or to attend a religious service or something. These things will leave bad effects on life.

Another case in *Tark al-Awla* is when you want to offer alms. Your brother or one of your relatives is in need of it, and the sum is enough to solve his problem. There is also a needy stranger. If you get your priorities right, you will give the money to your brother; otherwise, it won't be accepted. And because it is unacceptable, it will be ineffective too. Prophet Mohammad (pbuh) said:

---

[1] Man La Yahduruhu al-Faqih, vol. 1, page 376

«لَاصَدَقَةَ وَ ذُو رَحِمٌ مُحْتَاجٌ»¹

"Your voluntary charity to strangers, while your relatives are in need, won't be accepted."

Those related to us have the first claim on us because charity begins at home. It's an unremittable sin to neglect their affairs. What kind of charity is it to put a sheep to knife and give its meat to strangers when your brother is starving and embarrassed about his wife and children? A rich man had faced a problem, and did a strange thing to fix it. He bought two sheep and set them free for anyone to take! This is a service to the thieves rather than a charitable act! The one who takes the sheep does not know the intention of the owner. He thinks that they are stray sheep seperated from their flock. A virtuous person never takes them. Someone takes them who has no moral scruple. If that person had donated his money to two needy relatives, his problem would have been solved too.

A lot of things that we do are groundless and incorrect. We do not know how to conduct our affairs, how to care. A king, in days of old, asks a mystic to donate four hundred Dirhams to virtuous men in town on his behalf. The man takes his leave of the king, goes into town searching, and returns after a while. "I found no virtuous men, sir," he says. "How come?" The king retorts, "I know four hundred of them in this town!" The mystic replies, "The virtuous do not accept filthy lucre, and those who accept it are not virtuous." The king appriciates his reasoning.

Let's suppose you have dischared your duty in giving alms, but "without prioritizing" or have done "*Tark al-Awla*", what will be the outcome? Your good deed will be rendered null and void, and this nullity will lead to ineffectiveness in warding off evils. Therefore, disregarding priority can cause trouble. It is wrong to think that *Tark al-Awla* was for the prophets (pbut) only. No, devout Muslims can suffer due to it, too. Most of our work is *Tark al-Awla*. We often find ourselves in situations where we have to make a choice between "good" and "better". Distinguishing between the two is sometimes of utmost importance. Once we find which is which, we should simply shrug off the "good" and pursue the "better". If you are a shopkeeper and a customer comes into your shop to make a big purchase when it is time to say prayers,

---

¹ same, vol. 2, page 68

postponing your prayers to a later time, from the standpoint of jurisprudence, is not sinful, but according to Imam Ali (AS):

«لَايَتْرُكُ النَّاسُ شَيْئاً مِنْ أَمْرِ دِينِهِم لِاسْتِصْلَاحِ دُنْيَاهُمْ، إِلَّا فَتَحَ اللهُ عَلَيْهِمْ مَا هُوَ أَضَرُّ مِنْهُ» [1]

"If people give up something relating to religion to set right their worldly affairs, Allah will inflict upon them something more harmful than that."

Our key mistake is that we think there is a red line of distinction in religion, and everything will be fine as long as we do not pass the line, – just do the religious obligation *(Wajib)* and avoid the forbidden(*Haram*). The truth of the matter is that things are not as easy as this.

Anyway, you close the shop and come back home only to find that your child has some medical problem. You take him to the doctor's and spend your workday earnings and something more on the visit and medicine. However, instead of thinking that all this expenditure was due to the belated prayers, you will say, "Praise be to God that I made the money today to spend on my child's treatmet." We sometimes perceive things the other way round. Someone asked: "Why does the stork stand on one leg?" Another one answered: "If it does not stand on one leg, it will fall down." Getting things the opposite way is bad and problematic. If we enter a place where there is a virtuous man who holds no post–he is no more than a worker or a clrek–as well as a director general, then what is *"Awla"*? God says that we should greet the virtuous warmly with respct but the official, half-heartedly. Whereas we do the opposite; we commit *"Tark al-Awla"*. Actually, we fall in the trap of *"Tark al-Awla"* unknowingly all the time, and when we suffer setbacks, our first reaction is, "Why? What sin did I commit to deserve this?" We cannot get into the truth of our deeds–in fact, misdeeds–simply because we are infirm in insight, we are too dim-sighted to be able to see through things.

One day Prophet Mohammad (pbuh) asked the Companions in a desert to collect firewood[2]. They said, "This barren desert has no wood." Yet, he dispatched them to all directions saying, "Gather any piece of wood, twig, branch and straw that comes your way." When they returned, a hill of firewood piled up. The Prophet (pbuh), who missed no opportunity to preach people, reminded them, "Our little sins are, likewise, not noticible." Having encountered hardship, we moan, "What

---

[1] Nahjul Balagha, wise Saying 106

[2] Osoul-e Kaafi, vol. 2, page 288

have I done to deserve this?" However, when we rummage through the scraps of everyday life, we can spot numerous tiny sins that bring with them sufferings. It is said in a *Hadith* that **when a devout Muslim treads on an ant (unknowingly), God will put him to a little trouble.**

Relationship between Abandoning Good Deeds and Sufferings

Even abandoning good deeds may bring about sufferings. Charity, in a sense, is the opposit of justice. Justice means to act according to the rule of law. For example, Islamic law says that some of your property must be given as *Zakat* (a religious obligation for all Muslims who meet the necessary criteria of a wealth), or if you have some earnings surplus to your annual requirements, one fifth of it must be paid as *Khums*. So, if you pay *Zakat* and *Khums*, you have observed Allah's Law; therefore, devout Muslims and needy descendants of Mohammad (pbuh) will have no claim on you henceforth. This is justice, yet religion asks for something warmer and more human, the doing of good deeds even when perhaps they are not strictly demanded by justice, such as returning good for ill, giving people a helping hand, or sacrificing one's desires. For instance, law usually awards the custody to the child's mother until her daughter is seven and her son two years old. But after that, the divorce court tranfers it to their father if the parents are locked in a bitter battle for custody. This is the routine way of doing things in courts. Now, let's suppose the mother is so used to her children that she will die of grief if her children are separated from her. Blind justice does not care, but a charitable, sacrificing father does. He steps on his right and love and vouchsafes the custody to their mother. Charity is beyond law.

$$^1 ....إِنَّ اللهَ يَأْمُرُ بِالْعَدْلِ وَالْإِحْسَانِ$$

"Allah commands justice and the doing of good."

We think that everything will be over and done with if justice is done, whereas it is wrong to think so. Justice is incapable of improving societies on its own. It should go hand in hand with "Mercy" to do so. That's why abandoning it entailes punishment. Here are a few cases from the Quran:

---

[1] An-Nahl, *Ayah* 90

The First Case

In *Surah* Al-Qalam there is a remarkable Parable of the People of the Garden. The rich owners of the orchard wanted to steal a march at an early hour. Their father used to give the poor their share and wouldn't deprive anyone of his product. After the death of the father, the boys said, "Why do we toil and others eat?" One of the brothers warned the other two that they should continue the tradition of their late father. "That's why the garden is standing," he reasoned. When his advice fell on deaf ears, he came along and joined them in their unjust design–he was not necessarily a righteous man, but there are degrees in guilt. The Quran here says:

فَطَافَ عَلَيْهَا طَائِفٌ مِّن رَّبِّكَ وَهُمْ نَائِمُونَ * فَأَصْبَحَتْ كَالصَّرِيمِ ١

"Then there came on the (garden) A visitation from thy Lord, (which swept away) all around, while they were asleep. So the (lush garden) became, by the morning, like a dark and desolate spot."

Awakening from sleep, they were not aware that the garden had been struck burnt by lightening out of all recognition overnight. They couldn't believe their eyes. It was as if they had come to some place other than their own smiling garden. Their fond dreams were dispeled because they were in want of merciful hearts. Who says abandoning charity and goodness is not a sin? This is a complicated matter, but trust me that it is a sin, and bring to mind that God has commanded charity in the Quran. It is wrong to think that charity is just something recommended (*Mustahhab*) rather than obligatory (*Wajib*).

إِنَّ اللهَ يَأْمُرُ بِالْعَدْلِ وَالإِحْسَانِ...؛ **"Allah commands justice and the doing of good."**

How is it possible that a single verb, "command", reffering to "justice" should be obligatery, but reffering to "the doing of good" should be recommended? The "doing of good" must be obligatory too, because in a society bereft of mercy, everything, even justice will rot. Take this narrative:

مَنْ فَرَّقَ بَيْنَ الأُمِّ وَ وَلَدِهِ فَرَّقَ اللهُ بَيْنَهُ وَبَيْنَ أَحِبَّتِهِ يَوْمَ الْقِيَامَةِ ٢

---

[1] Al-Qalam, *Ayah*s 19-20
[2] Sharh Lum'a al-Dameshghiyah, the book of al-Talaq

"Anyone who separates a mother (divorced mother) from her child (albeit legally), God will separate him from his loved ones on the Day of Judgment."

Is it unlawful? With the permission of Sharia, the father has taken the child from his mother. The mother, sobbing her heart out, insists that she cannot get along without her child, but the father says, "Let's abide by the court decission." The Prophet (pbuh) says that Allah will treat this law-abiding man on the Day of Judgment quite lawfully (not mercifully). The rule of inflexible justice in societies makes for irreparable harm, but a subtle blend of justice and compassion will result in what the religion demands.

Living a life based only on civil rules and regulations does not fit into any Islamic community. Giving gifts, for instance, is a revocable contract in Islam. That is, if you regret having given somebody a gift, you are legally entitled to ask for it. But, do you ever do that? Do your personality, courtesy, and character ever allow you to take the gift back? I think not. After all, if you demand it, it is your right to have it back. There is a point, though. The recipient is not held responsible if the gift is not whole on demand. He can simply say, "You gave it and I used it. The gift was edible and I ate it. It was wearable and I wore it, but now it is worn and torn." It is not his duty to go and buy a new one, but it is his duty to return it, however it is. It is a religious rule, yet being rule does not necessitate enforcement. Rules, in many cases, are the minimum necessity.

Many things that are lawful (*Halal*) are detested by God. Isn't it in the *Hadith* that the most hated "*Halal*" before Allah is divorce? Misunderstanding religion, many people relinquish mercy, thereby rendering justice ineffective. Charity varnishes justice and guarantees its maintenance.

The Second Case
In the subject of inheritance, one of the *Mustahabbat* is "*To'mah*", which means giving a part of the property to the grandfather, who has no right in inheritance, who is now standing there, and you are dividing the

golds and silvers and the rest of the property. It is said that this To'mah is Mustahab. While dividing an estate, orphans and some relatives who have no legal shares (for example, in case the brother of the deceased has no legal right to the estate, by the same token the uncles, who are the third category of inheritors, don't either) must be taken into consideration too. The Quran says:

«وَإِذَا حَضَرَ الْقِسْمَةَ أُوْلُواْ الْقُرْبَى وَالْيَتَامَى وَالْمَسَاكِينُ فَارْزُقُوهُم مِّنْهُ وَقُولُواْ لَهُمْ قَوْلاً مَّعْرُوفاً»[1]

"But if at the time of division other relatives, or orphans, or poor are present, give them out of the (property), and speek to them words of kindness and justice."

Let's not treat anyone present at the division harshly. Let's not address anyone there, "Hey freeloader, what on earth are you doing here?" Ask anyone of the Islamic jurists you want; none of them will say that anyone else is entitled to the inheritance. But in the next *Ayah*, Allah takes a threatening stance on this:

«وَلْيَخْشَ الَّذِينَ لَوْ تَرَكُواْ مِنْ خَلْفِهِمْ ذُرِّيَّةً ضِعَافاً خَافُواْ عَلَيْهِمْ فَلْيَتَّقُوا اللهَ وَلْيَقُولُواْ قَوْلاً سَدِيداً»[2]

"Let those (disposing of an estate) have the same fear in their minds as they would have for their own if they had left a helpless family behind: let them fear Allah, and speak appropriate words."

The late Allameh Tabataba'i says: "If you speak harshly to the orphans present at the division and break their hearts, then misery will come upon your offspring." (And you will witness that in the Purgatory.) The question is: is it contrary to the law of *Sharia* if these children are not given anything? We say, "No, it is just a case of relinquishing mercy." So, it turns out that charity and goodness are necessary. «إِنَّ اللهَ يَأْمُرُ بِالْعَدْلِ وَالإِحْسَانِ...»; We are enjoined to do well but unfortunately we keep getting stuck in "*Wajib*" and "*Haram*". We have

---

[1] An-Nisa, *Ayah* 8
[2] same, *Ayah* 9

no scruples about doing what is prohibited and not doing what is obligatory, let alone doing benevolent acts. Sometimes we complain, "God, what did I do or say that such and such happened?" We must go back and see what wrong we have done, and what mistake we have made. Even, doing lawful actions that are in conflict with mercy and goodness will bring with them disasters. Yes, a lot of rules without the element of goodness are incompatible with mercy. For example, in Islam, an odalisque's child is bound to be a bondsman or bondsmaid. You may ask, "Is Islam not the religion of mercy?" If so, what kind of law is it then? This matter needs to be discussed, but not here, otherwise our main issue will go off the track. Anyway, despite the fact that this is an Islamic law, it is considered cruelty on the part of the slaveholder if he sells this child. There are three narratives about why the patriarch Hadhrat Ya'qub or Jacob (AS) suffered grief for being away from his son Joseph (AS): He had not fed a hungry man (giving food to the hungry is not an obligation like *Khums*, rather a recommendation); he had put a lamb to knife before its mother; he had sold his bondsmaid's child. Therefore, Allah seperated him from Joseph (AS), his best-beloved child, for years.

Let's Not Be Strict Disciplinarians

Islam says women should not leave home without their husbands' consent. Does it mean that men are allowed to practice force as much as they wish? Laws are passed according to necessities. Interpreting them without insight will result in disasters. That explains why a judge needs to be *Mujtahid*. Otherwise, anyone capable of reading books could be a judge. Insight is needed. Have you seen any doctor practicing medicine by merely reading books? Suppose your English is good enough, and you have a good command of medical terminology too, can you read medical books and treat people? Is this Medicine? Insight is the power to understand the nuances of issues and not just act according to books and templates; it is to know where to climb down, where to ignore one's rights, and at the same time to comply with the law, and this has proved to be very difficult. Why does Islam state that a woman must not leave home without her husband's permission? Is it to give the husband unlimited scope for refractoriness, to deprive his wife of the right to a visit of her parents' house? There must be a limit to every law.

Living a good life demands to learn how to live a good life. If you want to drive well, you have to learn how to drive well. If you desire to follow a hygienic style of life, you should learn health care methods. You will get nowhere without knowledge. Science is needed for every development. What fruit-bearing work have you seen without science and knowledge? We should give a lot of care to these issues in life. Any rule incompatible with mercy such as slaughtering a young animal before its mother deserves punishment. If you stretch your hand toward chicks, the cock will chase after you. This means he loves his babies. Cutting off a young animal's head before its mother is not forbidden *(Haraam)* in the Islamic law, yet it flies in the face of mercy and compassion. Have you heard that camels shed tears when you are about to slaughter them?! Destroying animals in view of other animals takes its toll on human life, but regrettably, we fail to take issues like these into account.

You may wonder why these rules, that are contrary to mercy and goodness, are passed in Islam. There are delicacies in them that are based on the principles of Islamic jurisprudence and Islamic law. This can be the subject matter of a fundamental discussion which is beyond our concern here. Islam, however, has asked us to enact laws through the channel of insight, only after thinking about them sensibly rather than strictly.

The Relationship between Corrupt actions (*Makruhat*) and *Sufferings*

Even some detestable (*Makruh*) deeds that we treat as trivial in our estimation could cause sufferings. It is said, for example, that if you sleep while you are in a state of ceremonial impurity, you will suffer imbecility. Foolishness, itself a sort of suffering, is the fountainhead of a lot more sufferings, isn't it? Who can dare say that abandoning *Mustahabbat* (recommended deeds) and doing *Makruhat* has nothing to do with the amount of suffering we have to bear? Therefore, let's give them due consideration and observe them at least when it is possible and easy.

A man goes to buy a bike,

Man: Is it possible to pay for the bike by monthly instalments?

Shopkeeper: Yes, it is.

Man: In how many months?

Shopkeeper: In three months.

Man: It's not fair.Three months was for the summer whose daylight lasts longer. Is it still in three months in winter whose daylight is shorter?!

Shopkeeper: You are right. Okey, you can have it in instalments for four months.

The deal is struck; the shopkeeper receives four checks, and the man rides the bike home. Passage of the time proves that all the checks are dud checks, and the man in response to the seller's complaints just gives him the roundaround. When things come to a head, the man goes up to the shopkeeper, "I have an idea. Aren't you the creditor in the deal?" he asks. The shopkeeper nods. "Alright, and I am the debtor. It is tit for tat, okey?" "Okey, it's a deal." And the shopkeeper returns the checks. NOT THE BRIGHTEST BULB IN THE PACK! Stupidity is painful.

Someone said that in Mecca one of the pilgrims, who was a factory owner, had a row with his wife over purchasing some cloth. To settle the family row, someone interfered, "You are a wealthy man, what is all this squabble about?" He replied, "The lady (pointing to his wife) has bought the exported fabric from my own factory a few times more expensively!" When it is said that doing some particular *Makruh* will bring about stupidity, it means that it will cause suffering. According to Rumi:

> Until the end, heart, sing my love-sick grief:
> Swear until in hardship, for relief!

Chapter Three:
External factors of suffering

1. People's jealousy

There is a series of external factors which are seemingly out of our control, but they bring sufferings with them. One of them is people's jealousy. What triggers jealousy? When you find any goodness and positivity with others, and you wish that they lost the thing. Now this question is raised: how can we prevent people's jealousy of us? Is it to say, for example, "Let them be jealous until they perish?" No, let's not say that, because a jealous person is evil and can harm. If he were not, the Quran would not have said: «وَمِن شَرِّ حَاسِد إِذَا حَسَدَ».[1]

"(I seek refuge in the Lord of the dawn)...from the evil of envious when he envies." Surely, the jealous can hurt. Satan was jealous of the honor that Allah gave to Adam, and harmed human big time. The Children of Israel were jealous of the Prophet (pbuh) and hurt him.

Adam's son (Cain) was jealous of his brother (Abel) and harmed him (committed fratricide), Joseph's brothers envied him and hurt him. Joseph was separated from his father for many years, and nearly thirty years of his father's life passed by without seeing him. Therefore, never underestimate jealousy because someone who is jealous burns both himself and others.

Now, what do you have to do not to raise the jealousy of others? Try not to show off any of the blessings that God has vouchsafed to you, except in times of necessity. If you are favored with a worldly boon or superiority, there is no point in letting everyone know about it. Even so, why does the Quran say?

---

[1] Al-Falaq, *Ayah* 5

«وَأَمَّا بِنِعْمَةِ رَبِّكَ فَحَدِّثْ» [1]

"But the Bounty of thy Lord—rehearse and proclaim!"

It is true that some people have given such a meaning to this *Ayah*, but when we refer to narrations, we see that it has a different implication from the surface meaning. The *Ayah* does not want to say we should proclaim whatever God has given us. In this regard, someone said: I went to *Beit Al-Haram* and asked Abdullah Bin Umar (son of the second caliph), "What is the meaning of this verse?" He said, "Tell the people about the blessings God has given you." Thereafter, I went to Sayyid al-Shuhada who was also circumambulating (doing Tawaf) to ask his idea. "God tells the Prophet (pbuh) to offer the people the religion that He has given him," he said. As you see, the meaning of the *Ayah* is quite different. In some narrations we see that the Messenger of Allah (pbuh) has said: «اسْتَعِينُوا عَلَى أُمُورِكُم بِالكِتْمان»;

Proceed with your work by concealing and covering the blessings God has given you, «فَإِنَّ كُلَّ ذِى نِعْمَةً مَحْسُود»; [2]**Because the recipient of any boon is the subject of jealousy.**

This *Hadith* is not compatible with Abdullah bin Umar's interpretation of the *Ayah*. If we translate «وَأَمَّا بِنِعْمَةِ رَبِّكَ فَحَدِّثْ»; as: But the Bounty of thy Lord– rehearse and proclaim, then why did Jacob say to his son Joseph:

«...لاَ تَقْصُصْ رُؤْيَاكَ عَلَى إِخْوَتِكَ...»; [3] **Relate not your vision to your brothers,**

«...فَيَكِيدُوا...»; **lest they concot a plot against thee?** Therefore, it turns out that sometimes boons and blessings should be left untold, and so should pains. Does it, on the other hand, mean that we should declare poverty? No, we ought to take heed not to fall from the other end, as our religion, Islam, calls for moderation in everything. If you talk with too much pride about wealth and other

---

[1] Ad-Dhuha, *Ayah* 11
[2] Tuhaf al-Uqul, page 48
[3] Yusuf, *Ayah* 5

things you are blessed with, the jealous will make a hell of your life. On the other extreme, if you pretend you are poor, life will give you a hard time. As Imam Ali (AS) says:

$$«مَنْ تَفَاقَرَ افْتَقَرَ»^1$$

"One who fakes poverty will be made poor."

It seems that God wants to say, "You who want to make a slogan, then do it for real."

2. Evil Eye

Another external factor is the evil eye. Is the evil eye a reality or is it a folk superstition? According to Islam, the evil eye is real. Experience, too, has approved it. The Quran says:

$$«وَإِن يَكَادُ الَّذِينَ كَفَرُوا لَيُزْلِقُونَكَ بِأَبْصَارِهِمْ لَمَّا سَمِعُوا الذِّكْرَ وَيَقُولُونَ إِنَّهُ لَمَجْنُونٌ»^2$$

"And the unbelievers would almost trip thee up with their eyes when they hear the Message; and they say: "Surely he is possessed!"

There are many facts and realities in the world that our science has not reached but they should not be denied because we do not realize or do not understand their causal interfaces. Yes, the evil eye is very effective. We must seek refuge with the Lord from such eyes through reciting the Surahs An-Nas, Al-Falaq and Ayat al-Kursi (The Throne Verse) (Al-Baqara, Ayah 255). There is also a prayer in *Mafatih al-Janan* for protection from the evil eye. Amir al-Mu'minin (AS) said:

$$«الْعَيْنُ حَقٌّ»^3$$

"Evil effect of sight is right."

---

[1] Tuhaf al-Uqul, page 42
[2] Al-Qalam, *Ayah* 51
[3] Nahjul Balagha, wise Saying 400

The best way is to seek refuge with the Lord and pray. Sometimes some evil eyes are so severe that make the sufferer miserable. There are some narrations in *Mafatih al-Janan* including one that says Peganum harmala, a plant known in Persian as "*Esfand*", has a mysterious effect on removing the effects of evil eyes. What effect does it have? Just God knows. Human science has not reached the point to explain the relationship between "*Esfand*" and the evil eye. After all, there are a lot of mysterious relations in the world not yet unlocked to man. The solution to this problem, (which I have heard here and there, and which has been backed up by my own experience, yet I have not heard any narratives about) is that if you take something from the hand of the person who has given the evil eye and give it to the afflicted one to eat, he will get rid of the effect(s). It has been proven by experience as one of the ways to eliminate the effects of evil eye.

Another point is that, a woman with child will give birth to a baby with evil eyes if she looks at a dead body. Pregnant women should be wary of shrouds, coffins, corpses, etc. during pregnancy. Because it is a deep experience and it has a real effect. To sum it up, the evil eye can cause lots of pains and sufferings, and to avoid it we should seek refuge with the Lord, and take Quranic verses as the bosom friend.

3. People's Envy

Another cause of suffering in life is people's envy. Envy is a state of mind and feeling to wish that you had someone else's house, possessions, position, abilities, etc. Envy is different from jealousy. When jealous, you will begrudge someone his holdings, and wish that he would not have them. However, when envious, you will complain why you do not have the same holdings. This attitude of people may leave bad effects in your life. If by showing off your property or perfection a heart breaks, it might well cause bitter effects in your life. The solution lies in avoiding luxury itemes. It is not wanted of us to adopt a lavish lifestyle that catches eyes; it makes life troublesome, absorbs others' yearning, and causes failure.

In the past, people followed a certain tradition. For example, when in a green grocery store, they would put the fruits in a paper bag or something not to be seen by anyone. In case the fruit was in sight, when they faced a child, an orphan, or a hungry person, they would give them some to satisfy their desirous hearts. Experience had taught them that the rueful look and sigh of the hungry and orphans will take a heavy toll on them.

You go to a family gathering, a party, or somewhere else where there is a childless father. Then your child comes by, you hug your child and say sweet things to him, and this reckless action of yours breaks that father's heart. When you leave the place, something sinister may happen to you. Here is what you should do: show no interest in your child. Say something like, "Go away kid! You are molesting me!" Seeing this that father would probably tell himself, "Even families with children have so much trouble with their kids." We should be attentive. It needs some tact not to make other people yearn for the things you enjoy. Showing off holdings is not a glorious move. It is, rather, bringing inconvenience into existence for you. You should never expose and show off the blessings Great God has bestowed on you if you want to live a life of ease. Taking these homely directives, like traffic rules, are easy but necessary. If you do not know the rules of driving, you will get into accidents. More often than not, breaking an oppressed heart may open the floodgates to so much pain that no amount of prayer can help it. As long as that heart burns, your life burns too.

There is an exception to this rule, though. And that is the implication of the criminal justice system. Suppose, for instance, someone has killed someone else, and bringing the murderer to justice will break the heart of his child and wife. It is not, for sure, a common sensical approach to let the killer be at large just because some hearts would break. Justice must be served. However, if there is a way to win people's heart, it must be done. There's no merit in breaking people's hearts.

Ne'er break a heart,
> it wends its way towards God
> With nothingness in the palm,
> the poor's heart sure has a trail to God.

It is of utmost importance to try to make nobody sigh due to what you say or do. A great many of our elders were observant to win hearts. I have seen people whose lives came to nothing because of a broken heart. Even though they did everything in their capacity to make up for their misdeeds and soothe the heart they broke, the consequences were not done away with.

A broken heart can destroy a life. Do not make people yearn, do not live a life that catches people's eyes. Do not assume an air of comfort so that people say what a wonderful life you live!

I saw a man who was very pleased with his life, and he let everyone know about it. One day I advised him that he should not acknowledge that everything was to his liking, that he was content with his wife, children, and life in general, for it might cause him trouble. I said if people asked how things were going in his life, he could half-heartedly answer, "Not bad, thank God." Then it could be interpreted in many different ways: it could be assumed that he was grateful to God because nothing was going wrong. It might also suggest that he had some problems; nevertheless, he was still thankful. It could have some other meanings as well, based on how he would say that and in what condition it would be said. I asked him not to say they had no problems and praise be to God everything was just fine, for it would lead to people's yearning.

However, whatever I said was just a waste of breath. It all fell on deaf ears. Later on, something happened that made his life a disaster.

4. People's Avarice

People's avarice is another external factor. The residents of Yazd (a city in Iran) have a proverb that goes: "The avaricious are worse than inheritors". The one who inherits something takes his share once and then leaves for good. However, a greedy man will not stop; if you have some riches and a generous heart, he won't leave you alone; he will keep coming back. One of these officials from a charity institution told me: "In the first quarter of the year, several hundred million tomans was paid to the poor and disabled." I suggested, "Tell the media so people will not ask where the money goes." He didn't embrace my suggestion, "Let them ask," he said. I wanted to know why. He used a logical argument to convince me, "If we announced that we have so much money, there would be a long line of paupers from such and such square to the entrance of the institute! Tolerating their swear words is easier! Why do we provoke people's greed? This way no one will know about our contributions. Furthermore, we know to whom we should give the money. If they found out that we have been giving things to people, they would end up coming one after the other and beg."

The fact that the Quran says: «...وَكَذَلِكَ جَعَلْنَاكُمْ أُمَّةً وَسَطًا»؛[1] **thus have**

We made of you an Ummat justly balanced. This indicates that we must, in essence, avoid all extravagances on either side because Islam is a sober, practical religion. In charity, like in other things, we need to take the middle path. We are advised to do it in a way that neither is the hope people have placed on us cut off (so no one would say you are not helpful), nor is the greed of greedy people provoked. The Quran in this regard says:

«وَالَّذِينَ إِذَا أَنفَقُوا لَمْ يُسْرِفُوا وَلَمْ يَقْتُرُوا وَكَانَ بَيْنَ ذَلِكَ قَوَامًا»[2]

"Those who, when they spend, are not extravagant and not niggardly, but hold a just (balance) between those (extremes)."

You have to take the middle path. Do your charities indirectly; most often, it is not necessary for anyone to know about them. If a person in need comes up to you for help, and you are sure that there are scores of eyes watching whether you help him or not, and finding out how generous you are they would keep coming too, tell him that you know a benevolent man and that you will ask for his help. Then sign a check, and via a middleman give it to him so that he won't know it was from you. This way you have carried out some benevolence without being disturbed by pushy alms seekers. Most charities should be carrid out secretly, yet some should be done publically in order to encourage other people. Both ways are needed. The Holy Quran says:

«الَّذِينَ يُنفِقُونَ أَمْوَالَهُم بِاللَّيْلِ وَالنَّهَارِ سِرًّا وَعَلَانِيَةً فَلَهُمْ أَجْرُهُمْ عِندَ رَبِّهِمْ وَلَا خَوْفٌ عَلَيْهِمْ وَلَا هُمْ يَحْزَنُونَ»[3]

"Those who (in charity) spend of their wealth by night and by day, secretly and publicly, have their reward with their Lord: on them shall be no fear, nor shall they grieve."

---

[1] Al-Baqara, *Ayah* 143
[2] Al-Furqan, *Ayah* 67
[3] Al-Baqara, *Ayah* 274

This way you will manage to steer the affairs. You will neither be grounded by the greed of the greedy nor will the hope of the poor be cut off. There were many people who devoted their lives to charitable works, but were trapped in insatiable greed of such fellows and ended up feeling helpless.

5. Laziness

Human does not like suffering. Suffering is considered a disturbing, troublesome, and imposed burden, but if a person does not suffer, he gets ill, an illness called chronic laziness. Maybe someone would say what is wrong with kicking around. I am eager to have such an illness. Maybe one would say it is no problem for me. However, here, I am going to mention the destructive effects of laziness in society:

1.   It is a barrier to duties. A lazy person cannot do his religious duties properly. He wants to go to the mosque, but he is not in the mood; he wants to pray, but he cannot overcome his laziness; he wants to recite the Quran, but he procrastinates. Laziness is an obstacle to attending to *Mustahabbat*. There is no such thing as a free lunch; as a Muslim, you need to pray, fast, and perform your obligatory duties as well as the optional ones (*Mustahabbat*). At night, when it is time for keeping a vigil to say prayers, he is not in the mood of praying. In addition, in the morning he does a quick half-hearted praying, and he is not in the mood of going to the mosque and saying supererogatory prayers. The same goes for pilgrimage. I wonder what kind of a Muslim he is!?

2.   Laziness leads to committing *Harams* (forbidden) and *Makruhs* (disapproved). Often a lazy person cannot leave committing a sin. This is also another bad effect of laziness.

3.   It is a barrier to giving obligatory rights. The spouse and children's rights cannot be paid. Sometimes, because of laziness, the sweetness of matrimony turns sour. The husband is not willing to help his wife; he expects everything to be done by her. He keeps commanding: bring this, take that, sweep here, and so forth. It is all caused by laziness and will lead to disagreements.

4.   Laziness is an obstacle to the fulfillment of commitments. An indolent civil servant cannot do his job well. What is the outcome? A clientele's request that can be answered

in no more than ten minutes makes him come and go for two months. He leaves people dissatisfied and corrupts the system.

5. Laziness causes harm to people: A person was injured and in need of immediate care. At 6 o'clock, they called the doctor to come to the hospital and see to it–apparently, the patient's body was infected. The doctor drowsily said, "I am coming," but he went back to sleep untill 10 o'clock. Meanwhile, the infection entered the patient's blood and he died. Had it not been for the doctor's sluggishness, the young man would not have died. Sometimes the judge needs to get up from his desk and go to the scene of the conflict so that he can judge more accurately. Someone claims bankruptcy, for example. The judge needs to investigate the case and ask a few people. If he remains seated at his desk, he may not be able to judge well. So laziness could lead to unfair judgements.

A fellow professor once told me: if I do not have a lesson plan for my class, I will call it off. I'd rather cancel my class than teaching badly. I told another colleague: if you only read through the textbook, your students won't learn a thing. He answered: "I do read the text and translate it, it is none of my business whether they understand it or not!" What would be the result of this attitude? The ill-informed, poorly-educated students just make passing scores, graduate and become lawyers, ministers, etc. and ruin people's lives. Who caused all of this? Mr. Professor.

Laziness is a great social pain. If you do not suffer pain, you will get lazy. Do not be afraid of sufferings. One of the good effects of sufferings is to purge the soul of diseases, one of which is laziness. Laziness is ruinous both to the life of the Present and to that of the Hereafter. Imam Baqer (AS) said:

$$«اَلكَسَلُ يَضُرُّ بِالدّينِ وَ الدُّنيا»^1$$

"Sloth does harm to one's faith and life."

No society has ever been benefitted from idleness. It has rather been the root cause of destruction and backwardness. Water, while in turmoil and hot, boils, turns to steam, and rise. But once cold, it distills and falls down. Laziness, by degrees, will manage to mould a different character in you. You begin to slack off on your commitment to faith and good

---

[1] Al-Amali, Book by Al-Shaykh al-Saduq, page 573

deeds; your ease and comfort will matter more than saying prayers and giving alms to the poor, needy and orphans.

The Companions of the Right Hand ask the sinners:

$$«مَا سَلَكَكُمْ فِي سَقَرَ»^1$$

"What led you into Hell-Fire?"

$$«قَالُوا لَمْ نَكُ مِنَ الْمُصَلِّينَ»^2$$

"They will answer: We were not of those who prayed."

They do not say they did not believe in saying prayers; they say they didn't pray.

$$«وَلَمْ نَكُ نُطْعِمُ الْمِسْكِينَ»^3$$

"Nor were we of those who fed the indigent."

Taking care of orphans, the weak relatives, and the dispossessed is called «اقْتِحَامُ الْعَقَبِه» by God. «اقْتِحَامُ الْعَقَبِه» means ascend the steep uphill road. You know how hard it is to ascend such a road. It is different from a straight, levelled one. It gives you a hard time. Is it possible to climb it up with laziness? A lazy man cannot obey God's command; he cannot obey his superior either. He is good for nothing in the army or at home. He cannot be a good husband, nor can he be a good student or a good child for his parents. He is a clumsy, awkward, and destructive element wherever he goes. He is like a loose hollow brick in a wall that puts the entire building on the verge of collapse. What would happen if a car's tire were underinflated? It would play havoc with the whole system of the car: the steering wheel would be hard to turn; the fuel consumption would be on the rise, etc. Laziness will bring calamities along wherever it penetrates.

Man's true mettle is known in adversity as gold is assayed in fire. Amir al-Momenin (AS) said:

---

[1] Al-Muddathir, *Ayah* 42
[2] same, *Ayah* 43
[3] same, *Ayah* 44

«وَ اِنَّ الْجَنَّةَ حُفَّت بالمَكارِه» [1]

"Heaven is wrapped in difficulty."

The path to perfection is through hardship.

Amir al-Mu'minin (AS) said:

«اَفْضَلُ الْاَعْمال ما اَكْرَهْتَ نَفْسَكَ علیه» [2]

"The best deeds (in worship) are the ones that you force your soul to do."

When you see it is hard for your soul to accept, compel it. Get it done by force. It is said in the narrative:

«اَفْضَلُ الْاَعْمال اَحْمَزُها» [3]

"The most virtuous deeds are the hardest ones."

One of the criteria by which deeds are approved and rewarded is the level of difficulty in doing them. The harder the work, the more rewarded it would be. Meanwhile, it also eliminates the soul from laziness. And when the human soul is saved from laziness, it will also be saved from the wretchedness of the Hereafter. Sometimes, even the human mind gets lazy. You know, it is not just the body that needs exercising. Get your muscels into hard work for a while, and they will get used to it. The same goes with the brain. Some people are nimble in doing physical jobs, but not so in thinking. The Arabic word for physical exercise is *"riadhah"*. The word *"riadhi"* meaning *"mathematics"* means mental exercise because math makes the brain vivacious and strong. People who are inactive in thinking suffer forgetfulness at the age of forty or so and learn no more. If you suggest that they go and learn something, they will answer, "Memory does not serve." However, those who are mentally active will be able to learn and memorize things up to the age of ninety or more. Have you ever heard anybody say that Imam Khomeini forgot something, or made a promise but it slipped his mind, or else he was at a loss about the number of *"rakaat"* in his prayers? One, who uses his mind constantly, will have intellectual vitality and therefore won't suffer mental retardation. Many social misfortunes originate from intellectual laziness. Someone wants to get married, for example, but laziness keeps his eyes half shut. After the deed is done, then he opens his eyes only to

---

[1] Nahjul Balagha, sermon 176
[2] same, wise Saying 249
[3] Bihar al-Anwar, vol. 67, page 237

see that he is living a miserable life. If he had treated such an important issue more seriously and thoughtfully, he wouldn't have had to suffer the dire consequences of a mishap.

Laziness Is Troublesome

After the Children of Israel believed in Moses (AS) and considered Allah as the only God, and after they turned in repentance to their Maker for the worshiping of the calf, the moment God sent the Taurat, they asked, "What is this?" Moses (AS) answered: "The *Taurat*." "What is *Taurat*?" they retorted. "It is a Heavenly Book in which you are comanded to enjoin good and forbid wrong, to worship none but Allah, to treat with kindness your parents and kindred and orphans and those in need, to be steadfast in prayer and give *Zakat*, and ...." (Maybe giving them orders all at once was also their punishment. God did not do so to the *Ummah* of Islam. He gradually decreed the rules). They started to put up feeble excuses, "O, Moses, it is very difficult to do all these things after all the toil and trouble. We do not have the mood to do them. We do not want them. Let everything be as it is." Moses told them it was for their own good if they took the scripture and followed it, but laziness overtooke them, and they moved heaven and earth to hold back the Book and its commandments. The Quran says:

«...وَجَعَلْنَاهُ هُدًى» "We gave Moses the Book", ; «وَآتَيْنَا مُوسَى الْكِتَابَ...»[1]

«لِبَنِي إِسْرَائِيلَ»[2] and made it a Guide to the Children of Israel.

This Book was the charter of prosperity in this world and in the world to come for the children of Israel. Instead of saying, "Sir, thank you, you gave us the key to dignity." They said, "We do not want it." Why? Because they were too listless to obey its decrees. Moses (AS) answered: "This is God's book, it is God's command, and you must take it and act accordingly." When they defied and flung the Sciputre of Allah behind their backs, God raised the Mount Sinai to the sky over their heads like a cloud. Moses (AS) said, "If you do not hold firmly to what I have given you and bring to remembance what is therein, this mountain will crash you all into the depth of the earth." Thus, they fell prostrate out of fear and grudgingly took the book. The Quran says:

---

[1]   Al-Isra, *Ayah* 2
[2]   same

«...اِلَّذِينَ حُمِّلُوا التَّوْرَاةَ ثُمَّ لَمْ يَحْمِلُوهَا»; [1]The similitude of those who were entrusted with the (obligations of) *Taurat*, but who subsequently failed in those (obligations)... «حُمِّلُوا» is a passive verb derived from the word «تحميل» meaning "charge, impose" that suggests the *Taurat* was impsed upon them. «ثُمَّ لَمْ يَحْمِلُوهَا» means: they did not follow it. A boy, half-hearted in faith, had said, "God, I say a Two-*Rak'at* prayer due to my father's force. Do not accept it. *Allah-o-Akbar*!"

The same people (Children of Israel) went up to Moses (AS) and said: "We need water." A vast number of people they were. If those 600,000 people had scratched the ground even with their fingernails, they would have reached the water in no time. You know, in the Mediterranean area, you can reach water in the depth of 4 or 5 meters. Even with sharp stones–assuming that they had no pickaxe or something–they could dig a number of water wells. But they were freeloaders, so they said, "Moses, we need water," and he assented.

e said, W"; [2] «...فَقُلْنَا اضْرِب بِعَصَاكَ الْحَجَرَ فَانفَجَرَتْ مِنْهُ اثْنَتَا عَشْرَةَ عَيْناً...» **"Strike the rock with thy staff." Then gushed forth therefrom twelve springs."** Somewhere in the *Surah* Al-A'raf, the word is [3] «...فَانبَجَسَتْ...» used instead of «فَانفَجَرَتْ» which signifies flowing out smoothly; whereas the latter word is derived from an Arabic word meaning explosion. Commentators believe that using these different words for the same purpose is not incidental. Apparently, God wants to tell them the first time they asked for water, It gushed forth explosively as springs, but they shouldn't be bold as brass and lazily expect the same amount of water over and over again. They should work for it.

It took Moses (AS) by surprise when they came back again and said, "Now we want garlic, lentils, onions, and so on." Wow, what lazy people they were! They were expecting God to send these things from the sky! Let's be fair in judgement; do you know any more dangerous attitude than this? However, the extent of the problem was disclosed when the fire of war broke out. These people whose faith was but

---

[1] Al-Jumua, *Ayah* 5
[2] Al-Baqara, *Ayah* 60
[3] Al-Araf, *Ayah* 60

lukewarm only cared about saving what they prized most, their own lives. They said: "Go thou, and thy lord, and fight ye two, while we sit here." Of course, all those 600,000 people were not all men, but there were at least 100,000 warriors among them. Nevertheless, only one or two accompanied Moses (AS) and his brother Aaron (AS) and stepped forward. Moses (AS) said:

$$\text{«...}\textarabic{وَأَخِي} \text{إِلاَّ نَفْسِي} \text{لاأَمْلِكُ} \text{إِنِّي} \text{رَبِّ} \text{«قَالَ}\text{»}^{1}$$

"O my Lord! I have power only over myself and my brother."

A person, who escapes from a small amount of suffering, will suffer from a large amount of it. It has always been this way. Lazy people suffer the most.

Getting Into Trouble by Fearing the Trouble

Lazy people, in the grip of ease, lose what they already have, just like greedy people. If you tell someone indolent, "Be satisfied with this little livelihood until you get more," he will say, "No, I want more even from the start. I want to be the master (head), what is that to be an apprentice?" This person will not get even that small amount. If you tell him, "Go, do some manual labor," he will say, "No, I do not have the strength". They need to be reminded that everybody who is anybody first set a goal and then had years of toil to make it come true. After all, no pain no gain. Where does this laziness come from? Do we have genes that code for laziness? No, the body will get used to the way it is treated.

I have a sad but instructive memory of the early days of captivity in Iraq, which, I think, is not void of grace to retail. We had a daily quota of one and a half loaves of bread (or "*Samun*" as the Arabs said), one and half cups of rice, and a glass of tea. Imagine the condition of those who had six times as much as this amount only for their breakfast! I remember that many pressed their hands on their stomachs and walked the floor overnight out of starvation. One day, before daybreak a fellow prisoner came to wake his friend up for the Morning Prayers. The moment he shook him to wakefulness, he began shouting: "Why did you wake me up?" the man answered: "It is time to pray. You always pray on time; why are you behaving like this?" He answered, "I had a sweet dream that I was in a sandwich bar, and I was savouring every mouthful of a delicious sandwich when you woke me up." (He was even pleased

---

[1] Al-Maeda, *Ayah* 25

with the dream of a sandwich). This dire situation lasted for two months. (The human body has a strange system. When it encounters inappropriate conditions it adapts itself). One day, representatives of the Red Cross came and registered the prisoners and heard out their complaints, among which the fact that we were not given enough bread.

They could convince the Iraqis to add half of a loaf to the quota, but by that time, we all had become light eaters, and this extra half proved to be a left over. Even the same guy who was always hungry couldn't eat the extra half. Once he did and he got sick. Our stomachs were used to the previous amount. May God bless Mr. Abu Tourabi; he showed me a fellow and said, "You see him? He did one thousand push-ups" (with the calorie of two loaves for twenty four hours)! That means a person can accustom his body to any condition. People in the old days had a proverb: The stomach, checked, is no bigger than a fist; left unchecked is larger than a plain. Other organs of the body are the same. Have you happened to notice how your eyes get used to the dark? When you go into a dark room, you cannot see anything at first. After a while, the pupils get larger. Perhaps then, you can even study in the same light. You will easily adapt to different circumstances, but if you are radically accustomed to living on Honey Street and Milk Avenue, you can no longer live anywhere else. Even if you wanted to do so, it would be too hard.

Therefore, the cause of laziness is courting the self's dalliance, and fulfilling all its desires: which furniture is more comfortable? Which carpet is thicker, denser and softer? Which car has more options and better seats? Which air conditioner is cooler? Will these things lead to human perfection? Of course, I do not deny the fact that these things are necessary, and when you spend money on something, you should be careful what you buy. What I want to say is, you shouldn't go all out for them, and make them your goal in life. The dangerous outcome of such an attitude is: A man who had a piece of bread in one hand and a gun in the other, defended his land alley by alley for God's sake, and ate his lunch at the same time, is now turned into a good-for-nothing idler, whose laziness has got the better of him, and has put aside all the values.

Laziness and Decadence
One of the commanders once said: In the battlefield no ono would say, "Here's a minefield, you go first." They would push each other back

and happily ventured onto the minefield themselves. One would say, "You should not go; what will become of your wife and kids after you? Let me go instead." Now, that same person fights over taking posession of a stall on the street! It's amazing what some of them do for gain now! Where do these unpleasant things come from? When the unbridled self turns to comfort and hedonism, things like these prevail. A portion of disbelief comes from laziness too. If your self yearns for something and cries over it, you should strain yourself and have patience against it. If as soon as the baby cries, you say, "what is wrong? What do you want darling?" and give him whatever he wants, he will get used to it and one day he will expect you to give in to all his demands. Then the spoiled baby will be totally out of control.

If you don't resist your self's clamouring demands and succumb to its longings, it is not going to leave you alone. It will rather impose itself upon your mind. Amir al-Mu'minin (AS) said:

$$«كَم مِنْ عَقْلٍ أَسيرٍ تَحْتِ هَوى أَميرٍ»^1$$

"Many a slavish mind is subservient to overpowering longings."

Then someone who knows that killing Imam Hossain (AS) will bring him misfortune, his comfort-seeking self makes him stoop low enough to do so. He says to himself, "I will be governing Ray (a city near Tehran, Iran) with all those holdings and glory, and my ego will enjoy it." With this reasoning in mind he goes and kills Imam Hossain (AS). The Children of Israel also evaded God's injunctions at the cost of comfort.

The people about whom God says, "We hold them in respect for they were the descendants of Noah's companions," are now despised by God. They were all from the generations of the prophets. [We are not like that, only some of us are the descendants of the Prophet (pbuh). In one respect, it can be said that *Sadat* are all children of Abraham without any exception. So what befell the Children of Israel? God says:

$$«فَقُلْنَا لَهُمْ كُونُوا قِرَدَةً خَاسِئِينَ...»^2$$

"We said to them, "Be ye apes, despised and rejected."

---

[1] Nahjul Balagha, wise Saying 211
[2] Al-Baqara, *Ayah* 65

This is the bitter fruit of laziness. If you are affected by some suffering, think of it as God's blessing. Some of the tribulations are given by God out of His grace and kindness in order to sublimate His servant. What is the fear for then? This is what Maulavi, the poet, says: "I shall not dread that my essence lessens by demise"

When a baby is born, he starts to cry as if to say, "I do not want this world." He thinks that little dark world is better for him. He still holds this misconception when he grows up. He thinks he will be worse off if he dies and goes to the other world. However, when the righteous meet their Maker in the Hereafter, they will say, "It is so comfortable in here; we were living in such a dark world!" God has created this system of existence in such a way that too much eases leads to perdition. Our age, however, has become the age of anodynes. Most of the medicines just reduce the pain or else keep it at bay instead of targeting the symptoms. A professor and surgical specialist once told me, "There are sixty of us surgeons in the city of Yazd who are constantly holding a scalpel in our hands. We only know how to cut..." (It's the expression he used; otherwise I do not intend to slight professors and those who serve in the medical corps). However, I want to say that today's major knowledge of ours is based on giving us a slight comfort at the cost of taking a greater comfort from us. For example, what is the use of these labour saving devices that keep us from moving our hands and using our muscles? What is the advantage of sitting idly and comfortably?

Inactivity will have frail muscles, diabetes, extreme obesity, heart attacks and many other medical conditions in tow. As the number of doctors gets more, so does the number of patients. What does it signify other than giving us a little comfort and taking from us some greater comfort? Where does science go? Why does it lead us astray? All the hardships we face through the insufficency of science are actually the forfeiture we pay because it (science) is in wrong hands. Because it is a version of science that comes from someone other than Imams (AS). The science that comes from the non-infallible is a pest. Therefore, seeking comfort and resisting pain is tantamount to courting self's dalliance, which has no better result than laziness. The Quran says:

$$«\ ...وَجَاهِدُوا فِي اللهِ حَقَّ جِهَادِهِ ...»^{1}$$

"And strive in His cause as ye ought to strive."

---

[1] Al-Hajj, *Ayah* 78

Jihad (striving) means hard work. The "*jihadi* thought" that the Quran has said is not just fighting. Fighting is but a part of it. *Jihad* means continuous pursuit of breathtaking work. There is an *Ayah* about *Jihad* in the *Surah* Al-Ankaboot, which was revealed in Mecca, while at that time there was no *jihad* in Mecca. *Jihad* was proclaimed in the year two A.H, fifteen years after the Prophet's Apostleship. It goes:

$$\text{«وَمَن جَاهَدَ فَإِنَّمَا يُجَاهِدُ لِنَفْسِهِ»}^{1}$$

"And if any strive (with might and main), they do so for their own souls."

The intended purpose of *Jihad* in this *Ayah* is not military action. Islam says: if you undertake to do some work, do it in a *jihadi* manner. If you work in the field of nuclear energy, do it in a *jihadi* manner. If you want to overcome difficulties and achieve success, you must work in a *jihadi* manner. Why is it said that someone is a "*Mujtahid*"? In Arabic language the word "*Mujtahid*" is taken from "*Jahd*" meaning "effort". The word *Jihad* is also taken from the word "*Jahd*". Perhaps the difference between "*mujtahid*" and "*mujahid*" lays in the fact that *Mujtahid*, no matter what, never abandons the responsibility which devolves upon him by God. Studying is not easy. Doing research and committing different material to memory is no cinch.

An Example of *Jihadi* Work

The result of the late Allamah Amini's entire life was eleven volumes of books. A ten-or-twelve-thousand-kilometer distance from India to libraries in London didn't hinder his pursuit of compilation *Al-Ghadir*. To do so, he felt obligated to take long journies and study more than ten thousand books. This is called *Jihad*. The Quran says: «وَجَاهِدُوا فِى اللهِ حَقَّ جِهَادِهِ...», do not hesitate to do *jihad* in the field of science, in the field of industry, in social issues, in everything. If the movement is a *jihadi* movement, it sure is successful. If you want to make progress, you must work in a *Jihadi* manner. Many students are quite well-versed in their majors, but, as soon as they stand on the platform as university lecturers and feel they do not have to take any exams, they start to forget

---

[1] Al-Ankaboot, *Ayah* 6

what they have learned. Someone had become a surgeon after years of hard work and perseverance, and then one day he changed his job. I asked him if he could still perform a surgery if given the scalpel. He answered, "No, I have forgotten all I learned."

Struggling For The Sake Of Comfort in This World Is Not *Jihad*

Some people endure hardships in the hope that they can have a lifetime of comfort, eating and drinking. A Persian proverb goes, "Resign yourself to bread and leek for a year, then you'll enjoy bread and butter for the next hundred years". This is a wrong outlook similar to another saying, "Why should I make a gift of an earthen bowl when there is no prospect of receiving a more generous gift of a better quality bowl?" What does graduation mean? Not opening the books anymore? No more studying and doing no research? Resting easy and enjoying the fruit of those few years of studying for the rest of life? This attitude is a far cry from what Islam wants from us. As far as seeking knowledge is concerned, there is no let-up. The Prophet (pbuh) remarked:

«أُطْلُبُ الْعِلْمَ مِنَ الْمَهْد اِلَى اللَّحْدْ»[1]; **"Seek knowledge from the cradle to the grave (from the beginning to the end of your life)."** A friend of Abu Rayhan Al-Biruni asked him, "You are about to pass away, yet you are asking a scientific question!" Al-Biruni answered: "I'd rather know and die than die ignorant. Tell me." He heard, knew, and died. If we change our view about sufferings, many of our problems will be fixed. A hard-working person can tolerate a difficult situation, but one who seeks comfort cannot.

Seek Comfort in *Jihad*

Hard working people are the winners of what is good in the world. Comfort of this world goes to those who do their work and duty diligently. This is the law of the world. About the pious and those who practice deeds of charity the Holy Quran says:

---

[1] Nahjul Fesāha, page 218

«...وَالصَّابِرِينَ فِي الْبَأْسَاءِ وَالضَّرَّاءِ وَحِينَ الْبَأْسِ أُولَئِكَ الَّذِينَ صَدَقُوا وَأُولَئِكَ هُمُ الْمُتَّقُونَ»[1]

Those who are firm and patient are manly on guard against pain, adversity, war and crisis (الْبَأْسَاء refers to external pain-inducing factors, and الضَّرَّاء refers to internal factors). Not anyone can meet the condition of becoming one of the righteous.

«وَلَكِنَّ الْبِرَّ مَنْ آمَنَ بِاللهِ وَالْيَوْمِ الْآخِرِ وَالْمَلَائِكَةِ وَالْكِتَابِ وَالنَّبِيِّينَ وَآتَى الْمَالَ عَلَى حُبِّهِ ذَوِي الْقُرْبَى وَالْيَتَامَى وَالْمَسَاكِينَ وَابْنَ السَّبِيلِ وَالسَّائِلِينَ وَفِي الرِّقَابِ وَأَقَامَ الصَّلَاةَ وَآتَى الزَّكَاةَ وَالْمُوفُونَ بِعَهْدِهِمْ إِذَا عَاهَدُوا وَالصَّابِرِينَ فِي الْبَأْسَاءِ وَالضَّرَّاءِ وَحِينَ الْبَأْسِ أُولَئِكَ الَّذِينَ صَدَقُوا وَأُولَئِكَ هُمُ الْمُتَّقُونَ»[2]

"But it is righteousness–to believe in Allah and the Last Day, and the Angels, and the Book, and the Messengers; to spend of your substance, out of love for Him, for your kin, for orphans, for the needy, for the wayfarer, for those who ask, and for the ransom of slaves; to be steadfast in prayer, and give *Zakat*, to fulfil the contracts which ye have made; and to be firm and patient, in pain (or suffering) and adversity, and throughout all periods of panic. Such are the people of truth, the God-fearing." These people are truthful. Lazy believers would not tell the truth. Laziness will make us wretched and ill-fated on the Day of Resurrection.

Perchance, you would say, "Now that you have said this much in favour of sufferings, we must crave them in our lives." No, this is not the case. I just meant to say: let's not make such a horrible figure out of sufferings in our minds. Kids are afraid of injections. As soon as they see a syringe, they start making such a fuss about it. I remember in schooldays, when the word was out that they had come to give us our shots, oddly enough, a handful of kids would make a tumult in the halls and eventually hide themselves in the restrooms. They preferred the

---

[1] Al-Baqara, *Ayah* 177
[2] same

horrible stink of urine, sweat, etc. there to taking the injections. However, a grown up man would plead to be allowed to have it first, because he knows enduring a tiny prick is far better than catching cholerae, which often causes death. If we cultivate our insight, sufferings will be tolerable for us. It is important to know how sufferings can benefit us. For example, if a father compels his son to dig the garden, the reluctant child will constantly complain that his hand is blistering, hurt and injured. If the father keeps insisting, "You have to work," the child will be very annoyed. However, if the father tells him calmly and sensibly, "Son, do you know why you have to dig? Here in this exact spot, there is a five tone solid gold statute to be unearthed." This time, however, he works for hours on end, and the father will have to keep nagging about his son's lacerated hands and that he needs to stop. Nevertheless, the child will not care anymore. Not only his numb hands but anything else will seem insignificant.

We are sick and tired of afflictions' "company"; that's why they stay with us. If we learn why they befall us, we can easily endure them. Then instead of escaping from them, they will escape from us.

May God have mercy upon the martyr Entezary[1], one of his brothers-in-arms had a lot to say about him, "Every day, he would seek martyrdom. Once he was informed that such and such a front was under the enemy's fire; he rushed there in no time. Always by the time he got there everything was settled down. He once said, 'I wonder why the more I crave death the farther it gets from me!' He loved martyrdom, but death would escape from him." Were it not for the *Jihad* of the *Mujahideen* (warriors) at the outset of Islam, there would be no trace of Islam nowadays. How much

---

[1]   Hassan Entezary, a young man of 21, was the courageous partisan commander of Imam Ali (AS) Battalion. Quite affable, obliging and considerate to his subordinates, he was a dignified man of few words. He enjoyed an acute mind (especially in military affairs). Despite being kind-hearted (a militiaman who was seeking ways to save people's lives rather than killing them), full of gentle pity and love for his fellow creatures, and humbly making time for candid and silent prayers, he was resolute and stout if the need arouse. Should a fresh person happened to make his way into the garrison, he would by no means be able to tell him from a soldier of the lowest rank. He would never give himself the airs of a commander, nor would he trifle with anybody. As a result, he soon gained favour with all fellow combatants. When he eventually won what he wished for, the crown of martyrdom, I saw his name in some Iraqi newspapers.

hardship Muslims suffered in the Mountain Pass of Abitaleb! How many fights Amir al-mu'minin (AS) took part in! Under what condition Hazrat Hamza Sayyid al-Shuhada (AS) performed *Jihad*! They all endured so much trouble. They stood up to armies ten times (or more) as great as theirs. They kept fighting until their energy began to flag. In the battle of Tabuk, for example, the number of Muslim warriors amounted to seven thousands. A number of them were hypocrites who had come out with Muslims to assassinate the Prophet (pbuh). With the grace of God, he survived three attempts on his life. A number of them, whose faith was but lukewarm, were looking forward to some chance to shirk and return to Medina. These are God's words in the Quran in *Surah* Al-Tawba. A number of them, however, were Muslims to the core. Recorded history says that on the other side of the battlefield, there were at least 200,000 armed-to-the-teeth trained warriors equipped with Roman weaponry. That is thirtyfold! Furthermore, if you compare the equipment and mobilization of the two sides, the whole thing will be utterly unbelievable. However, they were so consolidated, steadfast, and determined that the Romans were too scared to stay. If it were not for their *Jihad*, would still Islam be as it now is? If it was not for Hamza Sayyid al-Shuhada (AS) and Imam Ali (AS), would still Islam be here nowadays? Had the Prophet (pbuh) sat back behind the scene and had only ordered others to step forward, would there be any triumph? In the harshest conditions when the war went on unabated, and when the hearts sank and troops were forced to withdraw, the Messenger of Allah (pbuh) would use his dearest and nearest as a shield to safeguard his companions (he would not say: first my companions should go and then my beloveds. To alleviate the worry and fear, he would say, "Dear Ali, you go first").

Amir al-mu'minin (pbuh) in *Nahj Al-Balaghah* says:

«وَ كانَ رَسُولُ الله اذا اَحمَرَّ البَأسُ» ;[1]**"When fighting became fierce".**

«...وَ اَحجَمَ النّاسُ...» ; **"People began to lose ground"**, ﴿قَدَّمَ اَهلَ...﴾

«بيْتَه» ; **"the Prophet (pbuh) would send forward members of his family."** He is our exemplar.

---

[1] Nahjul Balagha, letter 9

«لَقَدْكَانَ لَكُمْ فِي رَسُولِ اللهِ أُسْوَةٌ حَسَنَةٌ لِّمَنْ كَانَ يَرْجُوا اللهَ وَالْيَوْمَ الْآخِرَ وَذَكَرَ اللهَ كَثِيرًا.»[1]

"Ye have indeed in the Messenger of Allah an excellent exemplar for him who hopes in Allah and the Final Day, and who remember Allah much."

When the enemy sent his strongest commanders to fight, the Messenger of Allah (pbuh) commanded his dearest family members to go and fight with those savages. Hazrat Amir (AS) addresses his companions: "Do you remember the day of Uhud, when that strong, big slave, whose eyes were like bowls of blood, came to fight? All of your breath was tied in chest. Then I went and cut him in two. In continuation Imam Ali (AS) says:

«فَوَقَى بِهِم اَصْحَابَهُ حَرَّ السُّيُوفَ وَ الْاَسِنَّه»

"Through them (his family members) protected his companions from the attacks of swords and spears."

Then the Imam (AS) says:

«...فَقُتِلَ عُبَيْدَهُ بْنُ الحارث، يَوْمَ بَدْرٍ...»; "In this way Ubaydah ibn al-Harith was killed on the day of Badr." Ubaydah ibn al-Harith was the Prophet's cousin who was killed on Badr day. (When the valorous men of Quraish came and said, "Where are your heroes?" The Prophet (pbuh) did not turn toward the *Ansar* and *Mohajer*. He said, "Oh Ali, you go." Ali (AS) was his cousin and son-in-law. Imam Ali (AS) had been trained by the Prophet (pbuh) himself and was his vizier. Then he said to Hamza, his uncle, and Ubaydah, his cousin, "You two go." Among all those people, he sent three of his close family members to the battlefield).

---

[1] Al-Ahzab, *Ayah* 21

Chapter Four:
Causes of Miseries (Calamities)

Where from do unwanted miseries come our way? If we repeatedly confront problems, does it mean we are dear to God? Poets, among others, have gone to town in this regard:

> The higher the devotee,
> The greater the adversity.

This is an oft-cited poem:

> No less than a sin in ardor court is innocence
> Incarcerated Joseph his guiltlessness.

And some people lay the blame on bad luck:

> A man of ill-luckc constract a Jameh mosque he may,
> The roof will crumble or else the qibla be off the way

What causes calamities? Are they coincidental? Are they something that just happen? Some people have gone to great lengths to find an answer: a small portion is incidental, some of them are by bad luck, some are due to our bad deeds, some miseries befall us because we are the elect, and yet, some are inflicted by God to test His slaves.

If you refer to *Ahadith* written in this regard, you will be astounded. A college student, who is now a professor, needed to chose a subject for his thesis. After giving it considerable amount of thought, he eventually decided to write about this subject at hand (causes of sufferings). I didn't leave him alone. I gave him an occational helping hand. After months of research, collecting data and material, he came up with a long face saying, "The supervisor says the material is all carelessly prepared, it is full of inaccurate and invalid arguments, and it includes ten insubstantial and fallacious points. He believes, as a result, that my research is only good for the waste-paper basket."

However, he wasn't through. Being a well-versed student, he did some more research, and I helped him in the process to clear ambiguities and find the answer to any probable question around the subject. He showed the professor the revised material and managed to convince him he was right. To put it in a nutshell, in the thesis presentation meeting, the professor was so impressed that he gave him a standing ovation, saying, "This is the best thesis ever written and defended at this university." After it was printed, this dissertation was introduced as the best book of the year among books written by students. The truth of the matter can be found in the verses of the Quran as well as the traditions of the infallible Imams (AS); the problem is we have misunderstood them.

Do We Suffer Miseries Merely Because We Are the Elect?

Who has said that? Where does this idea come from? Is it rom the surface meaning and appearance of some narratives or from some poems? So much exaggerated praise and eulogy is expressed in oral and written forms about grief-stricken people that it has become a popular belief that virtuous people with highly developed moral sense will suffer more. Does it not, honestly, get people farther and farther away from religion? Is it the right course of action to tell the youth that if they want to be virtuous, they must brace themselves for hardship? Where in the Quran can you find anything that God will make the life of those who are in the path of piety miserable? Whatever I, for my part, saw in the Quran was the opposite. For example:

$$\text{«وَلَوْ أَنَّ أَهْلَ الْقُرَى آمَنُوا وَاتَّقَوْا لَفَتَحْنَا عَلَيْهِم بَرَكَاتٍ مِّنَ السَّمَاءِ وَالأَرْضِ وَلَـكِن}$$
$$\text{كَذَّبُوا فَأَخَذْنَاهُم بِمَا كَانُوا يَكْسِبُونَ»}^{1}$$

"And if only the people of the cities had believed and feared Allah, We would have opened upon them blessings from the heaven and the earth; but they denied (the messengers), so We seized them for what they were earning."

It turns out that this blessing is material blessing, because it says, **"from the heaven and the earth"**. There are some other *Ayahs* in which God has reminded us of such material blessings:

$$\text{«... اسْتَغْفِرُوا رَبَّكُمْ إِنَّهُ كَانَ غَفَّارًا»}^{2}$$

"Ask forgiveness of your Lord. Indeed, He is ever a Perpetual Forgiver."

---

[1] Al-Araf, *Ayah* 96
[2] Nooh, *Ayah* 10

$$\text{«يُرْسِلِ السَّمَاءَ عَلَيْكُم مِّدْرَارًا»}^{1}$$

"He will send [rain from] the sky upon you in [continuing] showers."

$$\text{«...وَيُمْدِدْكُم بِأَمْوَالٍ وَبَنِينَ»}^{2}$$

"And give you increase in wealth and children."

$$\text{«يَجْعَل لَّكُمْ جَنَّاتٍ وَيَجْعَل لَّكُمْ أَنْهَارًا»}$$

"And provide for you gardens and provide for you rivers."

These are all material promises God has made.

If someone thanked you for saving his life from an impending doom and then he said, "I wonder how I can compensate for that deed of yours. I don't know how to show my gratitude and love to you. Since neither money nor gold nor anything else can make up for your kindness, I have made up my mind to slap you three, four times across the face!" What would you think of him? Would you not consider him an imbecile suffering from a paucity of intellect, a downright fool? If this is not expected to be heard from a normal person, how can be such things attributed to God, the Creator of Reason? It is realy outrageous to say that God has said: "My servant! I'm going to slap you because you are just too good." How can you justify it? Is it love? Is it imaginable that a lover says to his beloved: "Because you are so innocent, I need to harass you out of love!?"

Allah says in the Holy Quran,

$$\text{«وَمَن يَتَّقِ اللهَ يَجْعَل لَّهُ مِنْ أَمْرِهِ يُسْرًا»}^{3}$$

"And for those who fearAllah, He will make things easy for them."

$$\text{«...وَمَن يَتَّقِ اللهَ يُكَفِّرْ عَنْهُ سَيِّئَاتِهِ وَيُعْظِمْ لَهُ أَجْرًا»}^{4}$$

"And if any one fears Allah, He will remove his evil deeds from him, and will enlarge his reward."

---

[1] same, *Ayah* 11
[2] same, *Ayah* 12
[3] At-Talaq, *Ayah* 4
[4] same, *Ayah* 5

«...وَمَن يَتَّقِ اللهَ يَجْعَل لَّهُ مَخْرَجًا»¹

"And for those who fear Allah, He (ever) prepares a way out."

But there are some who say that if you follow piety (virtue), you will fall into trouble. What kind of mysticism is it?! We do not know any mycticism except the one advocated by the Quran and the *Ahlul-Bayt* (Prophet's household and progeny). We never approve of that kind of mysticism that says, "The law of love is that the virtuous need to be beaten." We do not accept this mysticism at all, because the Quran denies it. The Quran has emphasised in many *Ayahs*: Misfortune befalls on people who are indulged in sin and permissiveness. Deviation from this point of view in the name of mysticism is really bad.

Sometimes we do not pay due attention to *Ahadith*. We just read them superficially, interpret them as we wish, and use our interpretation as the basis for ideas and judgements. Then we put the stamp of religion on it, and disseminate it far and wide. Whereas what the infallible Imams (AS) had in mind had been quite something else. There is a host of *Ahadith* reiterating that whatever calamity befalls you is the consequence of your own deeds. They often make a reference to *Ayah* 30 of Sura Ash-Shura:

«وَمَا أَصَابَكُم مِّن مُّصِيبَةٍ فَبِمَا كَسَبَتْ أَيْدِيكُمْ وَيَعْفُو عَن كَثِيرٍ»²

"Whatever misfortune happens to you, is because of the things your hands have wrought, and for many (a sin) He grants forgiveness."

And now I will mention some of these *Ahadith*:
The Messenger of God (pbuh) said to Amir al-mu'minin (AS):

«تَوَقَّوُا الذُّنُوبَ فَما مِن بَلِيَّةٍ وَلانَقْصِ رِزقٍ اِلّا بِذَنَبٍ»

"Whatever disaster befalls man is due to his sins",

---

¹ same, *Ayah* 2
² Ash-Shura, *Ayah* 30

«حَتَّى الخَدش وَ النَّكَبَه» ١

"Even a hit on the leg with a thin stick or a scratch on the skin." In the narratives it is also mentioned that even an accidental hitting of your foot against a stone is the price you pay for a sinful act. Then the Messenger (pbuh) refers to *Ayah* 30 of *Surah* Ash-Shura as a proof to his statement. In another narrative the Messenger of God (pbuh) says: **O Ali, this *Ayah* is the best in the Quran.**[2] (Because it gets the point across and makes people cognizent that calamities are the outcome of their misdeeds and because it has a wonderful effect in improving their deeds and behaviour.)

Imam Sadeq (AS) said:

«امَّا اِنَّهُ ليسَ مِن عَرقٍ يُضرَب وَ لَا نَكَبَةٍ وَ لَاصُداع ولامَرَض إلَا بذَنب» ٣

"Beware! No blood vessel is cut, no head suffers a headache, and no foot is hit against a stone unless a sin has already been committed."

Technically speaking, 'sin' is an umbrella term here for all forms of sin.

The Holy Quran states: When a single disaster smites you, you will say:

«انى هذا؟»; **"Whence is this?"** Say to them: "It is from yourselves." you did something before and you cannot get away with it now.[4]

It is in the narrative that once Amir al-mu'minin (AS) went to visit Salman who was sick. (Unlike us, he wouldn't stand on ceremony; if we had been in his shoes, we would, most probably, have said: O Salman! You have got a higher position, so God has decided to tease you a bit). He said to him (to this effect): When our Shias commit a sin, God removes their sin by making them suffer pain.[5] Salman not only didn't get resentful, but he rose, kissed Ali's brow and said, "May I be thy ransome! If you *Ahlul-bayt*

---

[1] Al-Khisal, vol. 2, page 616

[2] Tafsir Ayyashi, vol. 1, page 20: «رُوِىَ عَن علىٍ(ع) أنَّه قالَ، قالَ رسولُ الله(ص) خيرُ آيه فى كِتابِ الله هذه الآيَه»

[3] Osoul-e Kaafi, vol. 2, page 269

[4] Aal-e-Imran, *Ayah* 165

[5] Teb-ol-Aeme, page 15

[Household of the Prophet (pbuh)] did not instruct us such things, who would?"

Imam Sadeq (AS) said in a *Hadith*: **Abu Dharr felt uncertain about Ali's religious authority for only one day, and God made him suffer a lingering death in Rabadeh Desert.**[1] Another narrative says that Salman cast doubt on Ali's religious authority for a moment (thinking: is this the man who knows The Great Name of God, yet he is taking his lumps while they are beating his wife and dragging him toward the mosque?) and a tumor appeared in his neck. The next day Amir al-mu'minin said to him, **"O Salman, that tumor of yours is the result of the fleeting thought that struck you yesterday."**[2]

I am too little, too insignificant to brag and boast about my affinity with God. Who am I to say that God entraps his friends, and since I am of the elect, I am in His trap too, and I am content with this condition of suffering. I never mean to say that man should not be content with the misfortunes that come upon him. That's a different story. Contentment in unfortunate conditions and events is a sign that not only is the man's sin cleared away, but he is also rewarded. However, let's not forget that misdeeds will bring about calamities. As Imam Ali (AS) said:

«...فَاخْزُنْ لِسَانَكَ كَمَا تَخْزُنُ ذَهَبَكَ وَ وَرِقَكَ فَرُبَّ كَلِمَةٍ سَلَبَتْ نِعْمَةً وَ جَلَبَتْ نِقْمَةً...»[3]

"Seal up your tongue as you seal up the scrip of gold and silver. Many a word that takes away riches and comfort and inflicts discomfort."

Imam Reza (AS) said:

«كُلَّمَا أَحْدَثَ العِبَادُ مِنَ الذُّنُوبِ مَا لَم يَكُونُوا يَـعْمَلُونَ أَحْدَثَ اللهُ لَهُم مِنَ البَلَاءِ مَا لَم يَكُونُوا يَعْرِفُونَ»[4]

"If people turn to unprecedented sins, then God will send unprecedented plagues."

---

[1] al ikhtisas, page 10
[2] same
[3] Nahjul Balagha, wise Saying 381
[4] Ilal al-Sharayi`, vol. 2, page 522

Where were SARS, AIDS, and the Swine flu in those good old days? Where was diabetes so widespread? A hypnotist once said that he had hypnotised someone and wanted him to ask Ibn-e Sina to recommend some medicine for a particular patient. Ibn-e Sina had answered, "This illness is not known to me. In my time, there were no such things."

Amir al-Mu'minin (AS) says in *Nahj al-Balaghah*: **By Allah, no people are deprived of the lively pleasures of life after enjoying them, except as a result of sins committed by them, because Allah is not unjust to His creatures.** [1] And usually, when He takes the blessing, it will not come back again. Some people believe, for example, that the elm tree bore fruit in the past, but now it has been barren for several hundred years. Furthermore, I have recently heard that almond and apricot trees do not bear fruit in a certain region of Yazd. Similarly, the sins people commit will make pleasures and blessings depart from them and calamities descend upon them.

Expressing Doubts

Following what was said, a few misconceptions might strike us:

1. How can we justify all the afflictions that came upon the Prophet's Household–considering their innocence–, that came upon the prophetsand Hadrat-e Zahra? What about all the pains and problems that the Warriors of Islam suffered in different battlefields?

2. How can we explain the sufferings of innocent children? What is their fault? How can we say that they are suffering as a result of sin?

3. What about the Divine Test? Do we not assert that some miseries and afflictions strike us because we need to be tested?

$$\text{«وَلَنَبْلُوَنَّكُمْ بِشَيْءٍ مِّنَ الْخَوْفِ وَالْجُوعِ وَنَقْصٍ مِّنَ الأَمْوَالِ وَالأَنْفُسِ وَالثَّمَرَاتِ...»} \,^{\text{٢}}$$

"And We will surely test you with something of fear and hunger and a loss of wealth and lives and fruits, but give glad tidings to the patient,"

---

[1] Nahjul Balagha, sermon 178: «ايْمُ الله ما كانَ قَوْمٌ قَطُّ فى غَضٍّ نِعمَهِ مِنْ عَيْشٍ فَزالَ عَنْهُمْ اِلاّ بِذُنُوبٍ اجْتَرَحُوها، لأَنّ الله لَيْسَ بِظَلّامٍ لِلْعَبيدِ»

[2] Al-Baqara, *Ayah* 155

4. There are a number of *narratives* that say: the more steadfast you are in your belief in God, the more calamities you are bound to suffer, like «البلاء «للولاء,[1] how are they accounted for?

These are all the antithetical arguments that are placed against the existing *Ahadith* on the matter, and they seem to be clearly contradictory. Nevertheless, in fact, there is no conflict. The problem arises only because attention is focused on the appearance of the narratives.

At the time of Imam Sadeq (AS), one of the believers in his pilgrim garb, in defiance of some pilgrims' advice, entraps a pigeon, kills and eats it in the Sacred Precincts. The offender, then again, kills and eats another pigeon. (According to the Holy Quran killng game in the state of pilgrimage a second time is beyond atonement. Allah, Lord of Retribution, will punish the offender in His own way: «...مِنْهُ اللهُ فَيَنْتَقِمُ عَادَ مَنْ وَ...»; [2]**"For repetition Allah will punish him."**) While this wretched man was circumambulating among the pilgrims, he was struck by lightning on the head and was reduced to a piece of charcoal.

Imam Baqer (AS) says: **If a believing servant is guilty but dear to God, He will give him a disease as punishment; otherwise, He will make him poor. If He does not do this, He will take his child from him; if not, He will make him die hard to get rid of his sins.** [3]If a servant is not dear to God, He will tell him, "Do whatever you would like to do, I will keep it in store for you." God says in the Holy Quran:

$$«...اعْمَلُوا مَا شِئْتُمْ إِنَّهُ بِمَا تَعْمَلُونَ بَصِيرٌ»[4]$$

"Do whatever you will; indeed, He is seeing of what you do."

Now, you can get the answer to many of the potential questions you may have from the above mentioned *Hadith*.

One of the most serious problems some of us encounter in dealing with the Quran and understanding its marvels is when we do not catch their drifts,

---

[1] Misbah al-Sharia, page 356
[2] Al-Maeda, *Ayah* 95
[3] Osoul-e Kaafi,vol. 2, page 444
[4] Fussilat, *Ayah* 40

instead of thinking them over and making the truth come out, we listlessly erase the problem. This way we manage to persuade ourselves that the deed is done. This behaviour of us is quite similar to that of a student who is asked to the board to do an equation far above his head. He just stands there scratching his head. Then suddenly, in a fit of bewilderment and dismay, he gets rid of the problem by erasing the board, believing what was supposed to be done is now done. If a question is raised about the basis of some religious belief or some Quranic verse, are we, Muslims, supposed to deny the question and give the verse an interpretation contrary to what the appearence of it says?

A Look at Some Verses and Narratives

Before answering the questions about the misconceptions, I would like to introduce a few reference books on *Ahadith*. Ayatollah Zainolabedin Tabatabai Abarghoui–one of the "Abdal" (an important group of God's saints)–who enjoys a high public profile for his piety and extraordinary works, in his book, *Velayatolmottagheen*, has mentioned some points:

Firstly, he offers a different interpretation of this *Ayah*:

$$...\text{«}...\text{إِنَّ اللهَ لاَ يُغَيِّرُ مَا بِقَوْمٍ حَتَّى يُغَيِّرُوا مَا بِأَنْفُسِهِمْ}...\text{»}^{1}$$

"Indeed, Allah will not change the condition of a people until they change what is in themselves."

You have always heard that this verse is used for revolutions and social changes. It is often interpreted like this:

People, if you do no rise to change your destiny, nothing will change." Whereas this is not the implication at all. If you pay attention to the context and check the verses around it, you will notice that this meaning is not intended. Unfortunately, giving the verses a cursory look has become common. Giving a quick opinion about the verses of the Quran, and saying the first meaning that comes to mind can cause misunderstanding. The word «غَيّر» in Arabic language signifies a change from good to bad, not from bad to good. Amir Al-Mu'minin, writes to Malek Ashtar «فإِنَّ ذَلِكَ

---

[1] Ar-Rad, *Ayah* 11

«يَدعُو اِلَى الغَيرِ»[1] **"If you oppress people, they will cause mischief, make bad revolutions. People rebel against you."**

«...إنَّ اللهَ لاَ يُغَيِّرُ مَا بِقَوْمٍ حَتَّى يُغَيِّرُواْ مَا بِأنْفُسِهِمْ...»;[2] **"Indeed, Allah will not change the condition of a people until they change what is in themselves."** That is, Allah does not convert the blessings that have been given to people unless they change their actions and behaviors (from good to bad).

Interestingly, there are several narratives in which the infallible Imams (AS) have interpreted and explained this verse, but some people fail to have a look at them. As a result, they give comments as they wish. The Quran says: **"Allah does not change the condition of any people from good to bad unless they themselves change their good deeds to bad"**. It is noteworthy that there are clues before and after. For example, the remainder of the *Ayah* says:

$$«...وَإذَا أَرَادَ اللهُ بِقَوْمٍ سُوءًا فَلاَ مَرَدَّ لَهُ وَمَا لَهُم مِّن دُونِهِ مِن وَالٍ»[3]$$

"But when Allah willeth a people's punishmen, there can be no turning it back, nor will they find, besides Him, any to protect." You may find this same meaning in many narrations. For instance, Amir al-mu'minin (AS) says in *Nahjul Balagha*:

«وَ ايمُ اللهِ، مَا كَانَ قَومٌ قَطُّ فِى غَضٍّ مِن عَيشٍ نِعمَةٌ فَزَالَ عَنهُم اِلَّا بِذُنُوبٍ اجتَرَحُوها لأنّ «اللهَ لَيْسَ بِظَلّامٍ لِلْعَبِيدِ»...»;[4]

"By Allah, no people are deprived of the lively pleasures of life after enjoying them, except as a result of sins committed by them, because certainly Allah is not unjust to His creatures."

It seems to mean that people would be the victims of opperssion if they got punished without committing any sins. Does God ever slap anybody on the face for no good reason!? It is interesting that God in some other place in the Holy Quran has taken this change as a kind of transformation to evil.

---

[1] Nahjul Balagha, letter 53
[2] Ar-Rad, *Ayah* 11
[3] same
[4] Nahjul Balagha, sermon 178

«ذَلِكَ بِأَنَّ اللهَ لَمْ يَكُ مُغَيِّرًا نِّعْمَةً أَنْعَمَهَا عَلَى قَوْمٍ حَتَّى يُغَيِّرُواْ مَا بِأَنْفُسِهِمْ»[1]

"Because Allah will never change the grace (to disgrace) which He hath bestowed on a people until they change what is in their (own) souls."

«...وَلَوْ أَنَّ النَّاسَ حِينَ تَنْزِلُ بِهِمُ النِّقَمُ، وَتَزُولُ عَنْهُمُ النِّعَمُ فَزِعُوا إِلَى رَبِّهِمْ بِصِدْقٍ مِن نِّيَّاتِهِمْ، وَوَلَهٍ مِن قُلُوبِهِمْ، لَرَدَّ عَلَيْهِمْ كُلَّ شَارِدٍ وَأَصْلَحَ لَهُمْ كُلَّ فَاسِدٍ...»[2]

"Then why, when Our punishment came to them, did they not humble themselves? But their hearts became hardened, and Satan made attractive to them that which they were doing."

Allah, all praise and glory be to Him has told us in the Quran:

«وَأَنِ اسْتَغْفِرُواْ رَبَّكُمْ ثُمَّ تُوبُواْ إِلَيْهِ يُمَتِّعْكُم مَّتَاعًا حَسَنًا إِلَى أَجَلٍ مُّسَمًّى...»[3]

"(And to preach thus), "Seek you the forgiveness of your Lord, and turn to Him in repentance; that He may grant you enjoyment, good (and true), for a term appointed...""

That is to say, ask God to forgive you the cause of all misfortunes, sin. Then turn to Him in repentance, that is, make a promise not to turn back to a life of sin anymore because seeking the forgiveness of Allah should be immediately followed by repentance. Asking forgiveness without repentance is a form of mockery, for it means: God, I can't promise not to return to sin. Then the upshot of it all is that He will grant you enjoyment, good and true, to an appointed time. There are two points in the phrase: «إِلَى أَجَلٍ مُّسَمًّى»

First point: The enjoyment of all good and true things in life refers to the present life with its limited term. We get this point from the fact that the final point for

«أَجَلٍ مُّسَمًّى» is «يُمَتِّعْكُم»; For example, when you say from now until Ramadhan you will do something, it means you will do it before Ramadhan. Therefore, "He may grant you enjoyment, good and true, for a term

---

[1] Al-Anfal, *Ayah* 53
[2] Nahjul Balagha, sermon 178
[3] Hud, *Ayah* 3

appointed" means the enjoyment of the present life from this moment to the end and not of the life to come.

Second point: Through your repentance and God's forgiveness, God will take away unexpected doom that your deeds have placed in your path and keep you in the world as much as possible. It is because many sins will cut life short and make you meet your Maker sooner. Relevant to this discussion, there is a narration from Imam Sadeq (AS):

«امّا اِنَّهُ لَيسَ مِن عَرَقٍ يُضرَبَ وَ لا نَكبَةٍ وَ لا صُدَاعٍ وَ لَا مَرَضٍ اِلَّا بِذَنبٍ» ١

"Beware! No blood vessel is cut, no head suffers a headache, and no foot is hit against a stone unless a sin has already been committed."

Then the Imam (AS) supports his claim by an eloquent testimony from the Holy Quran:

«وَمَا أَصَابَكُم مِّن مُّصِيبَةٍ فَبِمَا كَسَبَتْ أَيْدِيكُمْ وَيَعْفُو عَن كَثِيرٍ» ٢

"Whatever misfortune happens to you, is because of the things your hands have wrought, and for many (a sin) He grants forgiveness."

Imam Sadegh (AS) also said: **"Allah will never take back the blessings that He has given to anyone unless he deprives himself of them by sin."** [3] God's method is not to retrieve the blessings he has bestowed. Isn't it, therefore, really surprising how we let all these narratives go unnoticed?

«عَن اَبى عَبداللهِ قَالَ سَمِعتُهُ يَقُول كَانَ اَبى يَقُول»

Imam Sadegh (AS) said he had heard his father, Imam Bagher (AS), say:

«إنَّ اللهَ قَضَى، قضاءً حَتماً اَلاّ يُنعِمَ عَلَى العَبدِ بِنِعمَةٍ فَيَسلُبَها اِيَّاهُ حَتَّى يُحدِثَ العَبدُ ذَنباً يَستَحِقُّ بِذلِكَ النَّقمَةَ» ٤

"God has issued an irrevocable decree not to get back the blessings He has given to His servant unless he deprives himself by sin."

---

[1] Wasa'il al-Shia, vol. 15, *Hadith* 20565

[2] Ash-Shura, *Ayah* 30

[3] Bihar al-Anwar, vol. 6, page 56

[4] Osoul-e Kaafi, vol. 2, page 273

It is narrated when Imam Reza (AS) awarded a poet, the poet said: "Sir, I eulogized you in my poem out of love and not for the sake of lucre," and insisted on giving it back, but the Imam (AS) did not accept it. Then he, a man of open hands, dismounted from his horse, handed the poet the harness and said: "This horse is also for you. We, the household of the Prophet (pbuh), do not take back anything we have given to others." [1]The ethic-minded *Ahlul-Bait* were like this. God is wont to treat His servants in the same fashion, which is His attribute of absolute benefaction. If He, perforce, takes back the vouchsafed blessings, the reason, then, is no more than our sins.

A narrative goes: **a servant of God prays for something, God says to the angels to grant his wish. When the grounds are being prepared for granting his wish (because everything is done when the time is ripe), this man does a sin and God orders his angels not to fulfill it.** [2]

Imam Sadegh (AS) said: **Allah, all praises and glory be to Him, sent a prophet from His prophets to his people saying: "Tell your people that many a devoted and obedient man who undergoes a life of misery after a period of felicity, simply because he prefers his own desires to my desires and opts for a life of sin.** «فَأَصَابَهُمْ فِيهَا ضَرَاءٌ»; **Yet, when he turns his back to what I despise, I take his sufferings off him.** [3]

Imam Sadegh (AS) stated:

«إِنَّ الذَّنْبَ يَحرِمُ العَبْدَ الرزقَ» [4]

"Sin will deprive man of his sustenance."

There are some sins about which Imam Sadegh (AS) has said:

«مَنْ هَمَّ بِسَيِّئَةٍ فَلايَعْمَلْها فَاِنَّهُ رُبَّما عَمِلَ العَبْدُ السَّيِّئَةَ فَيَراهُ الرَّبُّ تَبارَک وَ تَعالى فَيَقولُ وَ عِزَّتى وَ جَلالى لا اَغْفِرُ لَکَ بَعْدَ ذلک اَبَداً» [5]

"Sometimes man perpetrates a sin about which God swears to His Might and Glory never to pardon it."

---

[1] Uyun Akhbar al-Rida, vol. 2, page 263
[2] Osoul-e Kaafi, vol. 3, page 373
[3] Thawab al-Amal, page 266
[4] Osoul-e Kaafi, vol. 2, page 271
[5] same, vol. 2, page 272

Of course, it does not mean that God will never forgive it. It, rather, means if the sin is not atoned for, He won't forgive it. In other words man must be punished for the sin first. However, because God is full of mercy to the believing men and women, He will forgive many of their sins. «...وَ يَعْفُو عَن كَثِيرٍ», Then Imam Sadegh (AS) ties his hands into one another and three times says: «...وَ يَعْفُو

عَن كَثِيرٍ»; for many (a sin) He grants fogiveness. In some cases, man does something unpardonable, then God not only does not grant forgiveness, but He also swears vengence. On the other hand, there are a number of *Ayahs* and narratives that indicate when man seeks forgiveness and asks for mercy, God shows mercy too.

Answering the Questionable Misconceptions

The First Misconception: Why did the Infallible Imams (AS) suffer? What was their guilt?

The same question was asked of Imam Sadegh (AS). Once, when he explained that sins would bring about sufferings, the narrator asked: what are you and your forefather Sayyid al-Shuhada (an epithet of Imam al-Husayn meaning Master of Martyrs) guilty of? Why do you, inerrant people, have to undergo sufferings, too?

The Imam said something to this effect: **we, the Prophet's Household, are made exceptions.**

Sufferings are divided into two categories: 1.Involuntary pains and sufferings that come upon us uninvited. 2. Voluntary sufferings, like those inflicted on someone who voluntarily goes to the battlefield to fight for the cause of Allah. A disabled war veteran of the Iran-Iraq War who is suffering from a spinal cord injury had gone to the front on his own will and now has to suffer too many difficulties.

These difficulties are not rooted in sin. Allah says in *Ayah* 120 of *Surah* At-Taubah:

$$...ذَلِكَ بِأَنَّهُمْ لَا يُصِيبُهُمْ ظَمَأٌ وَلَا نَصَبٌ وَلَا مَخْمَصَةٌ فِي سَبِيلِ اللهِ وَلَا يَطَؤُونَ مَوْطِئًا$$
$$يَغِيظُ الْكُفَّارَ وَلَا يَنَالُونَ مِنْ عَدُوٍّ نَيْلاً إِلَّا كُتِبَ لَهُمْ بِهِ عَمَلٌ صَالِحٌ...^1$$

"...becuse nothing could they suffer or do, but was reckoned to their credit as a deed of righteousness,–whether they suffedred thirst, or fatigue, or hunger, in the cause of Allah, or trod paths to raise the ire of the Unbelievers, or gain any gain from an enemy..."

That is due to hardships, sufferings, or injuries they endure, Allah will raise their degree in the spiritual world and have good deeds written for them, whereas no reward is granted to unasked-for sufferings. This kind of (unasked-for) suffering, on the other hand, will not only eliminate sins, but it will also be rewarded if the sufferer accepts it without complaining.

Suppose you have an accident with somebody who turns out to be your creditor. He comes up to you and says, "I am prepared to shoulder the blame because you had the right of the way, but I hope you have not forgotten that you owe me such an amount of money. I think that sum can pay for the damage to your car, so we are level." In a situation like this, if you don't lose your temper by crying out, "Why didn't you keep your eyes open?" or "What was getting into you?" or "The skid marks show you were driving too fast." or things like that, he may appreciate your magnanimous gesture, great soul and high-mindedness and even offer you a gift of money. If I may use such an analogy, pains and sufferings are a means to pay off our creditor, God. Furthermore, if we don't groan and moan in sferings and just grin and bear them, we will be rewarded.

---

[1] At-Taubah, *Ayah* 120

Amir al-mu'minin, peace be upon him, said to one of his companions during his sickness:

«فَإِنَّ الْمَرَضَ لَا أَجرَ فيه ولَكِنَّهُ يَحُطُّ السَّيِّئاتِ وَ يَحُتُّها حَتَّ الاوراقِ» ¹

"There is no reward for sickness, but it erases sins and makes them fall like (dried) leaves."

Sayyid ar-Radi explains this: Amir al-mu'minin is right to say that there is no reward for sickness as such because compensation is admissible in respect of the acts of Allah, the Sublime, towards His creatures such as grief, illness and the like, whereas reward and recompense becomes admissible against actions by the creature.

Endurance is considered to be a good deed. In sufferings, if you lose patience, sins are written off, but there won't be any reward because nothing has been done. Amir al-mu'minin, peace be upon him, said:

«وَ مَن ضَرَبَ يَدَهُ عَلَى فَخذِه عند مُصيبَته حَبِطَ عَمَلُهُ(أَجرُهُ)» ²

He who beats his hand on the thigh in his affliction ruins his good actions, because he hasn't shown endurance. Yet, if he endures pains without complaining and invokes God, "O Lord! I am content with what you want for me," he will be recompensed because he has shown endurance, which is regarded as a good deed. To sum it all up, reward is the result of patience not suffering. However, voluntary sufferings like those that come upon someone who fights or tries for the cause of Allah will be rewarded by Allah.

The Household of the Prophet, from the outset, opted for that kind of life themselves and were content with it. That is why the Imam (AS) says they are made exceptions. They also advised us

---

¹ Nahjul Balagha, wise Saying 42
² same, wise Saying 144

not to compare ourselves with them. (When some hardship befalls someone from among ordinary people, he immediately juxstaposes himself next to the Imams and says, "What should we expect from the course of life when it didn't look favorably even at the Progeny of the Prophet?" whereas their sufferings belong to a quite different type from ours.)

Amir al-mu'minin (AS) has said:

«لَا يُقاسُ بِآلِ مُحَمَّدٍ مِن هَذِهِ الأُمَّهِ احدٌ» ١

"None in the Islamic community can be taken at par with the Progeny of the Prophet (Al-e Mohammad)."

No one can be deemed their equal in sublimity and grandeur because their rank and dignity has roots in a different realm. When Grand prophets and the Prophet's Successors were punished for just once abandoning what was recommended, we are too insignificant to brag about love, and claim: we are suffering pain and hardship because we are the elect.

Some people who, in their own estimation, were indulged in mysticism, used to ask God for a plague, for a disastrous evil or affliction, only to find, later on, they were wrong. The late Molla Mahdi Naraghi said about someone who would pray, "God! I love you so much. I implore You to send me evil, nothing but evil and plague." God answered his call and afflicted him with a severe stomachache that was beyond his pain threshold. He left home, wandered about in the pathways and alleys calling for God's mercy to relieve the pain. Then he saw a couple of schoolboys and told them not to be a fool, as he was, to ask for pain and suffering.

It is truly silly to ask for pain. Once the Prophet of God (pbuh) was asked, "What is the best thing to ask God for if we are still

---

1   same, sermon 2

alive in the Night of Power (*Qadr*)?" He said, "*Afiah*."[1] (The best thing to ask for is *Afiah*, meaning to be free from all kinds of sufferings and agony in the body and soul, accompanied by welfare and the prospect of a happy life in the Hereafter). Is it mysticism, therefore, to wish for evil?! Mysticism is nothing but what the Household of the Prophet (pbut) said. What man in his right mind would ask for pain? Why not asking God for health, welfare and prosperity? It is a real problem that some people pull their hands out of the hands of the Prophet's Progeny, and put them in the hands of some others as wretched as themselves, thinking that they are treading the path of gnosis toward salvation. What did they (the Prophet's progeny) deny you? What mystery is left unsolved after them? Where are you going? Why are you following those who are stuck in the mud themslves scratching their heads? They just put on a knowledgeable front and use sweet words but they finally end up in byways.

The Second Misconception: How can sufferings and afflictions justify the Divine Test?

$$\text{«وَلَنَبْلُوَنَّكُم بِشَىْءٍ مِّنَ الْخَوْفِ وَالْجُوعِ وَنَقْصٍ مِّنَ الاَمْوَالَ وَلاَنْفُسِ وَالثَّمَرَاتِ بَشِّرِ الصَّابِرِينَ»}^{2}$$

"Be sure We shall test you with something of fear and hunger, some loss in goods, lives and the fruits (of your toil), but give glad tidings to those who patiently persevere."

If all of these hardships and calamities are tests, why is it said they are the upshot of sin?

Answer: There are two kinds of tests with God: sweet and bitter: wealth, poverty; health, sickness; power, weakness, etc.

---

[1] Mustadrak al-Wasa'il, vol. 7, page 458
[2] Al-Baqara, *Ayah* 155

Testing is an inexorable method of God, but its kind depends on your deeds. If you, for example, respect ties of kith and kin and give due consideration to your parents, Allah will test you with power, wealth, reverence and respect. Otherwise, He will do so with poverty, illness and wretchedness.

"Now," you may ask, "why, then, are some disbelievers better off than some believers? It must be the other way round."

Questions of this kind have made a great many people think the opposite way and let the relevant *Ahadith* go unnoticed.

Answer: If Allah decided to deal out justice to believers when the world ends, it would be a great loss for them. The fact of the matter is that, Allah is reluctant to chastise His believing slaves in the Hereafter, so He teases them a bit over here for their misdeeds. He paves the way for their entanglement in everyday conflicts, and then no matter how hard the struggle, they cannot writhe out of them. God says, "You need to suffer for some time." Meanwhile, if they seek forgiveness and satisfy those whose rights have been violated (or ask God to forgive them if they don't know them), the problems will go away sooner than what was appointed.

When you pray for God's blessing or say your prayers, don't forget to put up a prayer for those whose rights have been violated by you. It does wonders in bringing happiness and joy to your life and alleviating sufferings. It will lessen their claim on you if you ask God to shower His mercy and forgiveness upon them. For instance, in case of backbiting, if you think talking to the person about whom you have said unkind things, in order to satisfy him, may tarnish the relationship and give rise to indignation and dipleasure, don't do that; just ask God to forgive him his sins. God will forgive.

Allah punishes the believers in Here in order to cleanse them. The purport of what Imam Ali (AS) said to Asbagh ibn Nubata (a close and loyal companion of Imam Ali) is, **"Praise be to God that punishes my Shi'ites in this world. In the Hereafter when their accounts are given in their right hands, they see that no sin is recorded there..."** On the other hand, Allah is disinclined to reward the disbeliever's good deeds in the Hereafter; he will be recompensed here in this world. What about his sins? They are recorded in his account for the Resurection Day. What do you think the outcome will be? He will live a flashy, meretricious life, but you see the believer who slaves and drudges to make an honost living. Whereas, it is not really the case that disbelievers always live in the lap of luxury, and believers down in the dumps.

Where in Europe do people feel as secure as we feel here? People in our country come and go here and there feeling quite safe and secure. People are faithful and affectionate. If somebody gets hurt, they gather around him to help. It is something you cannot find in western countries. If we are afflicted by natural disasters, westerners are, too. How many years did the period between the Second World War and the end of Cold War last? Europe and America, rather the whole former Soviet and western blocs lived under the threat of nuclear missile attacks. Is it the meaning of peace and tranquility? When the volcano in Iceland came to life and spewed ash and lava, the damage to the airports alone was more than two and a half billion dollars! Tidal waves made nearly one million holiday makers and honeymooners from the local people, Europe and America disappear.

If you see that men of religious conviction are in difficulties, its secret is in what I said. As the Holy Quran testifies, hardships do not indicate that the person who is facing them is dragged to the lowest in the Divine Ranking, nor is comfort the sign of being elevated to the highest. It is actually God's manner to cleanse those He likes. By way of analogy, if your glasses get stained, you wipe them immediately. If your clothes get dirty you wash them every two three days. But when dust and dirt get into your carpet, you will leave it laid there for a whole year maybe, and then give it a good beating with a rod (this was the way people cleaned carpets from dust in the past). This is how Allah treats disbelievers, but with believers, His treatment is like glasses: as soon as they are covered with dust, He cleans them. Hafiz says:

Since with ringed ear I've served Love's house of wine,

Grief's gratulations have each hour been mine.

What comes to your mind by this poem? Those who fall in love with God must be annoyed by Him? Imam Bagher (AS) helps elucidate the problem in a *Hadith*:

عن ابی حعفر: «قَالَ إنَّ الله عَرَّوَجل: اذَا كَانَ مِن اَمرِه اَن يُكرِمَ عَبداً وَ لهُ ذَنب ابتلاهُ بالسُّقم» ١

"Allah, all praises and glory be to Him, has said: If I want to punish a servant, whom I have held in reverence, for his sin, I will make him ill."

No devout Muslim gets beaten for his piety. Allah, however, will beat your dust of guilts off your soul before it is overburdened with them on "the way to dusty death" and to the Hereafter–this is Divine Reception. In a sense, therefore, it is true that sufferings are because of closeness to God, but in this sense rather than the the way we think. He, in fact, says: I cleanse you of your sins Here; I don't let you bear them to the Next World because I love you. Yet, it's wrong to think that men get punished due to innocence.

Then the Imam (AS) goes on:

---

[1] Osoul-e Kaafi, vol. 2, page 444

«فَإِن لَم يَفعَل ذَلكَ له ابتلاهُ بالحَاجَهِ فَإِن لَم يَفعَل به ذَلكَ شَدَّدَ عَلَيه المَوت لِيُكافئه
بذلكَ الذَّنب» ¹

"Otherwise, I will strain his livelihood, and if I don't do that, I will make him die hard." At any rate, He doesn't let him carry his guilts with him to the Next World. This is the meaning of «البَلاءُ

That is, all these tribulations are rooted in amity. But if you «لِلوَلاءِ²

give it a different interpretation like: I (God) will slap you across the face a couple of times out of love, it isn't rational. If someone addresses such words to a good man, we will call him a psycho. How do you, then, expect God, who is the creator of mind, to have said such words?!

There is something destructive, something pernicious to this matter at hand: looking things on the surface. Superficial awareness and knowledge of the subject matter might well lead you to misjudgement and ill-treatment of the people around. Seeing someone having a pain in the leg, you may say, "It served him right for being so jealous, so selfish, for doing this, for doing that." It is, however, worthwhile to clarify the matter that the best people are to be sought among those who have the most problems. He who lives an anxiety-free type of life is not necessarily pure and immaculate. Nobody can claim his entire life has been free of guilt or shortcomings. After all, when you take a walk out, some dust may perforce settle on you. The catch is those who are fortified in faith, have a high suffering threshold; nothing, not even the worst plagues can get them carried away. Their reward is becoming cleansed Here.

---

¹ same
² Mesbah al-Sharia, page 356

On the other hand, some people are half-hearted in faith. They tend to get back from faith with the slightest blow. Therefore, Allah let them get away with their guilts Here. At the same time, Allah is unwilling to torture them in the Hereafter, so the only place left for Him to settle their accounts is Purgatory. There are, yet, a group of believers, according to Imam Sadegh (AS), who are in sheer bliss both in Here and in the Hereafter. Later on, I will explain how to reach this state.

$$\text{إِنَّ الَّذِينَ سَبَقَتْ لَهُم مِّنَّا الْحُسْنَى أُوْلَئِكَ عَنْهَا مُبْعَدُونَ * لَا يَسْمَعُونَ حَسِيسَهَا...}^1$$

"Those for whom the Good from Us has gone before, will be removed far therefrom. Not the slightest sound will they hear of Hell: what their souls desired, in that will they dwell."

The Third Misconception: What is the sin of minors who are vexed by illnesses and other problems?

Some narratives in this respect have put us wise. They say that siknesses and other forms of suffering would purge the guilt from their parents. Of course the kids themselves would be rewarded in exchange for the suffering. The parents of a kid who has a fever, for example, get into trouble, for which their sins would lighten.

A number of plights that afflict children are related to their future lives. In other words, the plights expiate their future guilts. The Omniscient God who already knows what they are going to do in the years to come, will have them recorded for the would-be sufferings. The relevant evidence is in the Surah Al-Kahf: Hadhrat Khidhr (AS) slew a boy. When Moses (AS) objected as why he slew an innocent person who had slain none, Hadhrat Khidhr (AS) responded, "If he had stayed alive, he would become infidel and would draw his pious parents to infidelity too. I didn't slay him on my own. I acted on higher authority. In return, his parents are

---

[1] Al-Anbiya, *Ayah*s 101-102

promised a better-behaved child who would be a credit to them."
[1] A *Hadith* says that they were given a daughter, whose progeny bore them a lot of prophets. Therefore, children, too, are punished according to some rules. Also in the Quran you can find cases in which the faults of the past and those to follow are forgiven. This fact is emphasized in *Ahadith* too.

"Isn't it a case of punishing a crime not yet committed?" you may ask. The obvious answer is "No." "Punishment of a crime not yet committed" is limited to the human world. In the realm of God, it is an inalienable right of Him to do what He wants to do, and this case is already obviated. Moreover, Khidhr's action was beneficial both to the young boy, for he didn't become infidel, and to his parents. Our knowledge and understanding is quite different from God's. We don't know who decides to do what, nor are we the proprietor of people, but God is, and his knowledge encompasses all. He is entitled to take any action deemed necessary. If a gardener breaks off a stick from a tree in his own garden, can anybody, in his right mind, say, **"he shouldn't have"**? Now that Allah, the Proprietor of the whole existence, has cut a stick and transplanted it somewhere else, who are we to daresay, **"He shouldn't have." It isn't necessary to talk about justice here.**

A Common Mistake Clarified By the Quran
A point to be mentioned here is that the Quran says:

«فَأَمَّا الْإِنسَانُ إِذَا مَا ابْتَلَاهُ رَبُّهُ فَأَكْرَمَهُ وَنَعَّمَهُ فَيَقُولُ رَبِّي أَكْرَمَنِ»[2]

"Now, as for man, when his Lord trieth him, giving him honor and gifts, then saith he, (puffed up), 'My Lord hath honored me.'"

---

[1] Al-Kahf, *Ayah* 74
[2] Al-Fajr, *Ayah* 15

If Allah tries man by prosperity (world's goods), he gets puffed up and says, "My Lord has honored me." Why? Because He gave me wealth, possessions and fortune.

«وَأَمَّا إِذَا مَا ابْتَلَاهُ فَقَدَرَ عَلَيْهِ رِزْقَهُ فَيَقُولُ رَبِّى أَهَانَنِ»[1]

"But when He trieth him, restricting his subsistence for him, then saith he (in despair), 'My Lord has humiliated me.'"

The Holy Quran negates both of these wrong attitudes wih one little word: **"Nay, nay!"**[2] It says: neither is "restricting subsistence" humiliating, nor is prosperity an indicator of honor. On the contrary, sometimes Allah honors His servant by restricting his subsistence and creating problems. Let's call to mind the aforementioned *Hadith* by Imam Bagher (AS): Allah, all praises and glory be to Him, has said: If I want to punish a servant, whom I have held in reverence, for his sin, I will make him ill. Otherwise, I will strain his livelihood, and if I don't do that, I will make him die hard in order to cleanse him of his sin. [3]So you see, sometimes restraints and hardships, rather than bounties and sustenance, are signs of glory and respect. On the other hand, Allah may happen to reward a sinner's good deeds Here, and reserve his sins for the Day of Reckoning, leaving the wretched sinner thinking that God is befriending him. The Holy Quran has elucidated these points with, **"Nay, nay!"** Pay attention, please, to these extremely important points.

Misunderstanding and ill-consideration of religion has given rise to too much inconvenience. More often than not, we manipulate simple problems into so complicated ones that even highly intellctual sages fail to understand them. After we are completely

---

[1] same, *Ayah* 16

[2] same, *Ayah* 17: «كَلَّا...»

[3] Osoul-e Kaafi, vol. 2, page 444

lost, we refer to the Quran only to find that our findings are incompatible with what the surface meanings of the *Ayahs* say. Then, perforce, we interpret the Quranic verses according to our taste or interest, and thereby, we are further lost. As long as the issue at hand is concerned, for example, the Holy Quran simply says: O people! If you show deep respect for God and religion, He will grant you comfort welfare, competent and pious children, rain, etc. On the other hand, if you turn to a life of sin, He will restrict your subsistence and gets back His bounty.

Emphasising a Point

Since there are indiscernible sins of all kinds, small and great, in the believers' lives, even the most eminent believers are not immunized against them. Those who are protected against them through knowledgeable care and vigilance are as rare as a winter pomegranate (narratives tell us even Salman and Abudhar were not exempt). As a result, the infallible Imams (AS) have pointed to this fact with the conclusion that believers are always afflicted. And we erroneously take afflictions as an exclusive sign of closeness to God. Whereas they are primarily due to our faults or shortcomings rooted in neglect, and secondly due to *vilayat*, as in the following narratives:

--Wherever a faithful Muslim settles, Allah will appoint a villain as his neighbor to vex him.

--The believer's affliction is proportionate to his belief and goodness of his deeds.

--Allah afflicts the people He loves.

--The faithful are afflicted to the extent of their piety.

--The more pious the faithful, the more they will suffer.

--The faithful are "gifted" by sufferings from God as a family is gifted by souvenirs from their father.[1]

Therefore, sorrows and sufferings are great treasures sent to people by Allah.

An Important Point: A close look at the narratives by *Ahlul-Bayt* (AS) will lead us to the point that the problems the faithful fall into may have their roots in three things:

1. Misdeeds: sins or deeds running counter to what *shariah* enjoins

2. Sometimes deeds do not apparently run counter to *shariah*. Yet with a little thinking you will get to know that they are not to God's liking. Getting involved in such things will get you into trouble too. For example, the *shariah* says: it is the father that will have the custody of his daughter from the age of seven in case of divorce. Now if the mother is so sentimentally dependant on her daughter that separation may well traumatize her or/and her daughter, the legislator will advise against its legitimacy, which is also judicious and humane. Laws in *shariah* are sometimes too general; (it is actually impossible to pass a specific law to every individual.) However, there are exceptions in enforcing them that *shariah* has left to our common sense and keen understanding of the religion. In the case of the custody, for instance, although the care of the daughter is given to the father, the *shariah* reminds us: whoever seperates the mother from her daughter, God will separate him from his dear ones on the Day of Judgement!

Of the same nature is what befell Jacob (AS). He turned a deaf ear to the request of Themyal, the mendicant when he asked for food to break his fast. Dejected, he retreated to a corner and slept with wet eyes and empty stomach. In return God afflicted Jacob (AS) with the rueful distress of separation from his favorite and best-liked son, Joseph. Clearly, people's properties are under their own commnd, according to *shariah* and Jacob (AS) did not owe Themyal a debt. However, common sense and tender feelings of affection do "know" that this rejection did not please God and was considered some sort of sin.

---

[1] Osoul-e Kaafi, vol. 2

3. Man's imprudent negligence in non-obligatory prayers and worship may also give rise to unfortunate circumstances. The matter is evidenced by a *Hadith* by the Great Prophet of Islam (pbuh), related as well by the seventh Imam (AS). He said: sometimes a believing and faithful servant of God potentially enjoys a high and special place in the sight of God, but the quality and quantity of his good and virtuous deeds are not fit for his place, are not as much as they should be to raise him to that high position. Perforce, God makes up for this shortcoming by some vexations, by making him face irksome situations before He elevates him to the level he is worthy of (God, in fact, makes Himself indebted to him.)! Yes, although failure in addressing oneself to *Mustahabbat* and positive traditions is not sinful, one will clearly be considered remiss in one's duty in God's view. As a result he/she may encounter consequences in this world not quite favorable to him/her. There are creditable documents to back this claim.[1]

---

[1] Wasa'il al-Shia, volume 4, page 75, *Hadith* 4553

UNIT THREE
The Effects of Sufferings

1. The Factor of Soul Excelence (*Nafs*[1]).

It is a truth universally acknowledged that "*Nafs*" achieves perfection only through suffering. This is the way Allah has created us. Any course of study, art, or branch of science can be learnt to perfection through sufferance. Which specialist, artist, or man of distinction (unworldly not worldly things) have you seen who has achieved success unalloyed by suffering? Have you ever seen a scholar who has achieved scholarship without suffering? Take, for example, Aghamirza Ali Akbar Hekami Yazdi, the master of mysticism and wisdom (knowing things as they are; philosophy), a scholar on whom Imam Khomeini took pride. He says, "I studied and taught in the Islamic Seminary in Isfahan (prior to the establishment of the Seminary in Qom, Isfahan was the center of religious studies in Iran) for forty years. Meanwhile I was so busy with studying math, theology, and philosophy that I had to go without all kinds of petty enjoyment and entertainment. The only paths I knew to move along were those of the bathhouse and school." It may seem an axaggeration to live forty years in a beautiful city and trample on all heart's desires, yet this kind of life implies work and discipline to achieve goals.

A prominent academic once told me, "I did some research that was ranked number one in the province. To do that, I needed to do something more than burning the midnight oil. Actually, I had to stay up all night every night. One day, my wife who had had enough of this situation came up, a hurt look on her face, and complained, 'The fact that you are keeping an all-night vigil has become a source of discomfort not only for yourself, but also for

---

[1] The term "Nafs" in different contexts implies different things like: self, psyche, ego, and soul.

the whole family. From this time on, you should go to bed by midnight,' she threatened. Being a family man and knowing the research was usurping her time and attenion, I gave in. I would go to bed at the imposed time, and after making sure she was asleep, I would take a small desk, books and things to the bathroom. I would hang a piece of cloth over the glass bathroom window to prevent the light out and turned the bathroom into a little private study. Shrugging off drowsiness, I worked on my research till fifteen minutes to the morning Azaan. Then I would go to bed and feign sleep. My wife, not knowing I was awake, would shake me to "wakefulness". After saying my prayers, I would take a nap and report to university." "How could you manage your classes without sleep?" I asked. "It was hard but manageable." he replied. This way he accomplished the task, and getting the first rank was the fruit of his perseverance and suffering. If you think success in anything is attainable with ease, try to shake yourself free of this thought.

A successful scholar has been related to have abhored falling into deep sleep. He would like to take a few-minute nap instead, and then rise to do his job. To do so, he would place a copper tray on some mud bricks and lit a candle beneath it. When he felt sleepy, he would rest his brow on the tray. After fifteen seconds or so, the tray, that was now hot, would jar him awake.

This is the world's rule. Have you ever heard anybody say, "I was an epicurean; I just ate and drank and had more than enough sleep, and then all of a sudden, I became a religious scholar, an artist, a scientist or a champion athlete? No way. Why should we be afraid of sufferings then? Why do we shun them? Why do we make a ghoul of them? It's wrong to assume them something horrible and threatening. If we are to repulse a thing, that must be comfort! Yes, you got me right; we must repel comfort. You may stop and wonder, "The average people see happiness in money, in prestige jobs, in college degrees and such like, and break into a trot to get them. Why do you say we must avoid them?" Are people always right?

2. TheHinder of Soul Decay (*Nafs)*

What gets us into trouble in everyday life is providing comfort for the *Nafs. Nafs* is very mulish! Leave it at ease, and it will create problems. Ease and pleasure bode well neither for the *Nafs* nor for the body. If you do regular workout, you will be in shape and healthy. Remaining stationary will leave you in a state of langour. Lack of physical activity will disturb the digestive system too. May God bless the great man who said, "*Nafs*, left at ease, will decay." What do you call the people who disobey the decrees their religion issues and run after sensual desires and animalistic pleasures? "Corrupt," you might say. A "corrupt" watermelon rarely decays other watermelons because of its thick rind, but a decaying orange, for example, may well decay all the oranges in the crate if they are not separated. Some people, likewise, are corrupt. Some others are not only corrupt themselves, but they also make others corrupt. In the stagnant water of a pond, algae, maggots and worms may grow, but the running water of a river that hits the rocks and moves over them is always pure. A man, who is always in sruggle against evil, will learn how to ward off the inciting *Nafs* and ascend the steep path to perfection.

If you consider the contemporary history of developed countries with all those breakthroughs in sciece, technology, medicine, etc, you will see that all of them have left behind a period of bitter and hard condition. Development and refinement in character goes through a period of hardship too.

3. Creating The Soul Sensitive

There is no reason to shun some pains and sufferings because we need them. For example, what would you do if you woke up one morning and found your hand in a state of numbness? You touched the hot stove, but it wouldn't burn; you gave it a cut with a knife and blood poured from it, but you wouldn't feel any pain; you pierced your palm with a nail, and no wince of pain would change the expression of your face! Would it be an enjoyable experience or something to be worried about? In all probability, I think, you would see a doctor and complain about painlessness. Pain, after all, is not bad.

It's quite a fortunate thing to have a sensitive soul. It is said of the people who drink themselves into a stupor that they behave abnormally due to the effects of alcohol. It is reoprted that they might even cut the flesh off their own legs, roast it and eat it. It is only after they have sobered up that they get to know what they have done to themselves. People who have made themselves insensitive to others' pains and sufferings do the same thing to themselves; on the Day of Reckoning, when the reality of our conduct and deeds dawns on us, they appear as limbless bodies. The angels, then, address them, "This is what you have done to yourselves." Yes, some pains are pernicious and must be killed as soon as possible. However, it is wrong to look for ways to blot out every kind of pain. Without some pains man will fall down from his state of humanity. If people's deprivation does not make you feel pain, you are not human. If you see that in a certain country some Muslims, or even non-Muslims, are hopeless, depressed, and starved, that in Palestine babies are born deformed, dangerously underweight, and anaemic, yet you remain unsympathetic, you have plunged into the pit of inhumanity. A mere feeling of sorrow for such people will be rewarded in the Hereafter because it is a sign of perfection.

The owner of a photographer's studio once said: before the Islamic Revolution when studios were not as equipped as they are now, a very old teacher with wrinkles all around his eyes and forehead came in for a picture. In order to make it look better and younger I carefully retouched the picture and cleared away every other wrinkle. After a few days he came for it. When I showed it to him, looking forward to a word of appreciation, he looked at it with eyes dilated with surprise and said, "Who is this?" "This is you, sir." I said. He took a look at his image in the mirror on the wall and said annoyed, "But my face is full of wrinkles and crow feet. Where are they?" "I have omitted some of them to make your skin look rejuvenated, sir." "You shouldn't have done that; they are the outcome of lifelong experiences. I want them back on my photo." he retorted. I worked on it again for some time. When he returned and saw it, he said, "Oh yeah, this is me." A smile of contentment appeared on his lips.

In the book "*Baran-e Hekmat*[1]" (The rain of Wisdom) Mohammad Reza Ranjbar, while relating the story of Hadhrat Yusof (AS), draws an eye-opening analogy between what Satan and a dentist do on human body. The dentist gives the patient a shot of anaesthetic. While the patient is unable to feel anything, he starts treating his tooth. He removes the decayed tooth material by drilling, cleans the affected area, and then fills the cleaned out cavity with a filling material. Satan does the same thing. First, he anaesthetises the heart and the mind with shots of lust and passion. Then he starts his drill work on the mind, heart and religion of his victim, and leaves a lot of cavities there like a piece

---

[1] Compiled by Hujjat al-Islam wal-muslimin Muhammad Reza Ranjbar

of wood eaten by a termite colony, but he never cleans the affected areas. All these things are done without the victim being aware what is going on. When the effects of the drug wear off in the Hereafter, it will dawn on him that he is quite helpless because he has no limbs.

قَالَ رَبِّ لِمَ حَشَرْتَنِى أَعْمَى وَقَدْ كُنتُ بَصِيرًا [1]

"He will say: 'O my Lord! Why hast Thou raised me up blind, while I had sight (before)?'"

قَالَ كَذَلِكَ أَتَتْكَ آيَاتُنَا فَنَسِيتَهَا وَكَذَلِكَ الْيَوْمَ تُنسَى [2]

Allah will say: "Thus didst thou, when our signs came unto thee, forgot them: so wilt thou, this day be forgotten."

Satan blinded him, but he didn't sense it. Moreover, he used to make fun of those who were deeply pained by the pain of others and call them names like: superstitious, jealous, etc. He even made fun of their chastity and tried to instil in them that being chaste was an encumbrance to them. He used to ask them to get rid of their chastity as one tries to get rid of pain in a painful situation, to get rid of one's sensory nerves, whereas it is bliss to have a fellow feeling. If a fellow in a corner of this wide world feels embittered, his embitterment diffuses rapidly in all directions and affects those who care. The waves of a mobile phone leave no effect on a tree or a brick. A tree does not ring upon receiving the waves of a mobile phone because it lacks the wherewithal to do so, but another cell phone does. Sad waves of pure hearts are spread everywhere; it takes a sympathising heart, not any heart, to receive them. Those who are callous to the pains of others do

---

[1] Taha, *Ayah* 125
[2] same, *Ayah* 126

not perceive these things until God makes them understand in the Hereafter when, alas, it's too late.

4. The Factor of Motiontoward Perfection

Some sufferings are sacred and are capable of sublimating man to the highest degree of human perfection. Allah, all praise and glory be to Him, addresses His Prophet (pbuh):

$$\text{لَعَلَّكَ بَاخِعٌ نَّفْسَكَ أَلَّا يَكُونُوا مُؤْمِنِينَ}\,^{1}$$

"It may be thou will kill thy self with grief, that they do not become believers."

Who does the Prophet (pbuh) grieve over? For a handful of Makkan pagans as why they could not be brought to believe in the Truth.

$$\text{لَقَدْ جَاءَكُمْ رَسُولٌ مِّنْ أَنفُسِكُمْ عَزِيزٌ عَلَيْهِ مَا عَنِتُّمْ حَرِيصٌ عَلَيْكُم بِالْمُؤْمِنِينَ رَؤُوفٌ}$$
$$\text{رَّحِيمٌ}\,^{2}$$

"Now hath come unto you a Messenger from amongst yourselves: it grieves him that you should suffer, ardently anxious is he over you: to the Believers is he most kind and merciful."

Allah, all praises and glory be to Him, here says: it grieves him that you should suffer. He praises His Prophet (pbuh) for not being indifferent to humans. Believers do no even afford to be indifferent to animals. They have feeling and sympathy for their sufferings, let alone be cruel to them. You won't like it if somebody flicks you on the cheek with his finger because your cheek is sensitive to even the slightest blows. If somebody gives the back of your hand a little prick with a needle, you will readily feel it because your skin is sensitive. Is this bad? That is excellent. Then if your soul is hurt

---

[1]   Ash-Shuara, *Ayah* 3
[2]   At-Taubah, *Ayah* 128

and you don't feel it is sick.it is problematic. Each horse in a stable minds its own manger. None of them thinks, "Now that I am eating from my full manger, do the other horses have anything to eat or not?" This kind of thought is meaningless to a beast. If man, likewise, minded his own stomach and became heedless of other people's starvation, then what would be the difference between him and a brute?

There was a man who, instead of saying grace after eating, would say: O God, now that I am no longer hungry, let all the hungry people die! Well, selfishness knows no bounds. A stingy person used to say to some other fellows like him: I find it too hard to share what I eat with other people. Actually, I feel I'm dying if I do so! His fellow companion said: I feel I'm giving up life to see somebody sharing food with somebody else! A third stingy person retorted: lucky you two! I cannot even stand seeing anybody eating his own food! I will die of grief!

If you go up to a *Marja Taqlid* and say that you are informed that on the other side of the world some land animals as well as the marine life are in danger and you have considerable expertise in dealing with the problem and that you know how to save them and then ask him what your religious duty is, he will say, "It behooves you to go and save them." What do we live for if we do not try to lesson pains and sufferings of others? This is a good sense to have. Otherwise, you would be in the dangerous state of numbness that even touching the hot stove would make you feel nothing. Painlessness is a great pain itself. Far be it from us!

These are spiritual attainments to be reached. Allah, all praises and glory be to Him, has told the Seal of the Prophets, the pick of creatures (pbuh):

«وَإِن كَانَ كَبُرَ عَلَيْكَ إِعْرَاضُهُمْ فَإِنِ اسْتَطَعْتَ أَن تَبْتَغِىَ نَفَقًا فِى الأَرْضِ أَوْ سُلَّمًا فِى السَّمَاءِ فَتَأْتِيَهُم بِآيَةٍ...» [1]

"If their spurning is hard on thee, yet if thou wert able to seek a tunnel in the ground or a ladder to the skies and bring them a Sign, (do it to convince them.)" As if Allah wants to mention there were many Signs of a divine mission in the Prophet's life and in the Message that he delivered. If these did not convince the Unbelievers, was it not vain to seek a miraculous Sign from the bowels of the earth or by a visible ascent to the skies?

When the earthquake seizes the Madyan people and finishes them at night, Hadhrat Shu'aib (AS) laments:

«...فَكَيْفَ آسَى عَلَى قَوْمٍ كَافِرِينَ» [2]

"But how shall I lament over a people who refuse to believe!"

Yet, he laments. There were too many cases in which different prophets (AS) cursed their people. Then the wrath of God came upon those refractory people and they were annihilated. And then God said to the prophets, "You made Satan, the enemy of my bondsmen, rejoice." When Hadhrat Yunus (AS) was disgorged onto the shore, Allah caused a plant of gourd to grow over him in his state of mental and physical lassitude so as to protect him from the heat of the sun. He was refreshed and strengthened. After a few days the plant withered and died. Hadhrat Yunus (AS) started to cry. Then Allah revealed to him saying: O Yunus! Why are you grief-stricken? He replied: My Lord! This plant was benefitting me. But now, as you can see, it has dried out. Allah said, "Oh Yunus, you cry for the death of a single plant, but you did not worry for a hundred thousand of my bondsmen? (I love my

---

[1] Al-Anaam, *Ayah* 35
[2] Al-Araf, *Ayah* 93

servants)." Then Allah admonished Yunus for not showing enough affection toward servants.

Sensitivity of the soul is one of the features of any believing Muslim. With it you are never at ease or settled. You are always worried about others. However, let's not forget that any bit of sadness you feel for others won't go unrewarded. So it is not to be afraid of because it does not cause any obstacle on the way to sublimity. On the other hand, let's not be bothered by a lack or shortage of what we think is the wherewithal of a comfortable life. This kind of want is good for self refinement. Living in want and fairly poor living conditions will, at least, make a little future comfort taste much sweeter, but a change from comfort to extra comfort has not only little or no effect on the palate, but it also makes sufferings look more acute.

Let's Not Be Afraid of All Sufferings

It was mentioned that sufferings and shortcomings, especially the worldly ones, would generally lead to perfection. In the past, when a seminarian, a student at the theological seminary, needed a book, he would probably have to rent a quadruped to take him to somebody to the other side of town whom he thought to have possessed the book in question, curry favour with him and pay him in order to have it for a few days. If the owner accepted to lend him the book, then he needed to promise to take utmost care of it lest it be damaged, torn or something. After he was done with it, he had to repeat the not-too-easy trip to return the book. Nowadays, the story is quite different. If you have a laptop with a DVD, you have a small or an average size library. Push a couple of buttons, and the needed reading material will be at your disposal. In return, forsooth, minds are getting lazier and lazier. In those days the pressure of want would make the student learn the entire book down pat and thus optimize the use of scanty resourses, because how many times could he go through the time-consuming, tortuous process of borrowing the book?

May God bless late Mr. Aboutorabi! He is told to have said that when Grand Ayatollah Khoei taught the highest-level classes (*darse kharej*) he would say everything from memory. He wouldn't take any notes with him to class.

It is said of Abu Jafar Mohammad Ibn Hassan known as Shaykh Tusi, "I know all the sourses of Shiite Jurisprudence by heart. Even if they were all to be cast into the sea, I would write them all over again." Wow, what memory! Now, if you snatch the lesson plan from some professors they cannot manage to keep teaching.

The students of a class go to the professor and ask him to call off the class for some reason, but the professor insists on holding the class that very same hour. As the dicussion over having or not having the class is heated, one of them slips his hand into the teacher's pocket and takes his notes. A few minutes later all the students are allowed to head for home happily!

Facilities of all kinds are everywhere, but memories are deteriorating. Why? You simply say, "The material is here on hand. Why do I have to commit it to memory?" Ironically, facilities are counterproductive. Since they are there at any moment, we assume we are entitled to use them. Whereas, going without some facilities will make you exert yourself in order to be successful.

«اذا احَبَّ الله عَبداً غَتّه بالبَلاء غتّاً» [1]

"In order to show affection to His bondsman, Allah indulges him in tribulation."

---

[1] Osoul-e Kaafi, vol. 2, page 253

In that case man's potentialities start to develop. An upside of sufferings is the strong sense of compensation. In other words one will say: now that this problem is raised, I need to do something to make up for it.

5. Suffering Will Make a Man from You.

A friend of mine, an Arab electrician from Khuzestan province, who is a released prisoner of war, once said, "I had been repeatedly eletrocuted by the domestic power supply voltage while working in different buildings. As a result, my body became shock resistant after several cases. From then on, I threw caution to the winds and I got more and more shocks. Then the war broke out and I went to the front. Not too long, and I was held captive by Iraqi soldiers. Once in captivity, I did something that was considered a breach of law by them, so they took me for electric shocks. Iraqis had recently used electric shocks as a method of torture, which caused tremendous horror among the prisoners. They would repeatedly ask the Iraqis to lash them instead, but their supplications would always fall on deaf ears. Anyway, they attached the electrodes to my ear lobes and switched the machine on. Electricity tickled me a bit, and I started to laugh. The soldier, thinking the machine wasn't working properly, manipulated the levers and knobs of the machine and delivered the shock again. I said, "It works." "But...you... feel no pain?" he asked. "Nope." I said. He stood there scratching his head, wondering how to torture me. A very low power supply voltage, say 12, is enough to jerk an average person. One who is away from any kind of sufferings cannot stand the slightest one.

Sa'di, the well-known Iranian poet, in *Gulistan*, narrates the story of two men who were convicted by mistake and sent to prison. One, a hearty eater by nature, the other one, an indigent who had a scanty meal once in two three days, if any. After seven eight days, they found they had made a mistake and went to the prison to release them. The greedy one had given up the ghost, but the poor man had sat there hale and hearty. Sa'di then says:

Tandoor of the belly to the tail,

It was a tragedy o miss the day.

It was for eating, but in other matters, the story is more or less the same too. If you have your *Nafs* (self) get used to comfort, it will make your life a misery when the shoe is on the other foot. Tolerating the not-too-good new situation might be too hard to survive. Therefore, let's not think that all good things come to those who live in pleasure, but, of course, it does not mean bringing yourself misery on purpose, which is tantamount to committing suicide for fear of getting sick. Both attitudes are wrong.

Not Every Kind of Suffering Will Make a Man from You

There are too many people who suffer idly. They spend their precious time on acquiring knowledge, art, and skill which benefits neither themselves nor the society. Once Amir al-mu'minin, peace be upon him, was proceeding towards al-Anbar. It did the heart of the countrymen of al-Anbar, who were near Persia, good to see Amir al-mu'minin and began to stomp. To welcome somebody, Arabs stamp one foot heavily and noisily down and raise the opposite hand up in a rhythmic manner called *Yazla*. If the ground is covered with dust, this rhythmic movement will raise a lot of dust up into the air. The countrymen of Al-anbar did it upon meeting Amir al-mu'minin (AS). He enquired why they were doing so and they replied:

«فَقَالُوا خُلُقٌ مِنَّا نُعَظِّمُ بِهِ أُمَرَاءَنَا» [1]

"This is the way we respect our chiefs."

---

[1]   Nahjul Balagha, wise Saying 37

Then he said:

«وَ اللهِ مَا يَنْتَفِعُ بِهَذَا أُمَرَاؤُكُمْ، وَ إِنَّكُمْ لَتَشْقُّونَ عَلَى أَنْفُسِكُمْ فِى دُنْيَاكُمْ، وَ تَشْقَوْنَ بِهِ فِى آخِرَتِكُمْ»

"By Alllah, this does not benefit your chiefs. You are belabouring yourselves in this world and earning misery for the next world by it."

Then he said something very interesting:

«وَ مَا أَخْسَرَ الْمَشَقَّةَ وَرَاءَهَا الْعِقَابُ، وَ أَرْبَحَ الدَّعَهَ مَعَهَا الْأَمَانُ مِنَ النَّارِ»

"How harmful is the labour in whose wake there is punishment and how profitable is the case with which there is deliverance from the Fire (of Hell)."

The Imam (AS) is, in fact, saying that what you do is an unjust hardship. If no advantage can be reaped from the hardships you are suffering, they must be removed from your life and replaced by those that are worth your while. People of sagacity, belief and piety face hardships. Similarly, rogues, scoundrels, and scamps suffer hardships too. A drug addict may suffer for not taking any drugs, but a man of God may suffer for failing to render a service or assistance to somebody. A fellow sinner had decided to commit a sin. The opportunity came and went and he failed to commit it. Years later, when he was breathing his last, kith and kin got around his deathbed and asked him to recite, "I bear witness that there is no god to be worshiped but Allah," instead, he recited a poem expressing regret for failing to commit that sin! We are enjoined not to regret over worldly concerns like economic and business failure. On the other hand, any sadness we encounter in the way of God will bring heavenly reward.

6. Transforming Suffering to Treasure

We are not supposed, of course, to escape sufferings, nor are we supposed to seek the panacea for comfort. This is a downright wrong attitude, for it is God's convention that the way to perfection should be through sufferings, voluntary sufferings, those we choose to go through with love rather than unwanted bad ones that involuntarily befall us. After all, isn't the world a place to suffer?

Successful people are those who make a ladder of sufferings to move up to perfection. In other words, these people can manage to change threats to opportunities. For example, during the Iraqi imposed war we made use of the intelligence the enemy had, even the spies they had appointed, to our own advantage. When it turned out that such and such a person was a secret agent, we would leave him alone to do what he wanted to do. However, we would give him burnt out or wrong intelligence, which get the Iraqis into trouble. We made the informer, in reality, work for us rather than work for them.

A Man of Exemplary Character

An Iranian teenager was taken captive by the Ba'ath Party at the age of seventeen. When he was set free after the war he was twenty seven. He was so highly motivated that late Mr. Aboutorabi commended him for half an hour. In captivity, he was always busy studying and learning. One of his achievements was memorizing the Holy Quran. I was his boon companion for years. One Ramadhan, he recited the Holy Quran forty five times from beginning to end by heart. He trained a hundred reciters. His command of the Quran was so good that he knew how many times each word was repeated, where and in which *Surah*. Which *Ayah* has the least and which has the most number of letters. Once to test him, a number of friends got together and started to barrage him with questions about the Quranic words (not interpretation). To their amazement, not a single question was left unanswered. They even asked him in which *Ayah* the letter "k", for example, is repeated most. He recited the Quran completely with Persian translation. If you asked him to recite it in English or French translation, he would eloquently do.

And yet there was another captive sitting in a corner lamenting why this should have happened to him. Sadness had taken its toll on him and given him grey hair prematurely! The one above had turned an extremely bad situation into an opportune chance, and this one, in order to avoid suffering would suffer more. Let's try, at all times, to manage to lever sufferings against themselves and prevail upon them. This is the way to achieve perfection. There is no condition in which one cannot make sufferings, even those that appear to be deadlocks, a means to perfection. Islam is here to teach us this same lesson. There are many examples in which the man made the suffering a way to his perfection.

A Second Man of Exemplary Character

A released prisoner of war, a friend, related, "A whole year in captivity had given me grey hair, so I went to the Red Cross clinic to see a specialist. He said, 'Go praise God that it is just your hair not your head, or you have to undergo amnesia. The only thing you can do is to somehow get rid of this suffering.' 'My heart is not here. It is in my beloved country. Soul and body are separated. No matter how hard I try, I cannot get them together,' I said. 'Engage yourself in something,' he proposed. 'How am I supposed to? My mind is already engaged 18-19 hours a day,' I retorted. 'You will perish this way. You need to find a way out of it,' he said. I thought I was interested in English. So I began to study English, although I knew it no more than a student in grade eight. The more I studied, the more interested I was until I found myself studying 18 hours a day. After the war I went to an institute to apply for teaching. They asked me what my graduation degree was. I said I was in grade 8. They laughed at me, thinking I had escaped from the giggle-house. They asked, 'What is the meaning of 'This is a book.'?' I gave them the meaning. They gave me a round of applause and said mockingly, 'Bravo! You are just the one we need.' And then they asked some more questions. They were very happy to have found an "idiot" to make fun of. I maintained a straight face though and wanted them to ask more difficult questions. 'We will. Just you wait,' one of them said. Then they asked about the meaning of a difficult word and I gave them the definition as Oxford dictionary had defined it. They were amazed and asked a lot more questions. When I gave true answers to all of them, they apologised and consented to have me as a teacher where I am still teaching."

If you now ask this man what has proved to be the greatest boon to him, he will certainly answer, "Captivity, which I most dreaded." There were too many people who were consigned to suffer, but instead of sitting and grieving over what had befallen them, they sought to find a way out of it and turn it to a means to perfection.

A Third Man of Exemplary Character

I had the honour to meet a mystic and enquire about something. In response he alluded to Sheikh Abu al-Hassan al-Kharaqani, a great mystic, and said, "Someone, who later on becomes his disciple, goes from town to town to meet him. He eventually arrives in the town he lives and finds his house. To his surprise he finds no guards placed about the house. He lifts the knocker and lets go of it. A woman hears the bang and opens the door of the ramshackle house. 'Is it Sheikh Kharaqani's house?' he asks. 'If you mean the impostor, he headed that way,' she says angrily. 'Why do you insult him?' he objects. 'I know my spouse well enough. He is a trickster and...' 'That's enough. I don't need his nicknames. Only tell me where he is gone,' he says in wonder and dismay. Not believing his ears, he goes off in the direction she points her finger. On the way, when he is wondering if this uncouth woman really is his better half, he suddenly spots a man hitching a ride on a lion, flogging its flank with a snake! At first, he gets frightened, but then seeing the Sheikh riding the lion, he rests asured that these beasts are under his command and cannot hurt him. When they get closer, he says, 'O Sheikh, I came here so you could satisfy my need. However, after seeing your wife, I'd rather not talk about my requirement. What a woman! May I daresay why you don't divorce her? Wave after wave of invectives poured out of her mouth. A man of your caliber and such miracles why should have married such a shrew in the first place?' 'She is not bad,' he says smiling. 'What do you mean she is not bad?' he asks. 'All the miracles Allah has bestowed upon me are because I supressed the natural instinct to complain, whether the vexation on her part was trivial or grave.'" As Hafiz says:

From this garden you don't pick any roses for yourself
Because of the thorns that now you avoid and degrade.

A Better Exemplary Character

After the Tragedy of Ashura Sayyidah Zaynab and her companions were taken to Ubayd Allah ibn Ziyad's place where he addressed Zaynab,

«اَلحَمدُلله الَّذى فَضَحكُم و قَتَلَكُم و اكذَبَ اُحدُوثَتَكُم»[1]

"Praise be to God who disgraced you, killed you, and belied your myth."

To which she responded:

«مَا رَأَيتُ اِلَّا جَميلاً»[2]

"I saw nothing except the beauty of God."

---

[1] Al-Irshad (Shaykh Mufid), vol. 2, page 115
[2] Al-Lohoof, page 160

She didn't merely want to take Ubayd Allah down a peg or two. What she said was rooted in her deep-seated faith. This is actually the way any believing Muslim looks at life's hardships. Allah in His Scripture says:

$$«فَإِنَّ مَعَ الْعُسْرِ يُسْرًا * إِنَّ مَعَ الْعُسْرِ يُسْرًا»^{1}$$

"So, verily, with every difficulty, there is relief: Verily, with every difficulty there is relief." You need to look for that relief. You are able to see the relief in medicine in your mind's eye. You say to yourself, "I tolerate the bitter taste of the medicine because relief is in its wake." you know that relief follows taking the medicine because you have experienced it times and times before, but relief in hardships is not as tangible. □□□□ □□□□□□□» «□□□□□□□ □□□□□□□□□, Apparently, the definite article in *"al-'usr"* is used in a generic sense and includes every difficulty. That is to say, Allah always provides a solution, a way out, a relief, a way to lead to ease and happiness.

Imam Ali (AS) says:

$$«وَ مَن ضُيِّقَ عَلَيه فِى ذَاتِ يَدِه، فَلَم يَرَ ذَلِكَ اختِبَاراً فَقَد ضَيَّعَ مَأمُولاً»^{٢}$$

"He who is afflicted with strained circumstances but does not perceive them as a trial will lose the coveted reward."

Therefore, sufferings do not matter a flip of the finger if they are looked at as God's presents and great boons. More often than not frustrations will bring talents that had lied dormant up to surface. Sometimes smaller setbacks you encounter in everyday life will have you find a way out of bigger and more serious ones. If you pour some gas oil on the ground and set it on fire, it takes some time before it starts to burn. Moreover, it burns very slowly and

---

[1] Al-Inshirah, *Ayah*s 5-6
[2] Nahjul Balagha, wise Saying 358

with a lot of smoke. And then when it is burnt completely it leaves a black stain on the ground. However, if you pour the same amount of gas oil into the tank of a truck with a twenty ton cargo, a few drops of it injected into the combustion chamber produces such a power that it moves the truck through a mountain pass, because the drops of gas oil are compressed in the limitted space of the cylinders. Are we aware of our talents? When left out of pressure, we burn incompletely and smoke, and think this is all what we are. By imposing sufferings on us, God seems to want to say: Oh my creature, you don't know what you are; you are not aware of your own capacity. Let me put you in a limited space and then you will see how powerful you are.

A Point

A fault we are blind to is the fact that we sometimes plunge into a permanent and real suffering for fear of an imagined one that we might come across in the future.

I asked a martial artist, who had decided not to go to the gym any longer, why he had stopped practicing. He said he had found it silly: all the jumping around. I asked if it was not good for self-defence. He said, "Sure it was, but the problem was that other practitioners and I were pitted against each other in combats and I was hit by opponents every day. So I thought to myself if I don't learn self-defence, I may or may not get hit by somebody in the street, but if I go to the gym I get hit every day." Many of the things we do are like this: for fear of probable future sufferings we get ourselves into real ones.

A similar case occurs in our families where a particular personality trait of a family member is not to our liking. Instead of turning a blind eye to it we start criticising, and the target member tries to throw the blame off himself. The outcome of all this is the spoiled mood and suffering of all for a personality trait which is kept at bay and may never get unveiled. The Holy Quran says some sufferings are our own deeds. Therefore, let's indulge in neither useless sufferings nor complete comfort.

«...وَسَطًا أُمَّةً جَعَلْنَاكُمْ كَذَلِكَ وَ»; [1]**"Thus have We made of you an *Ummat* justly balanced." The essence of Islam is to avoid all extravagances on either side.**

7. Suffering Strengthens Determination

A direct result of suffering is strengthening one's will power. Like Hindu ascetics who through self-discipline, austerities, and self-mortification practices can gain spiritual perfection, attain steely determination, and perfom extraordinary things. Comfort, on the other hand, weakens the will. Abstinence from *Mubah* (neutral) sensual pleasures is a way to achieve amazing spiritual powers. Great personalities and mystics, for the purpose of pursuing spiritual perfection would ban their selves (*Nafs*) from *Makruhat* (detestable deeds) and *Mubah* pleasures and make *Mustahabbat* (recommended deeds) incumbent upon themselves. This is a rule of thumb. If you look at sufferings from this angle, not only won't they look frightening, but you will receive them with open arms.

Somebody had to have his leg amputated. A team of six, seven physicians had decided there was no other way, yet a Yazdi physician in two, three sessions performed bloodletting on him and it worked. Many incurable diseases are treated by bloodletting. If you take a kid to the doctor's office with all those bloodletting instruments, he will be scared and may cry, yet you go there on your own and pay the doctor to take something out of your body, your blood. Or you take a saw and start pruning a tree. The tree suffers, but it does not know it will make it grow better and stronger. This is the case with man too. Sometimes God cuts off our branches. It hurts, so we say, "What's going on?" not

---

[1] Al-Baqara, *Ayah* 143

knowing this is the way to achieve perfection. We need to change our outlook. Amir al-mu'minin, peace be upon him, said:

«مَرَارَةُ الدُّنيا حَلَاوَةُ الآخِرَه و حَلَاوَةُ الدُّنيا مَرَارَةُ الآخِرَه» [1]

"The sourness of This World is the sweetness of the Next World while the sweetness of This World is the sourness of the Next One."

Even the *Mubah* sweetness that God bestows on us will diminish a part of our good deeds. So we say on the Resurection Day, "I wish sweetness had not been given to us."

Hedonistic Man!

A point that was discussed before was that we tend to look at sufferings in negative terms. Of course, sufferings belong to different categories, some of which cause deficiencies. Undoubtedly, the Self (*Nafs*) seeks comfort, enjoyment, and pleasure in all conditions. Nobody likes the summer's fierce heat; everybody likes to sit in the shade and keeps cool. Nobody likes to have an ugly companion. Or if you are told that there is a bakery that makes delicious but more expensive bread, you will head for it even if you have to walk a few kilometers, rain or shine, to get tastier bread. This is what we mean by hedonism. Why is man like this? Because he is a being given to attracting whatever is compatible with his Self and repelling whatever is incompatible with it. Does it always benefit the Self? Does it always lead to our well-being if we court the Self's dalliance? This is an issue that almost everybody in the world is misguided about. No crime against the Self is more serious than giving the passion free rein when it dictates something because each time you consent to answer the Self's request a part of your personality will be demolished. We fail; unfortunately, to notice that each time we

---

[1] Nahjul Balagha, wise Saying 251

give the Self the cold shoulder something good is added to our personality.

What should an athlete do to increase overal muscle mass? Trainers believe that in order to have stronger and bigger muscles you need to exert yourself until the muscles are sore. It is only when they are painful they start to increase in size. That is to say, you won't have a perfect body unless you put it under pressure. Have you ever heard anybody say, "I was well-fed and had more than enough sleep for a good many years in a five-star hotel and by the time I left it I had become a football superstar?" By the same token, the soul won't achieve any perfection if it is not under pressure. As a matter of fact a man's real personality has nothing to do with his body. Some learned men are scarcely more than forty kilos, but they are capable of managing the whole world. The late Allameh Tabataba'i was one from whom great men of knowledge, wisdom and philosophy were humble enough to learn and find answers to their intricate questions.

As the body grows when the conditions are met and shrivels when they are not, man's real personality or disposition, with which he should live eternally in the Hereafter, grows in some conditions and deteriorates in some others. Yet, the effects of his disposition are manifest in his behavior, deeds, and talks. As an example, let me cite Imam Khomeini's personality. Are you able to imagine his personality in your mind's eye? What did he have? Did he have military might, cannons and tanks? The former Soviet Foreign Minister, Eduard Shevardnadze had told Mr Larijani after meeting with Imam, "Sir, I have been a full-fledged diplomat and Foreign Minister for thirty years, yet I didn't know what would become of me when I got embarrassed. I had never tasted it before, but I was at a loss today in front of your leader!"

What made him awestruck? Imam used to wear plain garb. Was he impressed by his beard and turban? These were the things some others wore too. Or was he overawed by his humble adobe abode? What impressed and embarrassed him was Imam's personality. The question is: how does personality grow stronger and what may degrade it? What can sap personality's strength is providing the Self with what it desires. Do you give your kid whatever he wants? Any kind of food he likes?

The Self is like a sick person and we are like nurses. A good nurse, afraid for her patient, never feeds him to his heart's content. If she does, difficulties crop up at every step. It is a big mistake to think that well-being lies in getting what you wish for.

Necessity of Recognising the Self's Rights

As I said before most of the problems arise from paying undue attention to the Self. All the same, the Self is entitled to some enjoyments. Imagine someone saying, "I get pleasure from breathing, yet to face my Self down, I won't breathe!" What will happen to him? He will, doubtless, choke to death. The Self is quite within its rights to have some gratification. We humans, for example, love our children instinctively. We like to hug and caress them. Nevertheless, is it right to deny ourselves this right in the name of religion? Never is it. We are not allowed to shut ourselves off from pleasures entirely.

However, ascetics deny themselves many things and manage to mould different wonderful characters in themselves. In all probability you have heard that one of them had stopped a moving train by gazing at it. Another one had closed one eye and said he would never open it. Another had said he would stay silent for fifteen years to come. After that period of time, when people had gathered around him, he said he had come to conclusion not to speak for life. And yet a fourth one had clenched his fist and vowed not to open it, and he didn't until his nails had grown through his palm to the back of his hand.

Man has wonderful abilities. In the Next World they show these abilities to us by comparison. They show us a sea and tell us, "This sea was your abilities, but you didn't use it to capacity, actually you used only a drop of it and wasted the rest." But how do our abilities go to waste? They simply go to waste when the Self's desires are fulfilled. Take a look at the ascetics' lives. If what they do seems unbelieveable to us, it's only because we are too weak. A teenage boy sits in a hollow tree trunk for six months. He neither eats nor sleeps. He undergoes evacuation of the soul, an experience in which the soul is independent of the body.

Ayatollah Hassan Ali Nokhodaki's master asks him: why are you so pale and anaemic? He answers: master, I have had nothing for eleven days. The master says: "You have gone without eating for only eleven days and you look so pale and drawn? Even if you hadn't eatten for forty days, it shouldn't have given you such a white complexion." I don't want to say it's necessary to do these things. What I mean to say is how far one's Self can progress through a simple and strict way of living. The ascetic, for instance, holds his Self under pressure, bears it a grudge, stops catering for it, and manages to control it. Islam, nevertheless, doesn't approve of them living such a life that leads to a cul-de-sac. Nor does it approve of athletes who receive dangerous shots in order to have large stiff muscles in no time, but go infertile instead or suffer kidney failure. You think they are Rostam Zal (a legendary Iranian hero) by the look of them, but in reality they suffer a lot of sicknesses. None of these two methods are approved by Islam; it's an undeniable fact, however, that if the Self is kept on a leash, it will grow stronger. As Imam Ali (AS) states:

«اَلرُّشدُ فی خِلافِ الشَّهوَه» ١

"Growth lies in curbing *Shahwat*."

Shawat does not mean physical desire. *Shahwat* is defined as excessive desire. Any kind of desire is not called *Shahwat*. It must be beyond ordinary and very great in degree. Like excessive desire for overeating or excessive desire for a senior position. If you are able to contain your Self, you will gradually feel that it is completely harnessed. Then even when you are wrathful, you are capable of keeping a civil tongue in your head. In that case your tongue cannot, like a mulish horse, take you uncontrollably here and there until the dust settles, then sitting somewhere regretting what you have said.

Instructions in Islam Concerning the Self's Growth

In one regard, there are three spheres in *Ahkam* (practical laws):

The first sphere is that of *Moharramat*: they are the acts that are forbidden to the Self. For instance, the Self asks you to tell a lie, but you are to abstain from it, or you will be punished.

The second sphere is where it is incumbent (*Wajib*) upon you to give the Self what it wants. The Self asks for food, for example, and you should feed it. It asks you to kiss your child, and you should obey. Narratives say this act of yours will be rewarded in the next world. The Self, therefore, is entitled to a series of enjoyments, and one's perfection is rooted in their fulfilment.

Between these two spheres, though, there is a third wide sphere called *Mubah* or *Mustahab*. If you stick to what is *Wajib* and *Mustahab* and refrain from doing *Moharramat*, the least that will happen is that you won't go to Hell. But you won't achieve mysterious high positions. (By observing these points, of course,

---

1   Tuhaf al-Uqul, page 214

you will attain good enough positions that belong to veracious, honest believers: your prayers will be answered, and your breath will be sacred among other achievements). You will have special improvement, however, if you look at *Mustahabbat* as *Wajibat*. (Somebody had asked: how come the learned men of old would enjoy more Self-perfection than the contemporary ones? A scholar answered: that's because they considered *Mustahabbat* as obligatory as *Wajibat* and looked at *Makruhat* as abominable as *Muharramat*. This outlook will exert pressure on the Self and causes growth.

The Self always wants more; it is never satisfied. You have a motorcycle, for instance, and you wish you had a cheap car. Not too long after that, you buy one. Soon your Self recognizes that it does not have an air conditioning system. So you change it with one that has that system. A few days after that, you find out that it isn't equipped with Anti-Locking Braking System. So you buy a car that has it. And then a lack of other safty featurres like air bags will be matters of concern. And the story goes on and on until you see that you are driving a high model car but still have your eye on other people's vehicles. Where does the Self stop? What do you think will satisfy it? The point is it will stop at nothing. *Nafs-e Ammara* is like a little kid who knows nothing. If you ask him to take the medicine, he begrudges because it tastes yucky, he says. If you hold the picky kid and squirt the yucky, bitter medication into his cheek, he will gradually get used to it. Then as he grows up, he won't avoid taking medicine because he is now able to think in a sensible and logical way. As Maulavi says:

Being that my Lord be filled with elation,

I'm an ardent lover of my pain and passion.

Who can love suffering? The one free from want who has attained enough spiritual growth. One who has a troublesome cyst on his face goes to the doctor and says, "Pierce the cyst with a scalpel, doctor. I know I will suffer, but I don't mind." He pays for the small surgical operation too. Do you think he loves suffering? Not at all. He has no other choice to get rid of this nuisance.

As a matter of fact, there is no way to good save the one via suffering. Therefore, it stands to reason not to flee from it. Don't worry if you fall into suffering because your Self is being rectified. The more the Self rolls in enjoyment, the weaker your will power becomes, and your personality gets powerless, lowly, and abject. In all probability, you have seen wise, mature people behaving in an insensible way like crying over unimportant things. Their personality is nothing short of that of children because it is kids who sart crying when you take something away from them.

A released prisoner of war who is a friend of mine related some of his experiences to me: there were some captives who had given everything for their belief, and they were happy and smiling. Yet there was a civilian who didn't say his prayers because he believed in nothing. Somebody had told him in jest, "This captivity may last five to ten years." All of a sudden he burst into tears. I asked him what was the cry for, and he said, "Do you mean I cannot even drink a coke for the years to come?" There was another fellow, however, who was informed that a missile had hit his house and all of his family members had fallen martyrs, and he showed remarkable endurance.

Our personality needs "*Riadha*" to grow, which means tolerating the suffering. In Arabic lexicon the word "*Riadha*" means athletics. There is a chapter in Avicenna's five-volume medical encyclopedia, The *Canon of Medicine*: (*Al-Qanun fit-Tibb*), entitled: "Kitabu-Al-Riadha", which is exclusively about athletic movements. Mathematics in Arabic is also called *Riadhi* because it exercises the brain in order to do a problem. In Asceticism or spiritual exercise (*Riadhat-e Nafs*), the Self needs to be put under pressure (*Shari'a* must prescribe the method) to achieve the aim. Now, what are we supposed to do? We are not to abide by what the Self dictates: we should find out whether or not what it desires is according to *Shari'a* (it shouldn't cross the red line). As Imam Ali (AS) has asserted:

«الْمَالُ مَادَّةُ الشَّهَوَاتِ» '

"Wealth is the fountain head of passions."

A wealthy man may well say, "Now that I am made of money, I can do what I want to do: I can drive any car I want, I can live in any house I wish, and I can splash out if I want. I fail to see the logic behind this argument. I think this attitude is treacherous not only to himself but also to his family. "I'm in the money," is similar to saying: since my car runs up to 250 kilometers, I want to step on the gas. Is it logical? What about traffic regulations? It's true that your car is fast, but the mandated maximum speed is 120. A police officer stops a driver for speeding, "Why were you driving at the speed of 200 kilometers per hour?" "I've bought this car to enjoy driving at breakneck speed," the violater retorts. Money does not entitle anyone to do what they want to do. Call to mind what Imam Ali (AS) said: «الْمَالُ مَادَّةُ الشَّهَوَاتِ»; our great men hold themselves accountable for the way they spend their own money. Amir al-mu'minin, peace be upon him, said:

«أَفْضَلُ الْأَعْمال ما أَكْرَهْتَ نَفْسَكَ عليه» '

"The best act is that which you have to force yourself to do."

This leads to perfection, but man does not understand it. Muscles will become large and strong by tolerating the pressures

---

[1] Nahjul Balagha, wise Saying 58
[2] same, wise Saying 249

of exercise. Similarly, the Self will grow under force and personality grows stronger. A tall lanky person fails to carry a hundred kilo sackful of flour. If he does, he will get a slipped disk. An untrained soul or character is also weak and fails to tolerate silly, bullying or threatening words.

In this regard Sa'di narrates an anecdote: when I arrived at town square I saw a champion whose fame had gone far and wide. He had beaten all champions in different contests, and no one had ever been able to get his shoulders and back on the ground. But now he was wrathfully hollering and frothing at the mouth. Everybody was watching him from a safe distance. I asked someone what the problem was. He said that somebody's words have made him so angry. I said this ignorant guy can lift a load of two *Kharvars* (an Iranian unit for measuring weight equivalent to 300 kilos), yet he cannot stand people's unfair, illogical remarks?!

Strong personality is not necessarily in a strong body. Escaping from sufferings won't improve it. Great men, to grow, would impose sufferings on themselves.

Let's Not Be in Pursuit of Absolute Comfort.

It is in the tradition of the infallible Imams (AS) that performing *wudu* (ablution) with the water heated in the sun is *Makruh* (detestable, abominable). [1] You may ask: what's wrong with it? It is because the Self does not like cold water. Narratives assert this point too.

«اَفْضَلُ الْاَعمال ما اَکْرَهْتَ نَفْسَکَ عَلَیه»

"The best act is that which you have to force yourself to do."

Moderation must be followed. Great men achieve greatness because they do not give in to the Self. But, regretably, some people are slaves to the Self. What does a slave do? He is owned

---

[1] Man La Yahduruhu al-Faqih, vol. 1, page 7

by another person and is forced to obey orders. The master can boss him around at will. Are we supposed to be the Self's manager or its pupil? Everyone should look into himself to find out whether he is prudently in charge of the Self or has let the Self be in charge. Do we have authority over the Self or the Self is ruling us? If you are incapable of curbing your desires, you have allowed the Self to cotrol you. Imam Ali (AS) has said:

«اَلاَ وَ إِنَّ الْخَطَايَا خَيْلٌ شُمُسٌ حُمِلَ عَلَيْهَا اَهْلُهَا، وَ خُلِعَتْ لُجُمُهَا، فَتَقَحَّمَتْ بِهِمْ فِى النَّارِ. اَلاَ وَ إِنَّ التَّقْوَى مَطَايَا ذُلُلٌ، حُمِلَ عَلَيْهَا اَهْلُهَا، وَ أُعْطُوا اَزِمَّتَها، فَاَوْرَدَتْهُمُ الْجَنَّةَ» [1]

"Beware that sins are like unruly horses on whom their riders have been placed and their reins have been let loose so that they would jump with them in Hell. Beware that piety is like trained horses on which the riders have been placed with the reins in their hands, so that they would take the riders to Heaven."

King and Mystic

An overweening king cast his throne and crown in a mystic's teeth by boasting, "Of worldly material possessions what do you have? You rejoice in a handfull of superstitions and idle talk; you are indulged in whims and mislead people with ineffective instructions. Look at my realms, although you can never, by any conceivable stretch of the imagination, be aware how vast they are. They were not given us, though. We toiled for them, and now we have this kingdom and its accoutrements: large organized groups of warriors, retinue, time-enduring castles, and goods and chattels." The provident poor mystic requested, "May I take the liberty of saying what is in my mind?" When it was granted he said, "What is this self-glorification for? I care neither your position nor the possession. I will just let you know that I have two slaves under my command that rule over you." By this the king saw red. "Prove what you said, or I will have your head cut off," he said. "I'll

---

[1] Nahjul Balagha, sermon 16

prove it," he said "do you not comply with your heart when your desire or your wrath asks something of you, do you not kowtow to them?" The king was completely dumfounded. The mystic went on, "Well, wrath and desire that govern you are my bond servants." The hurt was more than the king could handle. He just dropped his eyes.

We are like this king. We need to train the Self while it is still a little kid. We should inform it about the necessity of perseverence when it confronts bitterness and ups and downs of everyday life. It should know that this world is not a suitable resting place because giving the self a rest is injurious not only to itself but also to the body. Move from the cool shade into the heat of the summer sun. Trickles of sweat on your skin are the sign that your fat is oozing out. Why do people go to sauna rooms and tolerate the hot temprature there? Because taking a sauna will help them lose weight. Winter cold must be tolerated, for it is beneficial to the body too. However, we move heaven and earth to protect ourselves from its cold. Winter comes and goes and not even once do we feel cold in our hands. Amir al-mu'minin, peace be upon him, in this connection says:

$$ \text{«تَوَقَّوُا الْبَرْدَ فى اَوَّله وَ تَلَقَّوْهُ فى آخِره، فَإِنَّهُ يَفْعَلُ فى الْاَبْدَانِ كَفِعْله فى الْاَشْجَارِ، اَوَّلُهُ يُحْرِقُ وَ آخِرُهُ يُورِقُ»}^{1} $$

"Guard against cold in its (seasonal) beginning and welcome it towards its end because it affects bodies in the same way as it affects plants. In the beginning, it destroys them but in the end it gives them fresh leaves."

In the past, when Ramadhan coincided with the hot summer days, it caused a lot of worry. Nowadys, however, there is not much difference between summer and winter because nobody

---

[1]   same, wise Saying 128

feels the heat. There is at least an air conditioner in almost every building. You leave home and get into a car equipped with another air conditioning system. Women in the past used to sweep the floor with a broom. They did the dishes and the laundry with hands. Doing the shopping and routine drudgery of life made them walk a couple of kilometers evey day. As a result, they did not have excess body fat nor did they get frequently sick. What's more, they were in good shape and maintained, unconsciously, a healthy weight. Nowadays, you can find a large percentage of women who are out of shape on grounds of excessive amounts of fat in their bodies due to a sedentary lifestyle. Why? The answer is labour saving devices: dishes are washed by dishwashers, the laundry is done by washing machines, the floor is swept by vacum cleaners, and so on. Fat, in the way in which they live, builds up to a dangerous climax. Then the women get pregnant and give birth to stillborn babies. One day, perhaps, they will have a baby. In the past our women used to have up to ten or more children and now that they are old, they walk well. Why is diabetes so ubiquitous? By working out regularly, even if you are susceptible to diabetes, you can ward it off for twenty years. So, suffering is not bad after all. Why escaping from it? Why don't we train our soul in such a way so that it cries out, "I abhor a lifestyle shorn of sufferings?" The grass roots of the society would formerly recite:

Rises a righteous man,

From travails and torments.

This is a truth reflecting a popular opinion. If almonds are not crushed into very small pieces between two hard surfaces, sweet, clear almond oil fail to materialize. If gold ore is not heated to very high temperatures and put in acid, we won't have solid gold. Iron by enduring high temeratures will change into strong hard steel. How can man expect to become highly distiguished by living a life of ease and comfort? No way. The basic system of the world is not structured this way. Hafiz has put all this in a nutshell:

The daintily nurtured in affluence took not the path to the friend:

The being a lover is the way of topers, calamity enduring.

Elsewhere he says:

In the stage where to fakirs the seat of wazirship, they give,

I expect that above all in rank thou art.

8. Sufferings Are Nurturing to The Soul.

I mentioned this narrative from Imam Bagher (AS) before:

»اذا احَبَّ الله عَبداً غتَّه بالبَلاء غتَّاً« ١

"In order to show affection to His bondsman, Allah indulges him in tribulation."

There is a similar narrative by Prophet Mohammad, peace be upon him: God feeds His believing servant with disaster and trouble as the mother feeds her baby with milk. [2] That is to say, suffering will elevate, nurture, and strengthen one's personality.

In another *Hadith* the Prophet, peace be upon him, said: The prophets are afflicted more than others, the second in rank are their successors, and then among other people, the better they are, the more afflicted they will be. [3]

There is no inconsistency, of course, between this and the earlier statement in which I said difficulties are due to sin. Allah loves truly devout men. He forgives them for the slightest lapse, but if their sins are not forgivable, He cleanses them promptly here

---

[1] Osoul-e Kaafi, vol. 2, page 197

[2] Bihar al-Anwar, vol. 78, page 195: »انَّ اللهَ لَيُغَذِّى عَبْدَهُ الْمُؤْمِنَ بِالْبَلَاء كَمَا تُغَذِّى الْوَالِدَهُ وَلَدَهَا باللَّبَنِ«

[3] Osoul-e Kaafi, vol. 2,page 259: »إنَّ فِى كِتَابَ عَلِىٍّ ع أنَّ أشَدَّ النَّاسِ بَلَاءً النَّبِيُّونَ ثُمَّ الْوَصِيُّونَ ثُمَّ الأَمْثَلُ فَالأَمْثَلُ«

in this World by punishing them just as fast as we clean our glasses when we notice a little dirty spot on them. Believing Muslims are like this; they are kept spotless. On the Resurrection day there are some who are as immaculate as the prophets (AS): no single sin is recorded in their book of deeds. They are happy, healthy and secure in the Purgatory and afterwards. Narratives tell us that their prayers are: «رَبَّنا أَقِمْ لَنَا السَّاعَه لِتُنجِّزَ لَنَا ما وَعَدْتَنا» [1] "Our Lord! Set up the Hour for us so You fulfill that which you have promised to us." At the approach of the Day of Judgement, they will have no qualm about the moment they are about to be raised. The Holy Quran says they burst into laughter.

$$«وُجُوهٌ يَوْمَئِذٍ مُّسْفِرَةٌ * ضَاحِكَةٌ مُّسْتَبْشِرَةٌ»^2$$

"Some faces that Day will be beaming, laughing, rejoicing."

In the pandemonium of the Fire of punishment amongst the groans and sighs of those who had rejected Truth and Right when evil sounds will drown every other sound, it would be meaningless for the virtuous to laugh. But why do they laugh? It is simply because they are not in the Hell. If in the purgatory they had been in the state of bliss, is it possible for them to be tortured on the Resurrection Day? Allah has told us in the Quran:

$$«إِنَّ الَّذِينَ سَبَقَتْ لَهُم مِّنَّا الْحُسْنَى أُولَئِكَ عَنْهَا مُبْعَدُونَ»^3$$

"Those for whom the good from Us has gone before, will be removed far away from that (Hell)."

In a number of instances Allah's mercy overtakes His wrath. Perhaps one of them where this happens is in the purgatory in

---

[1] Bihar al-Anwar, vol. 6, page 234
[2] Abasa, *Ayahs* 38-39
[3] Al-Anbiya, *Ayah* 101

which the virtuous are subject to Allah's mercy. Yet this privilege is not easy to attain. They must be purified before death. But how would it happen? One way is enduring sufferings without complaint. A second way is penitence–repenting all the sins. And a third way is doing good deeds. The Prophet (pbuh) said in the *Hadith* related by Imam Sadeq (AS):

«يُبْتَلَى المُؤمنُ عَلى قَدر ايمانه» [1]

"The believer is afflicted as much as his belief." However, some are not staunch believers, and if Allah punishes them here in this World, their faith will falter. Yet, He loves them and, therefore, is reluctant to chastise them in the Hereafter, so He punishes them in the purgatory where their faith will remain unblemished. In case of the virtuous, the first group, Allah will take pity on them and doesn't let them meet Him imperfect and impure. He purifies them with some pain or trouble. This group enjoys a high rank. There is yet another group who are left to their own devices. Allah does not care what they do, but on the Day of Reckoning, He knows well enough how to deal with them.

Then the Imam (AS) goes on:

«فَمَن صَحَّ ايمانُه وَ حَسُنَ عَمَله اشتَدَّ بلاؤُه وَ مَنْ سَخُفَ ايمانُه وَ ضَعُفَ عَمَلُه قلَّ بلاؤُه» [2]

"Staunch believers with good deeds suffer more; those of half-hearted belief and lighter good deeds do not suffer as much."

It is said in medicine: do not prescribe Adult Cold for kids; they cannot stand it. By analogy, these narratives do not mean to say the better you are, the more afflicted you will be. Let's not make a mistake: you are not afflicted due to goodness. What they mean to say is: because you are good Allah punishes your vice in this

---

[1] Osoul-e Kaafi, vol. 2, page 252
[2] same

world. Nevertheless, the door of forgiveness, narratives say, is still open. Joy of sin gives rise to some insufficiency in your personality. To counteract the effects of that joy, Allah will make you endure suffering and privation, which in turn, detoxify the body from that joy.

The following story is related by an athlete in *Pahlavani* and *Zourkhaneh* rituals about two renowned champions (*pahlavan*), a father and his son. One night a few wolves in sheep's clothing who had made an attempt on the son's life put a large tray full of pastries before him and play upon his feelings to eat them if he claims to be a real *pahlavan*. The inexperienced son, taking them for friends, accepts the challenge and eats them all and tears the copper tray in half to show them how strong he is, and then heads for home. Upon returning home he tells his father the story. The judicious father has a rude awakening, for he smells out conspiracy. So he takes him to the *zourkhaneh* (gym) and makes him do an overnight backbreaking workout until the sweat that was pouring off him makes the floor underfoot wet. "Do you see these beads of perspiration on your damp skin?" He asks. "They are poison. They intended to do you harm! Actually, they wanted to kill you!"

9. Sufferings, the Bitter Medicine of Shortcomings

As it was already mentioned some deficiencies are sometimes made in the believer's soul which Allah corrects, and returns the soul to its former condition by making him deal with the vicissitudes of life, thereby He does not permit the fault or flaw to leave a lasting effect on the soul. Immoderation even in *Halal* (lawful) joys may get us into trouble, which God imposes to compensate for the deficiencies of the soul. Suffering is good for spiritual growth, just as, in the opposite case, joy is detrimental to it. As suffering solidifies determination, joy weakens it. Joy moreover makes man lazy, unfeeling, and comfort-seeking, which is the root cause of a number of social blights. How numorous are the people who fell into the pit of devouring ill-gotten gains because of laziness! They were after easy morsel of food but ended up wandering in bad ways. How plentiful are instances of dereliction of duty because of indolence! These are the flaws that stem from a radical sense of pleasureseeking. When man goes to extremes in fulfilling even those desires that are allowed by religion, Allah makes him suffer in their wake in order for him not to get stuck in imperfections.

Sufferings, from a particular perspective, are divided into two categories: the first category is which we cause directly, and the second one is the sufferings which ways are paved by us. One of the causes of this second category of sufferings is the worldly joys. Even lawful joys done to excess may lead to deficiencies. Is it right to say, "Now that I have discharged my obligatory financial duties and have paid my debts off, I'd like to enjoy myself heartily?" Does it to the interest of a perfectionist believe Muslim? Does it bring perfection with it? Is Allah content with it? Do the verses of the Holy Quran as well as the traditions of the infallible Imams (AS) permit such an attitude and lifestyle? Later on, we will see that the law of *Shari'a* is something, and the fact that we are supposed to be a little more than law-abiding believers is something else (of course, the discussion is going to be a bit complicated). Indulgence in pleasures, even those prescribed by the religion can work against spiritual growth. To prevent such a problem, Allah inflicts sufferings. When the water in the pot begins to bubble, you pour a little water on it to stop the turmoil. When we start bubbling over with intoxicating pleasures, Allah pours a little water of suffering on us to make us sober again. We need to be sobered up after being intoxicated with power, pleasure, post, and property. Intoxication means not having any news of anybody. Intoxication means laughing apathetically when people around are moaning in pain. Intoxication means inability to think clearly. To lesson the effects of intoxication, Allah sometimes pokes us in the ribs with sufferings or has us take bitter medicines. What? Are you sick and tired of unpalatable medicines, of being poked and prodded? Then beware of any faults and weaknesses you may cause in the Self.

10. Suffering Will Bloom Dormant Talents

One upside to sufferings is that they bloom the talents that have lain idle and dormant. A college janitor goes to the professors' office to serve them tea. One of them, having his legs crossed, takes the cup of tea off the tray, but the cup feels cold to his touch, or maybe not as hot as he expected. He fails to keep his anger bottled up and gives him an earful for serving cold tea. The janitor, who feels badly slighted, decides this menial job does not worth his while. He puts the tray on the desk and washes his hands of the job in which he has to court different people's dalliance. The event in the office becomes his main motivation to pursue his studies until he gets his doctorate degree. And now he is taking up the same academic post as the one who insulted him. If that professor had gone easy on him, he wouldn't be an honour to his family and country now. Sometimes a mere nudge in the ribs is a blessing beyond compare. There are too many cases in which a setback or a matter of concern makes a distinguished scientist, a painter, or a poet of an ordinary person. The late Shahriar, the great Iranian poet, suffered unrequited love, so he turned to poetry to make him get his beloved out of his mind. Suddenly he discovers he has enjoyed a limitless poetic sense.

He, who had meant to become a physician, due to unreciprocated love, turned to poetry and became a poet of the first rank. The aromatic sandalwood, when burning, yeilds a sweet smell, but a mountain pile of it left somewhere is scaresly fragrant. It must burn to produce a pleasant smell. As Sa'di says:

Aloe is just a piece of wood.
Fire makes it smell good.
To understand this poem
Be baked on heat you should.

Allah intends to manifest your power, your latent talent by touching you with affliction. Why are you afraid of being cornered by Him?

Somebody said, "My brother had jacked up his car and managed to have it lifted off the ground by some bricks and was doing some repair work under it when all of a sudden the bricks toppled over and the car landed on my brother's leg. He gave out a cry of anguish, but nobody was there to help. Fraternal love made me catch the bumper and lift the car, and my brother could drag himself out. Later on, I heaved the same car with all my might but still couldn't budge it. Yes, in hard conditions that mysterious latent power awakes.

Let's not be afraid of sufferings as we are not afraid of bitter medicine, simply because sufferings demonstrate human power. A wise man does not lose heart in hard conditions. Joseph (AS) the prophet of Allah, in prison with its terrible conditions, among a lot of rabbles, changed the situation and was raised to honor in Egypt. Well rounded individuals are like this. In upcoming discussions, if Allah so wills, I will explain what you can do in different conditions to turn sufferings and hardships to your advantage, to burn in the fire of sufferings and rise purified like solid gold instead of being reduced to ashes like wood.

We have admirable role models like *Ahlul-Bayt* (the Prophet's infalible family). Despite all the serious problems they had to deal with in Karbala, they emerged triumphant because they were doing the right thing in a right way for a right purpose. *Hadhrat* Abolfadhl's highly esteemed place in the Hereafter will be the envy of all the world's martyrs and monotheists because he submitted himself to the will of Allah, discharged his divine duty, and chose the best course.[1]

If there are creases in the sheets of paper in a book, the bookbinder puts the book under maximum pressure. When the press is gone, you see the pages smooth and even. If you are out of true, you need the pressure of Time, (this is the way Time is structured to treat you). Why wailing? Allah intends to correct the crookedness of your soul. The creases in your clothes also need to be ironed out with a hot flatiron. Gold contaminated with other minerals is treated with heat in the furnace in order to extract purified gold. Grains of wheat in the sack are never changed into a good harvest, but when put in the dark of fertilized soil their natural ability come to fruition and wheat clusters will sprout.

Imprisonment is not always bad. Joseph (AS), the prophet of Allah, had an important mission. His calling was to go and save a country from a seven-year famine and deliver a nation from the evils of idolatory, but he couldn't accomplish the mission before the ground was prepared for it: He was subject to the brutish treatment of his hefty half-brothers. They mercilessly calumniated him after they threw him down to the bottom of the well. They sold him for a miserable price to a caravan of merchants (for something between six to twelve *Dirhams*, small silver coins). Then he had to bear insults and agonizing hardships in prison and

---

[1] Al-Amali, Book by Al-Shaykh al-Saduq, page 462

out, before he ascended the throne of dignity and honour, and before so many blessings poured out of him. What it all boils down to is the fact that we shouldn't look on life's hardships as impediments. If uranium is left unenriched, its huge potential energy won't get a chance to emanate. A believing Muslim, when afflicted with adversity, will have peace of mind that Allah did it for his own good. When the U.S-engineered sanctions were imposed against our country, Iran, everybody was concerned about the upcoming course of affairs and trade. Circumstances in which people lived and worked became harder and harder. The price of some goods increased manyfold in one week. People were in a state of panic because the country was experiencing economic free fall, they thought. Anticipating famine, some people started saving dried bread, and some saved gasoline in large tanks for the time of scarcity. The price of some goods skyrocketed upto twenty or thirtyfold. Obtaining some items was like finding a needle in a hay stack. Imam Khomeini, in that desperate situation said, with his great insight into things, something that many people thought he was saying in order to take America down a peg or two; they failed to recognize that he said it out of strong faith. He said, "If America renders the Iranians only one single service, it will be nothing but these sanctions."

After thirty years, his words turned out to be gospel truth. In order to destroy us, the enemy should have provided us with anything we needed for a low price. Then, we wouldn't have all these significant breakthroughs in different fields, nor would we be able to produce nuclear energy. Nowadays, the enemy is forced to admit that Iran is able not only to produce everything it needs militarily, but also to arm forty to fifty other countries. Today, high-tech weaponry: tanks, drones, missiles, torpedoes, etc are made here, whereas during the war, we couldn't even make barbed wire, nor would any country sell it to us. Once a country did, but the barbed wire was intercepted in Azerbaijan Soviet Socialist Republic. We had no landmines to place before the tanks of invading forces, nor were we able to produce any. If they had given us what we required, they would have hardly needed to wage the war against us; they could eaily bring us to our knees. The hardships the enemy imposed on us were a blessing in disguise. They, in fact, nudged us awake. They made us put aside our intimidation, use our gray matter, and think how to do things. Amir al-mu'minin, pease be upon him, said:

$$\text{«اَلرُّشْدُ فى خِلاف الشَّهْوَهَ»}^{1}$$

"Guidance is based on opposition to lust."

In order ro grow and flourish, you need to take the way which is the opposite of the one your Self pushes you. If you don't, you may live a life of ease but you won't thrive.

If a weak, timid person finds the modesty and virtue of his wife and daughters in danger, he may well stand up to ten people. Where is this courage coming from? There were too many people who were frightened out of their wits at the sight of a policeman but became heroes in the war. A friend of mine once said that he had seen a *Basiji*, a member of the Resistance Mobilization Force, was running after an enemy tank and the tank was getting away from him out of fear. What made him hardy was the hardship of war.

---

[1] Nahjul Balagha, sermon 147

UNIT FOUR
GUIDLINES

- Guidelines for warding off sorrows and sufferings
- Guidlines for quitting bad habits
- Guardlines for warding off the love of this World

Chapter One:
Guidlines for Warding off Sorrows and Sufferings

1. Patience

Amir al-mu'minin (AS) wrote to al-Hassan ibn Ali (his son, peace be upon them):

«أُطْرُحْ عَنْكَ وارِداتِ الْهُمُومِ بِعَزائِمِ الصَّبْرِ وَ الْيَقِينْ»[1]

"**Turn away the griefs of the past through decisions with good patience and certitude.**"

Sorrow is unable to bug patient people. Sadness cannot get well rounded individualls into trouble. Persevering people are strong and able to withstand seftbacks. If you show patience in the face of sadness, your character will be completed in the best possible way. Little by little you will be able to ward off the deepest sadness. In this stage, in other words, you will achieve the firmness of purpose in the conduct of affairs. In this connection Luqman says to his son:

«وَاصْبِرْ عَلَى مَا أَصَابَكْ اِنَّ ذلكَ مِنْ عَزْمِ الْأُمُور»[2]

"**And bear with patient constancy whatever betide thee; for this is firmnes (of purpose) in (the conduct of affairs).**"

What distinguished *Ulul-Azm* prophets (prophets of firm resolution) from other prophets? One of their distinguishing features was patience. People of firm resolution are patient too.

---

[1] Nahjul Balagha, letter 31
[2] same, letter 17

2. Belief in *Kismet*
Hadhrat Ali (AS) says:

«فى الزَّلازلِ وَقورٌ وَ فى المَكارِهِ صَبورٌ» ١

"He (a pious man) is dignified during calamities and patient in distresses."

Imam Ali (AS) asks us to protect ourselves from sadness with two shields: patience and certitude. But certitude about what? About the fact that what befalls us is our *kismet*, our destiny and fate; that it was decreed by Him. (It was mentioned before, of course, that our *kismet* accords with our past deeds not with predestination). If you know this, you won't complain why things happened as they did, nor will you blame your bad luck. Half of the distress will be gone if you know that what occured was supposed to occur. In this respect a tradition has come to us from both the Prophet (pbuh) and Imam Sadeq (AS) saying:

«فَانَّ الرِّزْقَ لايَسوقُهُ حِرْصُ حَريصٍ وَ لايَرُدُّهُ كَراهِيَّهُ كارهٍ» ٢

"Sustenance is not provided due to the greed of the greedy, nor is it withdrawn if one loathes it."

Your livelihood will reach you if it is supposed to, and there is no escape from it.

«وَلَو اَحَدُكُمْ فَرَّ مِنْ رِزْقٍ كَما يَفِرُّ مِنَ الْمُوتِ لَكانَ رِزْقُهُ اَشَدُّ لَهُ طَلَباً» 3

"If any of you escapes from his sustenance as he escapes from death, it will follow and reach him swiftly."

Will anyone, really believing in this, be ever motivated by greed? Will he ever do unsightly things?

Then the tradition goes on to say:

---

¹ same, sermon 193
² Osoul-e Kaafi, vol. 2, page 57
³ same

«وَ اَسْرَعُ اِدْرَاكاً مِنَ الْمُوتِ اِنَّ اللهَ تعالى جَعَلَ الرَّوحِ وَ الرَّاحَهَ فِى الْيَقِينَ وَ الرِّضا» [1]

"It (his sustenance) will reach him faster than death. Allah, all praise and glory be to him, has put comfort in certainty and contentment."

If you trust in divine providence, comfort will come to you as well. The elderly (of course, some of them) have beautiful sayings. For example: every sadness or joy that touches you is for your own good. On the surface, it does not seem to be well-documented, but it has great insight behind it. If all people's distress are placed next to yours and you are given the chance to take some up at will, you will reach and pick up your own distress because, by comparison, you find out it suits you most. In other words, you come to the conclusion that Allah has touched you with a sort of affliction which is the most expedient.

Of course, we do not accept *kismet* as something that was predetermined from the beginning. This deterministic view is untenable and rejected by *Imami Shias*. Actually, we do not consider determinists as real Muslims. It is in the *Hadith* that Libertarians (advocates of the doctrine of free will) are the Zoroastrians and determinists (believers in predestination) are the Jews of the *Ummat*. [2]Shiite does not accept the notion that what is supposed to happen was written from day one, nor does it accept that things happen haphazardly. Yet, we do believe that things come to pass based on what we do. When we do good deeds, good things will be recorded in our destiny, and when we do evil,

---

[1] same

[2] At-Tawhid (al-Saduq), page 382:

«قال الصادق (ع):إنَّ الْقَدَرِيَّهَ مَجُوسٌ هَذِه الأُمَّه وَ هُمُ الَّذِينَ اَرَادُوا اَنْ يَصِفُوا اللهَ بِعَدْلِه فَاَخْرَجُوهُ مِنْ سُلْطَانِه وَ فِيهِمْ نَزَلَتْ هَذِه الآيَهُ– يَوْمَ يُسْحَبُونَ فِى النَّارِ عَلى وُجُوهِهِمْ ذُوقُوا مَسَّ سَقَرَ. إِنَّا كُلَّ شَىْءٍ خَلَقْنَاهُ بِقَدَرٍ.»

what will happen to us in the future, will be evil. In other words, we are in control of our own destiny. This attitude was firmly advocated by *Ahlul-Bayt*. It is also clarified in the Quran:

«مَاأَصَابَ مِنْ مُصِيبَةٍ فِي الْأَرْضِ وَلَا فِي أَنْفُسِكُمْ إِلَّا فِي كِتَابٍ مِنْ قَبْلِ أَنْ نَبْرَأَهَا»[1]

"No misfortune can happen on earth or in your souls but is recorded in a Book before We bring it into existence."

«لِكَيْلَا تَأْسَوْا عَلَى مَا فَاتَكُمْ وَلَا تَفْرَحُوا بِمَا آتَاكُمْ وَاللهُ لَا يُحِبُّ كُلَّ مُخْتَالٍ فَخُورٍ»[2]

"In order that you may despair over, neither matters pass you by, nor exult over favours bestowed upon you. For Allah loveth not any vainglorious boaster."

There is no chaos in the world and its ffairs.

«...وَلَا رَطْبٍ وَلَا يَابِسٍ إِلَّا فِي كِتَابٍ مُبِينٍ»[3]

"...nor anything fresh or dry (green or withered), but is inscribed in a Record Clear (to those who can read)."

Nevertheless, the record is inscribed after your deeds. Allah first considers your deeds, and then He records your destiny: If you have respected ties of kith and kin, He will bestow longevity. If you hold your parents in high esteem, He will record honour in your destiny. You will want for nothing if you are charitable to people in need. God forbid, if you give people trouble, you will run into trouble. You will be disgraced if you disgrace people. What we know of *kismet* is this. We accept only this kind of destiny. No, managing of the world is not based on chance. When it is said that Divine Management and Lordship is absolute, it means that no haphazard happening, which signifies a state of utter confusion, exists in the world.

---

[1] Al-Hadid, *Ayah* 22
[2] same, *Ayah* 23
[3] Al-Anaam, *Ayah* 59

If in an office things happen out of plan and the manager fails to notice it, these can be taken as telltale clues of mismanagement, as signs that the manager is unaware of what is going on around him. But what about Omniscient God? Is it imaginable that things happen out of infinite knowledge, insight, management and calculations of Omniscient and Omnipresent Allah? No way, as it is not imaginable that God decrees punishment for a crime not yet committed. The truth of the matter is what the Holy Quran states: what we do determines our destiny. While it is true that your fate is predetermined at "Qadr Night", it is also true that your good deeds throughout the year may well obliterate the record of misfortunes that were supposed to befall you, and conversely, your bad deeds may erase the good things.

The traditions of the inerrant Imams (AS) state that sometimes a servant of God starts to pray (praying is a deed of goodness), and God wants the angels to answer his prayer. But before they do, he does some misdeed, and then God addresses the angels to stop. If you know this and believe in it, you won't be overtaken by grief. If something befalls you, it was written (determined) to befall you. If it does not befall you, it was written not to befall you. There is a host of *Ahadith* in this respect, about one of which Abdullah ibn al-Abbas says: Apart from the Quran and Prophet's sayings I did not derive greater benefit from any saying than this one by Amir al-mu'minin (AS).

«اَمَّا بَعْدُ، فَإِنَّ الْمَرْءَ قَدْ يَسُرُّهُ دَرَکَ مَا لَمْ يَكُنْ لِيَفُوتَهُ، وَيَسُوؤُهُ فَوْتُ مَا لَمْ يَكُنْ لِيُدْرِكَهُ...»[1]

"Let it be known to you that sometimes a man gets pleased at securing a thing which he was not going to miss at all and gets displeased at missing a thing which he would not in any case get."

---

[1] Nahjul Balagha, letter 22

Then the Imam (AS) goes on:

«...فَلْيَكُنْ سُرُورُكَ بِما نِلْتَ مِنْ آخِرَتِكَ، وَلْيَكُنْ اَسَفُكَ عَلى مافاتَكَ مِنْها»

"Your pleasure should be about what you secure in respect of your next life and your grief should be for what you miss in respect thereof."

What will happen to you in the Hereafter is not in your destiny; what counts then is your strife in Here.

«وَاَنْ لَيْسَ لِلْاِنْسانِ إِلّا مَاسَعى»[1]

"...that man can have nothing but what he strives for."

This *Ayah* is for the Resurection Day. The matter is clarified in the next *Ayah*:

«وَاَنَّ سَعْيَهُ سَوْفَ يُرَى»[2]

"That (the fruit of) his striving will soon come in sight, i.e. come in sight in the Hereafter."

In the time of the Prophet of God (pbuh), someone was late for the congregational prayer and couldn't catch up with the first *Rakat* (prescribed movements and words in a unit of prayers). After saying his prayers he went up to the Prophet (pbuh) and said, "O, Prophet of God, I was one *Rakat* late for the prayers. If I put a camel to knife and give it as *Sadaqah* (voluntary charity) in the way of Allah, shall I earn the *Thawab* (reward) of that *Rakat* that I missed out?" He said, "No." "What about two camels?" he asked. "No." "And three?" "No." And he kept on up to forty camels, for he was a well heeled man. Then the Prophet (pbuh) pointed to two mountains around Medina and said, "If they were of gold and

---

[1]   An-Najm, *Ayah* 39
[2]   same, *Ayah* 40

silver and you gave them in charity in the way of Allah, you wouldn't earn the *Thawab* of that missed-out *Rakat*."[1]

If we lose a banknote of little value, we spend the whole time it takes to say our prayers on finding it. We grieve for the lost money, but we don't grieve for the prayers not said on its own time. Amir al-Mu'minin (AS) said: Your regret should be for missing the reward of the Hereafter. Hafiz says:

Sage! If before you come sorrow or ease,

Ascribe not to other; for these, God makes.

Hafiz's view is not deterministic; he believes that what is involved is destiny, which is recorded according to our deeds.

In this regard, there is another *Hadith* in *Nahjul Balaghah*:

«اعْلَمُوا عِلْماً يَقيناً اَنَّ اللهَ لَمْ يَجْعَلْ لِلْعَبْدِ وَ إِنْ عَظُمَتْ حيلَتُهُ وَ اشْتَدَّتْ طَلَبَتُهُ وَ قَوِيَتْ مَكيدَتُهُ اَكْثَرَ مِمَّا سُمِّىَ لَهُ فِى الذِّكْرِ الْحَكيمِ...»[2]

"Know with full conviction that Allah has not fixed for any person more livelihood than what has been ordained in he Book of Destiny, (which is, of course, based on his deeds and behaviour) even though his means (of seeking it) may be great, his craving for it intense and his efforts for it acute;"

«...وَ لَمْ يَحُلْ بَيْنَ الْعَبْدِ فِى ضَعْفِهِ وَ قِلَّةِ حيلَتِهِ وَ بَيْنَ اَنْ يَبْلُغَ مَا سُمِّىَ لَهُ فِى الذِّكْرِ الْحَكيمِ»

"Nor does the weakness of a person or the paucity of his means stand in the way between what is ordained in the Book of Destiny and himself."

An Anecdote

Two paupers were standing next to Shah Abbas. One would say *"Ya Allah!"* (An invocation to God), the other would say *"Ya Soltan!"* (An invocation to the Monarch). The one who repeatedly used to say *"Ya Soltan!"* told the other, "How ignorant and stupid

---

[1] Mustadrak al-Wasa'il, vol. 1, page 448

[2] Nahjul Balagha, wise Saying 273

you are! Say '*Ya Soltan!*' and earn some money as I do." Yet his companion would again say "*Ya Allah!*" Observing all this, the king told his vizier, "You are used to saying that it is God who dispenses people's livelihood. But now I will show you that this is not the case by giving the one who says "*Ya Soltan!*" a lot of gold. Vizier said, "I have no idea. What I know is what is determined by Allah will certainly come to pass." The king went up to the chef and asked him to serve a plate of rice and chicken with a gold coin underneath the rice to the one who would say "*Ya Soltan!*" The chef obeyed and put the plate of food in front of him. The pauper took pride in king's favouritism and began to eat. When he was nearly finished, he pushed the plate of leftover towards the other pauper in order to humiliate him. The godly pauper didn't mind much and started eating the leftover rice when, lo and behold, he noticed the flickedring coin and quietly picked it and slipped it into his pocket. To thank Gracious God, now he said "*Ya Allah!*" more frequently. When his friend asked for an explanation, he simply wanted him to mind his own business and enjoy saying "*Ya Soltan!*" The next day the king asked the chef to put two coins on his plate, and then three, and then four etc. And thus all the leftover ended up in the other pauper's stomach and all the coins in his pocket. The more coins he got the more frequently and louder he would call out to *Allah*. After a few days he thought he had enough gold coins to set up his own business in town. He changed into a new set of clothes and went up to meet his fellow pauper. He told him that he had quit asking for alms and that he had a small store he could go to if he needed something. When the ungodly pauper asked him how he had gone from rags to riches, the righteous man told him the whole story. And thus, this ex-pauper who was mocked had the last laugh. Hafiz has artistically expressed this idea in a single *Beit* (line) of poem:

Content, the poor man's honour, I ask not to forego:
Predestined, tell the monarch, is what we need below.

Let's look on the world and its affairs from this perspective. If we do so, many things will get solved. Why does Abdullah ibn al-Abbas about the above mentioned *Hadith* by Imam Ali (AS) say: Apart from the Quran and Prophet's sayings I did not derive greater benefit from any saying than this one by Amir al-mu'minin (AS)? Simply because you will be relieved of many of your sorrows.

Let's suppose that someone is madly in love with a girl and thinks that she is the only one in the entire world that makes his heart flutter. Friends and relatives tell him that they do not match each other, but he ignores all their advice. Under this circumstance, what will happen to this young man if the girl ties the knot with someone else? If he doesn't die of grief, he will at least suffer for a long time that his would-be wife is now someone else's wife; whereas, she was not supposed to be his in the first place. Let's change our outlook and submit ourselves to the religion whose teachings have come to free us from these chains and shackles. The Holy Quran says:

$$\text{«وَيَضَعُ عَنْهُمْ إِصْرَهُمْ وَالْاَغْلَالَ الَّتِي كَانَتْ عَلَيْهِمْ»}^{1}$$

"He releases them from their heavy burdens and from the yokes that are upon them."

It is actually the responsibility of the Prophet (pbuh) and inerrant Imams (AS) to remove the iron collars from people's necks and deliver them from all the restrictions imposed upon them by ignorance. Amir al-mu'minin, peace be upon him, said:

«وَ الْعَارِفُ لِهَذَا الْعَامِلُ بِهِ، اَعْظَمُ النَّاسِ رَاحَةً فِي مَنْفَعَةٍ، وَ التَّارِكُ لَهُ الشَّاكُّ فِيهِ، اَعْظَمُ

---

[1] Al-Araf, *Ayah* 157

النّاسِ شُغُلاً فى مَضرَّه»`¹`

"He who realizes it and acts upon it is the best of them all in point of comfort and benefit; while he who disregards it and doubts it exceeds all men in disadvantages."

Somewhere else the Imam (AS) says:

«امّا بَعْدُ، فَإنَّ الْاَمْرَ يَنْزِلُ مِنَ السَّماء إلَى الْاَرْضِ كَقَطَرَاتِ الْمَطَرِ إلَى كُلِّ نَفْسٍ بِمَا قُسِمَ لَهَا مِنْ زِيَادَةٍ اَوْ نُقْصَانٍ، فَإنْ رَآى اَحَدُكُمْ لِاَخيهِ غَفيرَةً فى اَهْلٍ اَوْ مَالٍ اَوْ نَفْسٍ فَلاَتَكُونَنَّ لَهُ فِتْنَةً»`²`

"Now then, verily Divine orders descend from heaven to earth like drops of rain, bringing to every one what is destined for him whether plenty or paucity. So if any of you observes for his brother plenty of progeny or of wealth or of self, it should not be a worry for him."

What is destined for you is based on your deeds: recorded by your deeds and erased by your deeds. In other words, destiny in a calculated manner is at work. Therefore, if your brother enjoys a large family or plenty of resources and etc, don't look with envy at him. Praise Allah, instead, that Divine Destiny has smiled at him.

3. Writting and Reviewing Blessings

Write down all the things you are blessed with in a notebook. Do it once and see what effect it will leave. Make sure you haven't missed anything out. Once you do, you will soon find out that it is impossible because you will face an endless list of items in any field you think of. Go to the Medical Organization, for instance, and ask the specialists about the number of diseases one may suffer. They will say millions, one of which is cancer. Do you know how many kinds of cancer there are? A few hundred. Then write down those diseases you are not suffering from. "Wow! How blessed I am!" you will come to conclusion. When you are in the

---

¹ Nahjul Balagha, wise Saying 273
² same, sermon 23

grip of sorrow, open the notebook and run your eyes over the list. It will function as an elbow shaker to remind you of a forgotten or overlooked fact. Then you will certainly breathe a sigh of relief. Allah says in the Holy Quran:

$$«...وَإِن تَعُدُّوا نِعْمَتَ اللهِ لَا تُحْصُوهَا...»^1$$

"But if you count the favours of Allah, never will you be able to number them."

Is anybody able to count all the favours which a wise and benevolent Providence has given him? No way! This may be like a person whose pocket has been picked of a ten thousand toman banknote (the price of a hamburger), yet he is left a hundred million tomans in his bank account. However, he is sitting there wailing as if he were stranded in a different town and this bill were all he had on him. One amusing technique to avoid discomfiture and enjoy life is to call to mind what you are left rather than what you have missed (better yet, write it). The Holy Quran instructs us that this method will lead to salvation:

$$«...فَاذْكُرُوا آلَاءَ اللهِ لَعَلَّكُمْ تُفْلِحُونَ»^2$$

"Call in remembrance the benefits (you have received) from Allah: that so you may prosper."

4. It Could Have Been Worse.

Since imagination is a licenced trespasser, let's just imagine that your car, your only means of livelihood, is stolen from you. Sure enough it's a distressing situation. But it would be far more distressing to see your car tumbling off a mountain road with your whole family in it, and when you get there you see them breathe

---

1 Ibrahim, *Ayah* 34
2 Al-Araf, *Ayah* 69

their last. Experience teaches us that imagining a worse situation can cure the distrss of a bad one.

You might find mountain climbing hard if you are not physically in shape. Nevertheless, if you are made to carry a heavy load and climb a mountain at gunpoint, you will do it, simply because you are threatened to. Now suppose midway up, you are asked to drop the load. Then you will feel that you are in a state of weightlessness and can easily hop and leap up the mountain. Try to set a spiritual mood like this for yourself when you are in distress. Then you will find yourself weightlessly relieved.

It has been narrated that once a man was talking to his wife when he saw in the dim yard somebody moving. He asked her, "Can you see that white thing over there? I think it's a burglar. Just stay here and see how I settle my accounts with him." At the time that he was whispering to his wife, he took his bow and shot an arrow at the thief. Then he went to the yard and saw that he had shot his own shirt on the clothes line. When he immediately stood for prayers, his woman said, "What an untimely prayer!" He said, "Should I not thank God that I was not in the shirt?"

5. Comparing Oneself with the Disaster Stricken Not the Comfort Seekers

When you are struck by a disaster, look at people with greater disasters. A *Hadith* says: if you want to feel emotionally comforted when you are sad or disappointed, presume you have escaped from your grave. That is to say, think that you are dead and buried: in your state of helplessness you talk contritely to God that now you have come to know what the world was and what the Hereafter is, that you have made a lot of mistakes and you were a dead loss in your youth, that you lived a life like there would be no Resurection, and that you now know what you should do if you are returned to this world... How would you feel if God consented to your return? Would it be a matter of concern where your house is or how your clothes are? In all probability, your only apprehension would be how to collect provisions for the Day of Reckoning. Yes, with this presumption, that you have fled from the cemetery, your anguish would seem much less irritating. Some great men of God were like this. One of them was in the habit of going to the graveyard in the dead of night and lying down in the grave he had already dug out for himself in order not to forget the first night after death. After a few times he would get used to it and could undergo a sweeping change and simulate death under the impression of time and place. Then in supplication, he would beg God to forget his evil past, forgive him and return him to this world. After he recovered consciousness, he would say to himself, "Now that you have come back, let's see what you will do!" Then he would come back to civilization with a renewed mood for a more serious effort in doing good deeds.

When you are out of condition, look at people who are in a critical condition. I knew someone who was afflicted with Quadriplegia. He was inable to control and use his legs, arms, and body. If he had been mad, well, he wouldn't have understood anything. But (let's say, the problem was) he wasn't impaired in thought–he enjoyed a good enough level of cognition, his mentality was okay, and he could talk well. He lived a life like someone whose arms and legs were tied to his body for fifty years. He was stiff like a piece of dry wood. Ever since then whenever problems assault my mind, I just call him and his dire condition to mind. Thinking about him makes me forget all my problems.

There is an allegory which has become part of our folklore: a man is taking a rest upon a brooklet's edge when he spots a skull being carried by water. The skull repeatedly says, "May God prevents this bad situation from getting worse!" Upon hearing this, the man says angrily, "Could it have been worse than this? You were a man whose head was cut off. The only thing you are left is this skull, which is being carried by water. Isn't it already too bad?" suddenly the skull rolls toward a mill and the man hears it being crushed between the millstones. "Yeah, it went from bad to worse!" the man broods.

6. *Adhkar* That Eliminate and Ward off Sadness

1. The Holy Prophet of Islam (pbuh) said: the *Dhikr*, (meaning "mentioning", a short phrase or prayer which is repeatedly recited silently within the mind or aloud)

«لا حَوْلَ وَ لا قُوَّةَ الا بالله العلى العظيم» [1]

"Is a treasure of the Paradise's treasures that relieves 99 pains, the least unpleasent of which is distress."

2. A mystic said: if you repeatedly recite: ☐☐☐☐ ☐☐☐☐ ☐☐ *Ya Rasulullah*, Allah will either remove your sadness or give you enough forbearance, both of which are good. In other words, if you are not delivered from sadness, the mere increase in forbearance is good by itself.

3. *Dhikr Yunusiyah* (the call of Jonah), the same *Dhikr* that made the fish cast Yunus (Jonah) out ashore:

«...لا إِلَهَ إِلَّا اَنتَ سُبْحَانَكَ إِنِّى كُنتُ مِنَ الظَّالِمِينَ» [2]

"There is no God but Thou: glory to Thee: I was indeed wrong!"

Imam Sadeq (AS) is reported to have said, "It surprises me that one who is depressed fails to recite this *Dhikr*, for in the next *Ayah* Allah says:

---

[1] Wasa'il al-Shia, vol. 7, page 175
[2] Al-Anbiya, *Ayah* 87

فَاسْتَجَبْنَا لَهُ وَنَجَّيْنَاهُ مِنَ الْغَمِّ وَكَذَلِكَ نُنجِى الْمُؤْمِنِينَ [1]

"So We listened to him: and delivered him from distress: and thus do We deliver those who have faith."

It is proved effective in alleviating distress if you recite this *Dhikr* four hundred times while you are prostrating yourself. Don't give up if your request is not answered. Keep reciting until it is answered. Reciting as many times as seventy thousand is enjoined. It depends, of course, how serious your distress is. The more serious the distress is, the more the expenditure would be. Do you expect to have your son exempted from military service, and pass such and such an exam, and his problems in getting married get solved by giving two thousand tomans (the price of a stick ice-cream) to charity?! Of course intention, in doing things, with sincerity and good faith is an important condition; the current trend, however, is giving too little to charity. We tend to think of charity as giving a pittance. What's wrong with giving a million tomans if you have a billion? Moreover, let's not get rid of our junks and lemons as alms. It would be much less effetive. The Holy Quran says:

... وَلَا تَيَمَّمُوا الْخَبِيثَ مِنْهُ تُنفِقُونَ وَلَسْتُم بِآخِذِيهِ إِلَّا أَن تُغْمِضُوا فِيهِ ... [2]

"And do not aim at anything which is bad, out of it you may give away something, when you yourselves would not receive it except with closed eyes."

7. Cheering up People's Hearts

The most important factor in warding off distress is cheering people up, whether they are faithful Muslims (*Mu'min*) or infidels (*Kafir*). Of course, those who are resistant to *Haqq* (*Muanid*) are

---

[1] same, *Ayah* 88
[2] Al-Baqara, *Ayah* 267

exceptions; there is no virtue in cheering them up because they have no happiness short of annihilation of Haqq (truth) and disintegration of good people's lives. However, if you take a measure to alleviate the suffering of a non-Muslim, it can be effective in alleviating your distress, let alone the person is a believer in Almighty God and submissive to *Haqq*. Amongst the pure not all of them are in the same level: the more purified and better the person, the more *Thawab* will accrue from cheering him up. Cheering children is better and easier, because first they are without sin and second it doesn't cost much to please them: a bar of chocolate, a story book, a nice word (e.g, what nice handwriting you have! How beautifully you've written your composition!) will immediately gladden their hearts. If you see a child in the mosque for the congregational prayers, for example, encourage him and give him an affectionate pat on the head. If he is an orphan, patronize him by buying him shoes, shirts or by even becoming his guardian. There are too many ways to please children unlike adults–who are hard to please. A net curtain sways gently in the breeze, but it takes a gust of strong wind to move a thick, heavy curtain. A kid's heart is like that net curtain: it leaps with the slightest breeze of affection.

But the heart of a man is like that thick, heavy curtain; it must be quite windy before it leaps. Nonetheless, men's hearts too can be captured by words. You might well express words of sympathy for them. If they have lost a dear one, for instance, put on a sad front, offer your condolences, attend the wake, the funeral, and/or other services, and thereby reduce their burden [unfortunately, contrary to the policy of noninvolvement of the bereaved, which is enjoined by religion, all the burden (involvement in funeral rites, preparing lunch, dinner, fruit, cupcake, etc) is borne by them]. These measures, to a large extant, can lighten up their distress.

However, gladdening children not only doesn't take that much effort, but it is also bought at a higher price by Allah. Someone once said, "I had a dream that a relative who had passed away insisted on preparing a meal or pastry and give it in charity, and then he insisted that children must be fed first."

Somebody else told me, "My brother had terminal cancer and died in the hospital. A few nights after his death, I had a dream that I was taking a walk in the street. Suddenly I saw him coming toward me with some food or bread in his hands. When he got closer I asked him: would you give me some of that food? He said: okay, but you should first give me the pistachios in your pocket. I slipped my hand into my pocket and took out the pistachios. They were ten. I gave them to him and he gave me the bread in return. When I woke up in the morning I could remember the dream but I couldn't make head or tail of it. Anyway, I got dressed after a while to go to work. When I left home, I saw some little kids playing in the alley. I put my hand into my pocket to see if I had anything to give them. There were exactly ten pistachios. My dream was interpreted. I gave them to the children on my brother's behalf." As this dream indicates we need to make a little more effort in delighting kids. The *Thawab* (reward) accrued from delighting *Awliya Allah* (the chosen friends of Allah) is even more than that accrued from delighting children. However, gratifying them is more difficult; you cannot please them by nice words or by the lure of filthy lucre. What makes them happy, though, is obedience to Almighty God. The traditions of the Infallible Imams (AS) state that comforting even nonhuman beings, namely animals will work wonders in alleviating your distress. A poacher, for instance, has trapped a young animal. Its mother is, for sure, annoyed by this. (Although some may say that animals do not get sad the way we do, they certainly get vexed in situations like this.) Releasing this young animal and relieving the mother's anxiety can relieve your anxiety. Many people whose esteem was raised by God for a mere loving care to an animal.

Once a *Mu'min* (believing Muslim) dreams about someone who has passed away. He asks the *Mu'min* why they don't give anything in charity on his behalf. He says that they are not very well off. The deceased says: you do not have to lay the table in charity; just toss the bones in the leftovers before a dog. Experience has shown that being kind and caring to animals may bring about salvation. Mulla Salih Mazandarani who was praised with attributes, such as "knowledgeable" and "insightful" was once asked, "How come you have such a good memory for the information and skills you get through education?" He said, "At first I was a dull seminarian with a memory like a sieve, then I did an animal good and God opened the floodgates of His grace and blessing to me."

Some poor mystics, when in their spiritual journeying and wayfaring faced impediments, would get some grains of millet, ground them and placed them next to ants' nest. Then they would start to pray, "O God, we helped these weak creatures of thine, in return we ask thee to solve our problems."

It is said that Allameh Tabataba'i was so tenderhearted that he didn't permit the chickens in his house to be slaughtered. The poultry in his house would grow bigger and bigger until they died a natural death. Allameh used to say, "These animals have taken refuge in my house." I don't mean, of course, that you should follow suit, nor is God going to punish anybody who slits an animal's neck. What I mean to say, though, is that we should take care not to hurt any harmless animals. We are walking along the alley, for example, and we see some ants wandering innocent as the dawn; we should be careful not to accidentally step on them.

There are a number of traditions from the inerrant Imams (AS) stipulating that if a believing Muslim tramples an ant underfoot while walking in a lane, God will touch him with some distress.

One narrative from among all narratives suggesting why Jaccob (AS) was afflicted by being away from his beloved Joseph (AS) is one that says he slaughtered a lamb before its mother. Therefore, we should keep away from teasing and hurting animals, for they have sentiments too. I saw with shock a poulterer putting to knife and skinning chickens before other hens and cocks on customers' demands. It can cause extreme horror among other chicks not yet slaughtered. I have heard, maybe you too, that camels understand they are about to be killed and shed tears in fright before they are hamstrung.

Annoying animals, physically or mentally, overburdening them or making them pull heavy things will leave bad effects in the owner's lives. Traditions of the infallible Imams (AS) reiterate commitment to the need of animals and avoiding mistreatment. Rasulullah (pbuh) in this regard said:

«لا تَضرِبُوا الدَّوَابَّ عَلى وُجُوهِها فَاِنَّها تُسَبِّحُ بِحَمداللهِ» ١

"Do not hit animals in the face, for they praise and glorify Allah."

In no religion are people advised as vehemently as in Islam to treat animals well.

In the period of mass starvation and disease in Iran, a famished man manages to obtain some food with considerable difficulty. On the way home a hungry breeding bitch attracts his attention and pity. He puts the hard-gained food before the dog lest the famine-stricken beast, whose newborn pupies might starve to death due to reduced milk production to total failure, die of hunger. When he arrives home, his neighbour dashes toward him and says, "Please

---

[1] Osoul-e Kaafi, vol. 6, page 538

help me; a splitting headache is killing my wife." He suggests some medicine out of the blue and goes in. After a while the neighbour comes back and asks, "Where did you study medicine? Your prescribed medicine was highly effective. It was actually a wonder drug." "I just said something by chance," he says. "It's not necessary to humble yourself before me!" he exclaims. "No, I'm not humbling myself; I know nothing of medicine. I'm not an apothecary," the man says, a bit touched by anger. When he looks up, he sees some other people standing around and insisting on being visited. He repeats what he has said before, but no one believes he is not a physician. "Well, if I suggest some substance, some herbal drink or something with no tangible physical effects, they will soon see the reality that I'm not a doctor and will leave me alone," he thinks to himself. However, the course of events, ironically, happen just the opposite of what he expects and wishes for. The suggested substances prove to be quite effective, and soon groups of patients and disabled people from all walks of life mill around his house. Soon, in those deadliest years on record for the Iranians, his sure-fire remedies tie him up at home for long and unsocial hours as a popular doctor. He goes up to a great man of God and says, "I have absolutely not the slightest idea what is going on, but this is the whole story." He talks about his miraculous power in healing the sick of their diseases. The man of God says, "It seems to me that you have done a great job favourable to God." when they go back in time and review the recent events together, they reach the feeding-the-dog incident. "Yeah, that's it," the man of God suggests. "The healing power of your tongue stems from pleasing that dog."

Now think! If pleasing a mongrel is so meritorious, how much more meritorious it will be to please a human, and yet more to please a *Mu'min* (a believing Muslim), and yet more than that to please a purely sincere Muslim. The traditions of the inerrant Imams (AS) tell us that all the blessings of the world cannot recompense that deed. There are more than a hundred A in this regard, one of which is by Imam Sadegh (AS): a Mu'min who has gladden people's hearts, especially those of Mu'mins, will see some good-looking being before him, on whose hills he treads in the Life to Come. That being will give him a helping hand on hard-to-tread paths and precipices and accompanies him until he reaches the Paradise. Then he says his farewells. But before he leaves, the Mu'min asks him, "Who are you? You were so helpful to me!" "I am the embodiment of that happiness you gave such and such believing servant of God," he answers.[1] As I said, there are a lot of Ahadith in this respect. Therefore, one of the important ways to alleviate your distress is pleasing saddened hearts.

Amir al-mu'minin, peace be upon him, said to Kumayl (He swears by God): "O Kumayl, direct your people to go out in the day to achieve noble traits, and to go out in the night to meet the needs of those who might be sleeping, for I swear by Him Whose hearing extends to all voices, if someone pleases another's heart, Allah will create a special thing out of this pleasing, so that whenever any hardship befalls him, it will come running like flowing water and drive away the hardship as wild camels are driven away."[2] That's a very important point we should pay heed to in our lives

8. Rendering Relief to the Deprived

One way to remove distress from your heart is to share the burden of those burdened with grief.

Amir al-mu'minin, peace be upon him, said:

---

[1] Osoul-e Kaafi, vol. 2, page 190
[2] Nahjul Balagha, wise Saying 257

«مِنْ كَفَّاراتِ الذُّنُوبِ الْعِظامِ اغائَةُ الْمَلْهُوفِ وَ التَّنْفِيسِ عَنِ الْمَكْرُوبِ» ١

"To render relief to the grief-stricken and to provide comfort in hardship means the atonement of great sins."

It is not a good thing to be immerced in one's own life of ease and not pay due attention to others. Human world is not the world of indifference. Human beings are like the parts of a whole, like the branches of a tree. If a part or a branch is afflicted with pain, other parts or branches will suffer too. If man's soul is healthy, he will be irritated to see people suffer. He won't ever say, "It's none of my business. That's not my problem." He won't seek his own ease. Unfortunately, a serious problem in our society is to shun responsibility, put its burden on others, and call it successful management. In an organization, for example, you can see that things are done without much bureaucracy and without wasting too much of the clientele's time. Then the manager decides to streamline the system and prune out any unnecessary paperwork. When it is done, you see that now the clietele have a rough time in doing their jobs. What has happened, actually, is taking the burden off the clerks' shoulders and putting it on the heads and shoulders of the clients. Is it successful management? Is it what Islam asks from us? The Prophet (pbuh) said in a *Hadith*:

«مَلْعُونٌ مَلْعُونٌ مَنْ أَلْقى كَلَّهُ عَلَى الناسِ» ٢

"Cursed be the one who puts his burden on the shoulders of other people."

Many of us are not aware of the problems we cause for others: we just drive off, oblivious of the the problems we make for other people. The same goes for walking, gardening, socializing, car-washing, etc.

---

¹ same, wise Saying 24
² Man La Yahduruhu al-Faqih, vol. 2, page 68

Once I went to an organization and asked the manager to allocate one of the offices, temporarily, for some job I needed to do. He readily consented without giving me the slightest runaround. Later on, I talked to someone about this, "May God bless the manager: I asked for some room, and he immediately equipped an office for us." An office worker who was standing nearby overheard what I said. Snickering, he stepped closer and said, "We were already pressed for place. The manager made our condition worse by taking that office and giving it to you."Is is correct to provide comfort for someone at the cost of difficulty for others?! What do we call this? There should be a name for this kind of misbehaviour. If red tape for getting an official document, a permit, or a licence used to waste two days of your precious time, now it takes ten days. There is a computer on every office desk; state-run organizations are equipped with them and other devices out of the public purse, but what noticeable change have they brought about in facilitating clients' affairs?

I am telling you all this in order to work together to find out where the catch is and how to facilitate referrals. Office equipment is on the rise, desks are getting wider and longer, computers and other electronic equipments are getting ubiquitous, but office referrals are taking the same amount of time as before (sometimes they take longer and sometimes they take shorter, but put together, they take as much as before). Concerning the time it takes, what difference has been made, now and past, in getting a driver's license? If it doesn't take longer, for sure it doesn't take shorter either. So what is the effect of billions upon billion tomans' worth of equipment and devices that the Traffic Department uses? The story is almost the same with getting a construction permit or a business license. In the past you could get a business permit in two days, but now you should wait for six months. Is this way of doing things Islamic? Not at all.

I asked someone, "Has the computer facilitated your job in any way?" He was rather dubious about what he wanted to say. "The abacus has put the computer to shame!" he said. Maybe he is right, maybe not; but I daresay technology hasn't solved our problems in most fields. If you delve into it, you will see that your problem is solved, but the essence of the problem is still there; somebody else is suffering! In driving, for example, there is some etiquette to adhere to: considering the right of other motorists in traffic jams, using turn signals before making a turn, yielding right-of-way to other vehicles, etc. Failing to stick firmly to these rules will be tantamount to getting people into trouble and loading them with the burden you were supposed to carry.

The call of Islam is to share people's burden, to deliver them from embarrassment, and to solve their knotty problems. But unfortunately the current trend, especially in state-run organizations, is a far cry from what the religion asks of us. These organizations sometimes drive you up the wall by the time you manage to get the signature of somebody in authority. Several years ago after my studies at Tarbiat Modarres University were completed; I went there to apply for my degree certificate. They gave me a few forms to fill out and sign. I said, "Is that all?!" Prasing Allah that it could be done in no time, I started filling them up. Then I was told that I needed to get somebody's signature who worked in another building, the top floor of a five-storey building. So I went there, but there was a long line of clients waiting for the elevator. I thought it would be a waste of time to ride it, so I took the stairs instead. I found the room, but before I could get one of the forms signed, I had to refer to fifteen other office workers in different buildings. Anyway, at noon I felt a stinging pain in my heel and I thought I could walk no more. When I took off my shoes to perform ablution, I found a big blister on my right heel. I call God to witness that I had to go back to my hometown, Yazd, and return to Tehran again and again four times before I could get all the signatures and complete the tortuous process of getting my degree certificate, which seemed a piece of cake at first. I went up to the Education Administrator and suggested, "These clerks and authorities here that give the clientele the runaround and cause so much pain must be flogged according to the rules of *Sharia*." Who are all the traditions of the infallible Imams (AS) for?

Who is the addressee when Imam Ali (AS) says?

«مِنْ كَفَّارَاتِ الذُّنُوبِ الْعِظَامِ اِغَاثَةُ الْمَلْهُوفِ وَ التَّنْفِيسِ عَنِ الْمَكْرُوبِ» ١

"To render relief to the grief-stricken and to provide comfort in hardship means the attonement of great sins."

If an employee goes to the office and starts work in the name of Allah with the best of intentions and tries as much as possible (provided that he doesn't violate God's law) to solve people's problems, his mere breathing will be an act of wordhip. Sometimes the client needs to make a phone call. Since he is not supposed to use the office phone, it doesn't hurt if you lend him your own cell phone. But who takes it upon himself to do these things?

If you relieve the oppressed and downtrodden people of their burden, unpleasant feelings and pains; Allah will recompence by forgiving your grand sins. Once the grand sins are forgiven, grand problems and sufferings will be removed too. If somebody comes to you for help, never get tough with him by saying, "Why do you suppose I am as hard as the nether millstone (not in the Biblical

---

1 Nahjul Balagha, wise Saying 24

sense, but as one who bears the burden of others)? Why do you always come down on me like a ton of bricks? May God keep your evil far from me!" consider people's turning to you for help as a blessing from God. One of the blessings from Allah is people's referral to you. Imam Ali (AS) in this regard has said: the fact that people ask you for help is to be considered as a blessing from Allah. So try to meet their needs and don't get tired. [1]This way, God will remove many of your problems and sufferings.

9. Du'a

Du'a (invocation) is an effective act of worship for the fulfillment of a need or the removal of some harm. A group of traditions of the infallibl Imams (AS) even say that the Devine Destiny descends from the sky, then a servant of god starts reciting *du'a*, and God revokes what was going to happen, although Destiny is said to be irrevacable. «لَا تُرَدُّ وَ لَا تُبَدَّلُ»;[2]

The people of Yunus (Jonah) recited *du'a* and cried in repentance and God forgave them. You are enjoined to shed tears while offering *du'a*, even if (the infallibe said) the drop of tear is no more than the weight of a fly's wing[3]–especially when you are prostrating yourself. You can also sit facing the *Qiblah* (the way you sit while performing *Salat*) and raise your hands in invocation. Offering *du'a* in congregation is especially emphasised in Islam. We Muslims should appreciate *Du'a Kumayl*. However, when it is recited in congregation it should not take long lest people get tired. The reciter of the *Du'a* is advised to bring it to an end soon, so

---

[1] Ghurar al-Hikam wa Durar al-Kalim, page 238: مِنْ نِعْمَةٌ إِلَيْكُمْ النَّاسِ حَوَائِجَ إِنَّ»

نَقَماً. فَتَتَحَوَّلَ تَمَلُّوهَا فَلَا فَاغْتَنِمُوهَا عَلَيْكُمْ الله».

[2] Osoul-e Kaafi, vol. 2, page 472

[3] same, vol. 6, page 61

one of the secrets of salvation is *du'a*. *Du'a* will help you get rid of disasters.

Du'a for Mu'minin

One effective way to get relief from worries induced by human deeds is *du'a* for *Mu'minin* (believing Muslims). There are tens of *Hadiths* that indicate if you perform *du'a* for forty believing Muslims and then for yourself, your prayer will certainly be answered by Allah. That is why we are asked first to perform *du'a* for forty believing Muslims in the *Night Salat* and then seek forgiveness from Allah (*Istighfar*). This is for the fact that our *Istighfar* to be effective.

One of the companions of Imam Moussa al-Kadhim (AS) says: in Arafat (a plain and mountain near Mecca) I asked Abdullah ibn Jundab, the great companion and transmitter of *Hadiths* of Imam Moussa al-Kadhim (AS), who was blind in one eye, "You have cried so much in supplication that you are about to get blind in the other eye too." He answered, "I have not called upon Allah for myself; all my supplication had been for the *Mu'minin* because I heard from my *Maula* (master) that Allah asks the angels to give the supplicant a hundred thousand times as many as he has asked for others.[1] Another *Hadith* says: whoever makes *du'a* for *Mu'minin*, a hundred thousand angels ask Allah to answer his own requests. [2]

There are some *Ayahs* (verses) in the Quran indicating that angels recite *du'a* for *Mu'minin*. It's really surprising that angels recite *du'a* for them. Nowhere in the Quran can you find an *Ayah* saying that angels call upon Allah for themselves; however, they

---

[1] same, vol. 2, page 508

[2] same: «قال الكاظم (ع): اَنَّ مَنْ دَعَا لِاَخيهِ بِظَهْرِ الْغَيْبِ نُوديَ مِنَ الْعَرْشِ وَ لَكَ مِائَةُ اَلْف ضِعْف».

make *du'a* for *Mu'minin*. *Du'a* for *Mu'minin* is not only very effective, but it is also some sort of practice in repulsing egocentricism and paying attention to what other people need or want. You cannot always turn your back on society and its problems, and indulge in your own Self. It is pure selfishness to call upon Allah for your child, your property, your life, your body, your health, etc. Try to go beyond the scope of Self. Broaden your horizons and make *du'a* for your neighbour, your brother, your friend, and all the believing men and women. Call to mind, in this respect, the *Hadith* by Amir al-mu'minin, peace be upon him:

«مِن كَفَّارات الذُّنُوب العِظام إِغاثَةُ المَلهُوف وَ التَّنفِيسُ عَن المَكرُوب» ¹

"To render relief to the grief-stricken and to provide comfort in hardship means the atonement of great sins."

The grief does not need, necessarily, to be worldly. Those stricken with grief can be in the Purgatory. If they had been virtuous, render relief to them by doing some good deeds in their behalf, put up prayers for them: say in supplication, for example: O God, remove the sufferings of all *Mu'minin* who are suffering in the Purgatory! As you can see, it is really an easy way to help them. More than ten *Hadiths* are related on this issue by the inerrant Imams (AS) that if you perform *du'a* for forty *Mu'mins* before you perform *du'a* for yourself, your *du'a* will be met by acceptance. But if you neglect the affairs of other *Mu'minins* and put up a prayer only for yourself, then you will have to repeat it forty times before it is accepted by God. Now you may compare these two ways. Which one is better? In the first way you have both prayed for others, which is liked by God, and you have got your own prayer accepted.

There are two types of *du'a*: the first type are those that have come down to us through narration from the Prophet (pbuh) and infallible Imams (AS); the second are those we make and utter, like: O Allah! Forgive them their sins, treat them with clemency, shower your bounties on them, resolve their problems, bless them with plenty, heal their patients, pay off all their debts, provide them with

---

¹ Nahjul Balagha, wise Saying 24

decent clothes and pure food, remove the indignation they feel toward each other, and so on. You can also pray for a particular person, yet if you get into the habit of reciting *du'a* for *Mu'minin*, you won't need to make *du'a* for yourself. There might not be an apparent familial bond between you and another *Mu'min*, there is yet another bond which is stronger than family relationship, and that is faith. If he is not your brother, he is your broher in faith instead. Therefore, if there is a Gordian knot in his life, camaraderie behooves you to shed tears while praying for him in supplicaion. Our Prophet (pbuh) is reported to have stated: **Allah said to Moses (AS): put up prayers and call on Me through a tongue not yet fallen into sin.**[1] Moses asked: how am I supposed to do that? Allah answered: through the tongues of others (eg, ask others to pray for you, or behave in such a way, that others pray for you out of love). If you find a *Mu'min* in real trouble, stand in *salat* for him in a corner, shed tears and put up a prayer for him. The effect it leaves might be equal to forty, fifty, or a hundred times the effect his praying for himself leaves. Then not only will all the rewards and blessings be yours, but your problems will also be resolved.

10. Avoiding Deeds That Induce Sadness

In Al-Khisal (The Book of Characters) Shaykh al-Saduq writes that once Imam Ja'far al-Sadeq (AS) said: **one day when sadness befell Amir al-mu'minin (AS), he said, "I wonder what the reason of my sadness is; I'm sure I didn't sit on the threshold in the doorway, nor did I go through a herd of sheep or cow, nor did I put on my pants standing, and nor did I dry my face and hands with the edging of my garb."**[2] This *Hadith* clearly shows that these four actions can induce sadness:

---

[1] Wasa'il al-Shia, vol. 7, page 109
[2] Al-Khisal, vol. 1, page 226

Chapter Two: Guidlines for Quitting Unpleasant Habits

1. Being Open to Criticism

First of all we need to identify our unpleasant habits, yet it is not always easy to do so. Since it is actually imposible for us to discover all our flaws, we should be grateful if other sets of eyes, ears and tongues take out the time to point them out. If people dare not give us feedback, we are to blame, because we have already behaved in such a way that they scare to point out our mistakes. But if we do not shut out criticism, nor make it a point to brush constructive criticism off, nor prepare points for a rebuttal, they will mention our mistakes and thereby enable us to easily spot them. Even if what they say about us is ninety percent wrong, it is still worth not taking a defensive position, and react openly and positively for the sake of the remainder (ten percent right). Otherwise you will be like a smoker whose foul breath disgusts the people around but not himself; like someone whose breath smells of garlic, but he does not notice; like someone who suffers a noticeable blemish on the face, but his own eyes cannot see it. We need a mirror to see our flaws. We should appreciate others if they reflect our shortcomings.

«المُؤمن مِرآة المؤمن»[1]

"The believer is a mirror to his faithful brother."

---

[1] Bihar al-Anwar, vol. 74, page 414

2. Inculcation

The second way to kick bad habits is inculcation. If you, through repetition, instill the idea that you can do something good or that you can avoid doing something evil, then the way will be paved for your cast of mind to change the situation. The Holy Quran sometimes uses this method to implant positive attitudes:

«وَلَا تَهِنُوا وَلَا تَحْزَنُوا وَأَنتُمُ الْأَعْلَوْنَ إِن كُنتُم مُّؤْمِنِينَ»[1]

"So lose not heart. Nor fall into despair: for ye must gain mastery if ye are true in faith."

If the idea of superiority over the problem is impressed on you, you will emerge victorious; if you rank yourself low, you will lose big time. Nonetheless, inculcation may get pesty: if the problem is inculcated to be too little or unimportant, then you are doomed to be defeated by that problem. You must be inspired in such a way to say that the problem is serious, but I am strong enough to resolve it, or the problem is very serious, but I am not the one to give in; I will work hard until the problem is no more. With this attitude you can even fight incurable diseases.

A friend once said, "Someone who lived in the vicinity of my shop got skin cancer in 1981. As a result, awful boils and malignant tumors occured on his skin especially on his face and neck. Doctors believed he would give in to the disease in two, three months. One day this idea struck me that 'inculcation therapy' may work, so some fellow shop assistant and I devised a plan. The next morning when he was passing my shop, I called him in. 'Have you got your prescription changed?' I looked him at the face and asked. (Incidentally, he had.) 'Yes, why do you ask?' he said. 'Nothing, I just think you look better today, praise be to God,' I said. He left my shop and continued his walk. The next

---

[1] Aal-e-Imran, *Ayah* 139

door shopkeeper also told him he looked healthy–or words to that effect. And then the next one and the one after that, so he believed that he was getting better. It is now almost thirty years that inculcation has kept the cancer in check–if not healed it completely." Instilling a positive idea strengthens the soul.

It is said that somebody was once bitten by a snake; thinking it was a wasp, he survived the bite. Another person was stung by a wasp; he thought it was a snake and passed away.

One of my friends said, "Someone decided to donate blood, so I went with him to the blood donation clinic. At the sight of blood he fainted. They had drawn only two or three millilitres of his blood, but he thought they had drawn all. That's why he had lost consciousness."

Inculcation will leave wonderful effects in alleviating pain. Those who claim to be able to heal patients by energy therapy, actually use "inculcation methed". (I wonder whether energy healing is science or pseudo-science.) A cancer patient visited one of these people. He thought that the healer could really channel healing energy into him. Nevertheless, his mere belief in the healing power of the method cured him. Ever since then the healer used him as a means to promote his job and convince the sceptical who sought to cast doubt on his healing method. What makes the method workable, though, is the patient's belief in its workability not the method itself.

A veteran of the Iran-Iraq war related what happened to his brother-in-faith in the military action. He said that his fellow combatant had been shot eight times in his chest and stomach. At the crack of dawn, when his khaki was already covered entirely with blood, he was shot once again in his stomach. He pressed his hand on the fresh wound and knelt down. I knew if I looked worried before him, he would most probably succumb to his wounds. "Come on man! It's nothing; look at that guy over there: he's got thirteen shots in his body." I said. Meanwhile I gripped him and pulled him up. He looked me in the eyes and stood on his feet. Then we ran slowly back to safty. Later on when I stated the account of this event to someone with the emphasis on the fact that the combatant was still alive, he told me that he knew someone who survived nineteen shots in his body! Judged by our own standards, stories like this are indeed hard to believe, yet what kept them up and about is their powerful souls. Consider the loyal companion of Sayyid al-Shuhada (AS) in Karbala; a single arrow shot from the enemy's bow was enough to make him yield but he resisted seventeen of them until the Imam (AS) brought his prayers to an end. Of course, what he did was beyond inculcation, because inculcation may give rise to belief, but he stood the arrows because of faith, which is much stronger than belief.

A friend of mine who is a doctor and used to be a prisoner of war in Iraq worked in the infirmary there. He said: one day a fellow inmate came to me complaining that poor nourishment and scarcity of vitamins were killing him. He said he felt pain in his joints all over his body. I guessed some fear has been instilled into him, so I told him, "The Red Cross doctor has brought a kind of ampule that does wonders. If you inject it into a dead man, he will stand alive. I will give you injections for three days, and you will be up and about for seven, eight years. But I don't want anybody to know about it, so mum's the word! OK?" "All right," he agreed. The next day he came to the infirmary and I gave him an injection of sterile distilled water. I gave him another injection the day after and yet another one the day after that. The following day he came up and said, "O doc, I am here to tell you that I feel so agile and energetic that I can climb up a whitewashed wall."

3. Finding a Suitable Substitute

A third way to break bad habits is to find an appropriate substitute. You need to replace bad habits with good. For example, if you are used to uttering offensive words against your wife, neighbours, or colleagues, try to cut it out and use good words instead of the swear words. If you are interested in gambling, turn to sport and stick to it. If you like to listen to a type of music which is not allowed by religion, make it your habit to listen to beautiful Quran recitation or melodies allowed by religion. Needless to say, deleting bad habits and replacing them with cleaned-up alternatives take time and effort, but mostly they take perseverance.

4. Gradual Quitting

Bad habits should be tapered off. In the age of Aristotle somebody went up to him and said, "I am addicted to a plant. What I want to know is how I can give it up." Aristotle didn't answer–actually one day of the week he wouldn't talk to anybody. Instead, he leaned a ladder against the wall and climbed it up and down. The man in a state of confusion left him and went to Plato, his teacher. He told Plato that Aristotle didn't answer his question. Plato asked, "And he didn't do anything?" "He just climbed up and down a ladder," the man answered. "He did give you the answer," Plato said. "But what did he mean by that?" the man enquired. Plato said, "Aristotle meant to say you got addicted rung by rung and you need to stop it rung by rung. You cannot jump down from the top to the bottom rung; you may break your leg."

A smoker who has been enslaved by cigarettes may suddenly be fed up, tear and crush his packet of cigarettes and vow not to smoke anymore, but relapse into his old habit of smoking after a while when a fellow smoker offers him one. Yes, there is always an increased risk of relapse when he hangs out with smokers. It often starts with one cigarette– and this cliche that a single cigarette won't make you an addict–and then adds up to more. One coping strategy, therefore, in quitting smoking is to practice saying, "No, thank you, I don't smoke anymore." However, if you accept the offer, you will soon be disappointed and lament that smoke is more powerful than you. Another coping mechanism is to stop gradually rather than stopping it cold turkey. You may cut a cigarette in three and smoke each portion with a cigarette stick. This way if you smoke even ten times a day, you won't have smoked more than three cigarettes by nightfall. You do not have to think about quitting forever. That can be overwhelming. Too much deprivation is sometimes bound to backfire. I suggested this last method to someone. He took it and successfully managed to get rid of it forever after a year. His success brought this idea to mind to recommend to cigarette factories to curtail their cigarettes to half its normal length or even shorter. When the smoker's cravings will pass in the first two centimeters, I don't see why cigarettes must be four to five centimeters long. Every year billions of tomans are spent on manufaturing cigarettes in our country. Do you know how much will be saved if this idea is actualized? Well, I don't either, but I know it's a lot.

Islam and Step-By-Step Training
The method of Islam in canonizing ordinances was the same. If Islam, from the outset, had ordered people to establish *salat*, to fast, to give *Zakat* and *Khums*, to go on pilgrimge to Mecca, to fight against enemies, to enjoin good and forbid evil, they would have said: practicing *Shirk* (polytheism or joining gods with Allah) is better than practicing Islam. The first order was just: say there is no god worthy of worship except Allah and you will be successful.

«قُولُوا لا اِلهَ اِلَّا اللهُ تُفْلِحوا» ١

Although the Arabs were used to doing forbidden things (taboos), Islam avoided confrontation. At first there was no talk of taboos and forbiding them. However, in different occasions things became obligatory or forbidden. For instance, *Jihad* was made obligatory in the second year of *Hijra* and total prohibition of intoxicants was decreed nineteen years after the Prophet's apostleship. That is to say, for nineteen years many Muslims would attend the congregational prayers in the mosque when they were drunk. The first *Ayah* that implicitly indicated that wine was evil was descended from heaven in Mecca.

«وَمِن ثَمَرَاتِ النَّخِيلِ وَالاَعْنَابِ تَتَّخِذُونَ مِنْهُ سَكَرًا وَرِزْقًا حَسَنًا...» ٢

"And from the fruit of the date-palm and the vine, you get out strong drink, and wholesome food."

"Strong drink" is juxtaposed with "wholesome food" to suggest it is unwholesome and harmful. And then in Medina this *Ayah* was descended from Allah:

«يَسْأَلُونَكَ عَنِ الْخَمْرِ وَالْمَيْسِرِ قُلْ فِيهِمَا إِثْمٌ كَبِيرٌ وَمَنَافِعُ لِلنَّاسِ و...» ٣

"They ask thee concerning wine and gambling. Say: in them is great sin, and some profit."

There may possibly be some benefit in it, but the harm is greater than the benefit. As a result, some Muslims avoided indulgence in them. One day one of the Muslims was reciting the Sura Al-Kafirun in his *salat*. But he was too drunk to recite it correctly. He left out all the 'ﬆﬆs, (*Nor*'s and *Not*'s) and spoiled the meaning:

---

1 Bihar al-Anwar, vol. 18, page 202
2 An-Nahl, *Ayah* 67
3 Al-Baqara, *Ayah* 219

«أَعْبُدُ مَاتَعْبُدُونَ وَ أَنْتُمْ تَعْبُدُونَ مَا أَعْبُدْ»

I worship that which you worship and will you worship that which I worship.

This paved the way for some other Allah's decree:

«يَاأَيُّهَاالَّذِينَ آمَنُواالَاتَقْرَبُواالصَّلَاةَوَأَنتُمْ سُكَارَى...» [1]

"O ye who believe! Approach not prayers in a state of intoxication, until ye can understand all that ye say."

Then nineteen years after the prophet's Apostleship a bitter incident gave rise to the descent of this *Ayah*:

«يَاأَيُّهَاالَّذِينَ آمَنُواإِنَّمَاالْخَمْرُوَالْمَيْسِرُوَالْأَنصَابُ وَالْأَزْلَامُ رِجْسٌ مِّنْ عَمَلِ الشَّيْطَانِ فَاجْتَنِبُوهُ لَعَلَّكُمْ تُفْلِحُونَ» [2]

"O ye who believe! Intoxicants and gambling, sacrificing to stones, and (divination by) arrows, are an abomination, – of Satan's handiwork: eschew such (abomination), that ye may prosper."

This is the way that Islam advocates, the gradual approach. Islam didn't reveal everything from the beginning. The advent of Islam did not coincide with issuing all the decrees. We need to adopt the same approch in breaking bad habits. But first we should get to know what our flaws and bad habits are. We are to take time and make a list of them and then set our heart on dealing with them immediately. Suppose breaking one bad habit takes a year. Then how many years would it take to break all bad habits? So procrastination is not allowed. Considering the fact that after a certain age habits will become harder to overcome, that will power gets weaker, it makes it even more necessary to start now.

---

[1] An-Nisa, *Ayah* 43
[2] Al-Maeda, *Ayah* 90

It is like straightening the crooked trunk of a strong tree. A sapling is much easier to straighten.

«فى التَّأْخِير آفَة»; **"Things get pesty with tardiness."**

Maulavi says:

Corybant, bestow a goblet of wine upon me,
Speak not of morrow wherein exists sorrow.

5. Religious Vow

By taking a religious vow (*Ghasam*), you make it obligatory upon yourself to do an act or to avoid an act for the pleasure of Allah. Taking a vow will make it possible for you to do things automatically and with ease [after all, if you don't, you have broken your vow, and you have to make expiation (pay *Kaffara*)]. Great men of God would, this way, make non-obligatory good deeds obligatory upon themselves.

When you make something obligatory upon yourself, you will get a strong will power to do it. If you decide not to eat or drink anything during the day, you will find it really hard to stay on your decision. But you easily fast in Ramadhan, simply because it is *wajib* (obligatory) to fast. If you like to get into the habit of doing good things, just make them *wajib* upon yourself for a few days. This is the way in which great men get into the habit of doing *Mustahabbat* (recommended deeds).

6. Display

What is display? Is it to be taken as duplicity? Of course not. They are two different things. Display means making something known in order to seek the pleasure of Allah. It is like giving obligatory alms (*Zakat*) openly, so that people see and follow suit. We are enjoined to give obligatory alms openly and non-obligatory alms covertly. We are recommended to go to the mosque and display the daily prayers in congregation. Show that you are fasting during Ramadhan. Even if you cannot go on a fast, at least you should pretend that you are fasting by your behaviour and look. Some people think that feigning something which is not part of your character will amount to double-dealing. I assure you it is not true. It is approved by psychologists too. They believe that if you assume some quality, that quality will become your second nature after a while. For example, if you put on an air of cheerfulness, you will soon become cheerful. Amir al-mu'minin, peace be upon him, said:

«إِنْ لَمْ تَكُنْ حَلِيماً فَتَحَلَّم، فَإِنَّهُ قَلَّ مَنْ تَشَبَّهَ بِقَوم إلّا أوشَكَ أَنْ يَكُونَ مِنهُم» [1]

"If you cannot forbear, feign to do so because it is seldom that a man likens himself to a group and does not become as one of them."

A captive in a Nazi concentration camp feigns madness in order to gain freedom. Thinking that he is mad, they release him. After the war his friends go to see him and find him really mad in a loony bin.

Once, a sergeant is taken to a mental hospital by mistake. Interesting enough, the one who is really ill and some other people take him there. After three days they know they have made a mistake. They immediately go to the hospital to discharge him, only to find that the poor sergeant has really gone mad.

Displaying a quality is closely linked with inculcation. In a movie directed and starred by Mehdi Fakhimzadeh, a thief, Reza, is caught burgling. He is then subjected to a bizarre 'selection process' by SAVAK (the intelligence service of the Pahlavi regime). It transpires that they are seeking a doppelganger for a political leader, Tohid, and Reza's resemblance to him is uncanny. The investigators use the resemblance to their advantage, and,

---

[1] Nahjul Balagha, wise Saying 207

with Reza as their prize prop, proceed to destroy Tohid's social influence and reputation. In his new role as a political pawn, Reza undergoes changes far more drastic than he could ever have believed. Tohid dies, but a new revolutionary Tohid is born. He gives lectures, disgraces Shah (Mohammad Reza Pahlavi), and causes uprising. When SAVAK find out their malicious plan is having the opposite effect to the one which they intended, they execute him too.

In fact what Amir al-mu'minin, peace be upon him, says:

«إِنْ لَم تَكُن حَلِيماً فَتَحَلَّم»; has got mental and spiritual roots. When movie stars play the role of noble and dignified people, they really become dignified and live a life of sanctity and high-mindedness for some time. What do they do in their role? Is it more than a mere display, a false front?

The essential step, therefore, to improve conduct and good behaviour is to follow the example of those who enjoy it and hold onto it until it integrates into your nature. The secret of this *Ayah*: "Ye have indeed in the Messenger of Allah an excellent exemplar for him who hopes in Allah and the Final Day, and who remebers Allah much," lies in the fact that believing Muslims liken themselves to the Prophet (pbuh) in talk and conduct. This will make them take in some excellent characteristics of his.

Chapter Three:
Guidelines for Repelling the Love of This World

To sum up the root cause of all sufferings in one short phrase, we would say it is the love of this world below; as Rasulullah (pbuh) believed:

«رَأْسُ كُلِّ خَطِيئَةٍ حُبُّ الدُّنيا» [1]

"Love of this world is the root of all evils."

There are some ways to drive this kind of love out of the heart. Toothache or tooth pain is caused when the nerve root of a tooth is irritated. But if the nerve is removed, the tooth can be pulled out with forceps without feeling any pain. By way of analogy the root of the worldly love, which is the source of all problems, needs to be removed. There are five ways to help:

1. Contemplation

By contemplating the verses of the Quran as well as the traditions of the infallible Imams (AS) we get to clearly recognise the real face of the world beneath its beautiful facade. You may like and befriend a person as long as his badly burnt face is hidden beneath a beautiful mask. Once the removal of the mask brings home to you what the face is really like, you might well be scared off. The Quran and *Ahadith* do the same thing. They show us the unmasked world. If they do not completely take the love of this world out of the heart, they will at least make it less intense. By pouring cold water in a boiling pot, you may not get it cooled,

---

[1] Osoul-e Kaafi, vol. 3, page 766

but it won't be bubbling and boiling anymore. Thinking about Quranic verses will lower the heat you feel toward the world:

مَّن كَانَ يُرِيدُ الْعَاجِلَةَ عَجَّلْنَا لَهُ فِيهَا مَا نَشَاءُ لِمَن نُّرِيدُ ثُمَّ جَعَلْنَا لَهُ جَهَنَّمَ يَصْلَاهَا مَذْمُومًا مَّدْحُورًا ١

"If any do wish for the transitory things (of this life), We readily grant them–such things as We will, to such persons as We will: in the end have We provided Hell for them: they will burn therein, disgraced and rejected."

As you can see the wicked may not be provided with what they wish, but with what Allah wishes for them and even if they are provided, it is not just because their recipients wish for them, but according to a definite plan of Allah. And then Allah will provide Hell for them. Why? because they asked for a lease of life and luxury for a time, which was granted as the reward of their good deeds. Yet their wickedness, which has not been punished here, has not escaped notice. As a result, on the Day of Reckoning not only will they not be left any rewardable virtue, but they will also have just punishable vice. Where will vice be paid for except in the Hell?

And in *Surah* Hud:

مَن كَانَ يُرِيدُ الْحَيَاةَ الدُّنْيَا وَزِينَتَهَا نُوَفِّ إِلَيْهِمْ أَعْمَالَهُمْ فِيهَا وَهُمْ فِيهَا لَا يُبْخَسُونَ * أُولَٰئِكَ الَّذِينَ لَيْسَ لَهُمْ فِي الْآخِرَةِ إِلَّا النَّارُ وَحَبِطَ مَا صَنَعُوا فِيهَا وَبَاطِلٌ مَّا كَانُوا يَعْمَلُونَ ٢

"Those who desire the life of the present and its glitter,–to them we shall pay (the price of) their deeds therein,–without diminution. They are those for whom there is nothing in the Hereafter but the fire: vain are the designs they frame therein, and of no effect are the deeds that they do!"

---

[1] Al-Isra, *Ayah* 18
[2] Hud, *Ayahs* 15-16

It is noteworthy that none of these verses is exclusively about infidels. They include Muslims too. Surprisingly, all the *Ayahs* of the Quran that deal with the love of this world are absolute and inclusive. If man cogitates on these *Ayahs*, which are not small in number, he won't be infatuated with this world below.

In a sermon, Amir al-mu'minin, peace be upon him, describes the situation of the Prophet of Allah (pbuh): he took the least share of this world. He did not lay one stone upon another (to make a house) till he departed and responded to the call of Allah. Of all the people of the world he was the most empty of stomach. He loved that the world's alluremets should remain hidden from his eyes. The world was offered to him but he refused to accept it. Then Amir al-mu'minin (AS) says: Now, one should see with one's intelligence whether Allah honoured Mohammad—the peace and blessings of Allah be upon him and his descendants—as a result of this or disgraced him. If he says that Allah disgraced him, he certainly lies and perpetrates a great untruth. If he says Allah honoured him, he should know that Allah dishonoured the others when He extended the (benefits of the) world for them but held them away from him who was the nearest to Him of all men.[1] This is how Imam Ali (AS) sees the world. But unfortunately our society is getting farther and farther away from these values. We are getting unmindful of them. In some cases the situation is even worse: values are getting so devaluated that those who are mindful of them are considerd dupes.

If someone sticks to the beliefs and principles of religion, behaves ethically, and lives a clean life, he will be taken as crazy. Amir al-m'minin, peace be upon him, said:

---

[1] Nahjul Balagha, sermon 159

This house (the World) is the closest to the displeasure of Allah and the remotest from the pleasure of Allah [of course what Imam Ali (AS) meant was the evil face of the World not its divine face]. At the end of this sermon, he mentions a point which is worthy of contemplation: Friendship with Allah's enemy (the World) is enmity with Allah.[1] That is to say, the World is Allah's enemy; if you wish to be a friend of the World, you have loved Allah's enemy. Therefore, you have made yourself an enemy of Allah. Suppose someone was diametrically opposed to us (you and I). At the same time someone else made friends and kept his loving contact with him, what would you think of him? Whould you befriend him?

How to Look on the World
In a sermon Amir al-mu'minin, peace be upon him, said:

«مَن أَبصَرَ بها بَصَّرتهُ وَ مَن أَبصَرَ اليها أَعمَتهُ»[2]

"If one sees through it (this World), it would bestow him sight, but if one had his eye on it, then it would blind him."

When you are having your glasses on, either you can see to them or through them. If you focus your sight through the glasses, you can see all the things around. But if you adjust your sight on the glasses, you will see just the glasses rather than the objects around. You cannot have it both ways. A friend said while his glasses were resting on his nose and ears, he was looking for them all around the house. Yeah, when you have them on, you cannot feel them. The similitude of the World is also like that of the sun. The sun will help you see things. However, if you keep your eye on it, you will go blind. Let's try to see through the World, through the nature as the Quran enjoins:

---

[1] same, sermon 160
[2] same, sermon 82

ٍ«أَفَلَا يَنْظُرُونَ إِلَى الإِبِلِ كَيْفَ خُلِقَتْ * وَإِلَى السَّمَاءِ كَيْفَ رُفِعَتْ» [1]

"Do they not look at the camels, how they are made?–And at the sky, how it is raised high?"

Many a scientist embraced monotheism by seeing through the nature and discovering its rules. There was a documentary on TV about the Big Bang theory and its compatibility with what the Quran says (It's one of the scientific wonders of the Quran.) in this regard. It was said in the program that some materialist sientists turned to the belief that there must be only one God. However, on the other end of the spectrum there are those who lead a pretty mundane existence and have a materialistic outlook of everything in the world. A cherry tree for them, for example, is no more than a means to gorge them on.

Destroy yourself coming upon gratis property,

It is a transaction made extremely rarely.

Allameh Tabataba'i, by contrast, once saw a cherry tree; stood still before it, lost in thought for a while; started to shed tears; and recited, "There is no god but Allah." If one sees through it (this world), it would bestow him sight, but if one had his eye on it, then it would blind him.

Let's not gaze at the world! It will win our hearts. Why do you think the Prophet (pbuh) asked Ayesha to get the floral curtains off his sight? Because the mere look at this World's finery and trappings can cause heedlessness. All the luxuries, welfare, and glittering ornaments of this World, for whose possession, there is a constant competition and rivalry, and the fact that brotherhood, friendship, and neighbourliness are all being sacrificed for them, all show the stark reality that the current situation is way out of control. What we can do, though, is to avoid hankering after them

---

[1] Al-Ghashiya, *Ayah*s 17-18

and pay heed to the traditions of the infallible Imams (AS). Of course, there is no paucity of verses of the Quran that say: for those who desire the life of the present there will be nothing in the Hereafter.

These warnings will help distract our attention from this World. If your beloved friend is always talked ill of as avaricious, jealous, haughty, selfish, stingy, and bad- and hot-tempered, little by little you try to drop friendship with him. Friendship, moreover, may even turn into animosity. Then you will even change your way not to accidentally meet him. By the same token, if you pay attention to what Allah, the Prophet (pbuh), and the Imams (AS) have said about the life of this World, it cannot attract your attention as much.

2. Making the Hereafter Your Goal

Another strategy that diminishes the love of this world is to make the Hereafter our objective, or in Imam Ali's words "To be the son of the Next World", to know that we are departers not stayers. When you are out on an excursion or something, you may make a campfire, unroll a rug near it, stay there for a while and take a rest. But it will never escape your notice that in the afternoon you should go back. Now, if you forget that you are not supposed to stay there, and take two sleeping pills and have a restful sleep, when you wake up, you will feel quite desperate. Hafiz says:

Departed, the caravan; and, in sleep, thou, and the desert in front:

How thou goest; where thou goest; what thou doest; how thou art.

Then Hafiz goes on:

On account of time's grief, the liver of blood how long, how long art thou?

How long do you want to be in grief because of this World? It is not becoming for the heart, which is the shrine of Allah, to grieve for it.

So one of the effective ways to erdicate the fondness for this world is to know that we are living a probationary life down here in order to be prepared for a sublimated life up there, to know that this lowly World is not worth giving credence to. Amir al-mu'minin, peace be upon him, said:

«فَكُونُوا مِن أَبنَاء الآخِرَه وَ لَا تَكُونُوا مِن أَبنَاء الدُّنيا» [1]

"You should become sons (followers) of the Next World and not become sons of This World."

That is to say, you must remain faithful and never relax your efforts in doing things for the Day of Judgement. If this world is not supposed to be your goal, why should you bother yourself for it? Of course, this target is attainable only to staunch believers in the Hereafter who sincerely (and with certainty) serve Allah, rather than to those whose belief is alloyed with doubt in the World to come, nor those who have completely forgotten it. Also the strong faith to Hearafter can be reached through pure worship:

«وَاعُبُد رَبَّكَ حَتَّى يَاتِيَكَ الْيَقِينُ» [2]

"And serve thy Lord until there come unto thee certainty."

Purified acts of worship, prayers, fasting, anything at all done to gain the pleasure of Allah will raise the level of faith. These things not only will be rewarded, but they will also elevate you to certainty. If you achieve that level, you can easily forgo this World for the sake of the Next World. A farmer's working on his land might be seen by a child as, "How strange! This man is throwing

---

[1] Nahjul Balagha, sermon 42
[2] Al-Hijr, *Ayah* 99

grains of wheat onto the land." But a wise man would say, "How juditious the farmer is! He is throwing wheat seeds on the ploughed land to have sustenance next year." Unfaithful individuals see believing Muslims who expend their money, energy, effort, prestige, well-being and even life in the way of Allah as ignorant fools, but insightful people say:

«فَلِأَنْفُسِهِمْ يَمْهَدُونَ»,[1] "They will make provision for themselves." Do you ever hesitate to buy shares of a company whose price will sure go up ten fold? If this world is not what you are after, it will make no difference to you whether you gain it or lose it.

Life is full of struggles. On such a thorny path called life, it is only hope that keeps us moving forward. If someone, whose son is dead, is told that his son was being held incommunicado in prison for six years, he will get discouraged and suffer grief, yet he will tolerate the situation. But if the ghastly truth, the son's death, dawns on him, he will lose hope and suffer much more although in both suppositions he won't be able to see his son for the time being. In a similar assumption, if he is told that his son has gone abroad and won't be back for ten years, he will feel relatively at ease by thinking that he is studying or working there. But the news of his son's death will break him. Hope is what keeps us going in life.

Islam is here to fill the man of faith with hope when he is suffering hardships, whereas for the man without faith, who has no hope of a life, good and pure, in the Hereafter, hardships are devastating. The Holy Quran says:

«...إِن تَكُونُواْ تَأْلَمُونَ...»; [2] "If ye are suffering hardships,"

---

[1] Ar-Room, *Ayah* 44
[2] An-Nisa, *Ayah* 104

«...فَإِنَّهُمْ يَأْلَمُونَ كَمَا تَأْلَمُونَ...»; **"They are suffering similar hardships."**

«...وَ تَرْجُونَ مِنَ اللهِ مَا لاَيَرْجُونَ...»; **"But you hope from Allah, what they have not."**

The difference between you and them lies in the fact that you are full of hope in Allah, but the men without faith have nothing to sustain them.

3. Recognizing the Real Nature of the World

The third way that helps stop loving this world is getting to know that being rich means dealing with different problems. Amir al-mu'minin, peace be upon him, said:

«مَنْ ظَفِرَ بِهِ نَصِبَ وَ مَنْ فَاتَهُ تَعِبَ»[1]

"Whoever is successful with it encounters grief and whoever misses its favours also undergoes hardships."

What the Imam (AS) means to say is that if you are not wealthy, you are gripped by grief whenever you look at the lives of the rich, because it appears as if they have it all. However, if you become a billionaire, do not think your problems will be solved. Wealth will make you an easy target. Those who are the nearest like children will covet your riches. They will think, "For sure we will be unhappy if Dad passes away, but at least we will come into his wealth by means of an inheritance or other windfall." Some children even vocalize this thought in jest.

It is really distressing to think that your own children are looking forward to your death, to think that people you trust can be anything but trustworthy. Being wealthy does not mean distrusting everyone who offers a smile, but you have to be on the lookout for fake friends–people who, like wasps landing on a piece of meat, only come around when they need something. You have to be

---

[1] Nahjul Balagha, wise Saying 72

careful about fraudsters, burglars, and kidnappers too. (Some time ago when a rich Yazdi and his wife return home late at night, they see a man with a gun in the yard. He threatens to kill them if they refuse to give in to his demands. In another case the son of a wealthy man was abducted. They asked for ransom in exchage for releasing the boy.) And then the nagging wife who would like to renew all the household appliances according to the latest models comes. In short, everybody around him demands something. The situation will become so unbearable that he wishes he did not have so much money!

The childless couple envy families with children. After months or years of anticipation Allah vouchsafes a baby. The couple who used to sleep like a log is now likely to become "on call" parents who have to get up in the night to calm the crying baby. As the baby grows up, they come to realize that raising a child, after all, is not that easy. It requires resources, time, effort, and commitment. In his early teens, when he knows his right hand from left, he calls his parents fuddy-duddies. To have, or not to have children, that's the question. Now I ask you; does a wise, well-rounded person ever poke his finger into a beehive for a little honey? We get into trouble because we tend to see the sweet side of things. We see only the flower not the thorns. The heart of the matter is the words by Imam Ali (AS):

«مَنْ ظَفَرَ بِهِ نَصِبَ وَ مَنْ فَاتَهُ تَعِبَ»[1]

A relative of mine once said that his grandfather used to sleep on the roof. He would roll over in the open air and say the king was not enjoying himself as much as he did. He would also say, "I'm not living under constant assassination threats, I have no throne and no money to be worried about. I'm not responsible for

---

[1] same

fixing the mess after a flood. I do not have to be concerned about the country's territories or the enemy's advance. I sleep like a baby and in the morning I resume work refreshed." Let's have such a relaxing outlook on life. Why would you like to be a boss, a manager, a high-ranking official? Just to have others bow before you?! Haven't you heard the offensive, indecent language against them in the Islamic Republic?! Haven't you seen the inappropriate, insulting words thrown at them in newspapers and websites?

When you feel envious, it often helps to step back and look at the bigger picture. When you take a holistic view of things and people, when you try to see good and evil, both advantages and disadvantages, you will see things to which you were previously blind. A lot of our sufferins grow out of our erroneous outlook. A change of it will change everything.

A passenger was arguing with the airport ticket agent over missing the flight. "It was all because of you that I didn't make it in time to get aboard; if you hadn't shilly-shallied in issuing the ticket, I would now be flying over the Persian Gulf. If you...," he was crying when all of a sudden the phone in the agency intterupted him. The agent took the call and listened. A few seconds later he went deathly pale and looked as if he might faint. "The plane is not above the Persian Gulf; it is in it!" he said. "May God bless your father for not issuing the ticket!" the passenger heaved a sigh of relief.

History says that once the despot, Hajjaj bin Yousef gave a banquet. All the ravenous people took part in it. He asked them to start the meal when he gave them a hint and not to begin otherwise. Then he gave the permission. But before they reached for the food, the bloodthirsty potentate said, "If you touch the food, I will have your head cut off." With this, their hands locked together instantly. However, a glutton from among them didn't give a damn to the threat and started to eat ravenously. Most probably he had thought to himself, "I'd rather eat myself to death than just sit and watch!" He swallowed tasty morsels of food one after another while addressing Hajjaj, "Don't worry about your children! I will take it upon myself to teach your children and make scholars of them." (When you eat and talk at the same time, you will make yourself a laughing stock.) It is said that Hajjaj laughed himself to tears and fell on his back to see the gluttonousness and carefree attitude of the man! And then he ordered his men to give him some currency.

A man, visually impaired, goes to a shop to buy a water glass. The shop assistant turns one upside down and hands it to him. He touches the glass and says, "I'm sorry sir. It has a big hole on the bottom. Oh, and the top is closed!" The assistant says, "There is nothing wrong with the glass; turn it right side up and it'll be okay." Sometimes we, too, look at the world topsy turvily.

The Wealthy on the Day of Judgement
On the Day of Judgemnt a voice is heard:

«أَيْنَ الفُقَراء»; Where are the poor? Some people rise and say, "We had nothing; we were poor before we came here." So their accounts will be taken by an easy reckoning and they proceed towards the Paradise (of course the faithful poor ones). These believing Muslims are among those who go into the Paradise before others. At the entry, the angel treasurers ask them who they are and where they are going. They say: □□□□» «□□□□□□□□□;

We are the poor. And they welcome them warmly.[1] Traditions of the infallible Imams (AS) even say that they will be given permission to intercede for whoever they like. At this moment the wealthy resort to beggary. A lot of things that make us anxious will be gone if we look at the world from this particular angle. Once I asked a country man of seventy five if he still worked. He

---

[1] Osoul-e Kaafi, vol. 2, page 264

answered he was a farmer. He was still enjoying good health and his look didn't show he was that old. Then he showed me a snapshot of his mother's grandfather, well and standing, taken at the age of one hundred and twenty seven! Yeah, in the past people worked hard and enjoyed themselves.

4. Contentment with Divine Guardianship

Rabb is one of the appellations of Allah. He is the Lord of the Worlds. Despite His absolute authority over the world, He has a reformational tendency. As the Most Gracious and Most Merciful reformer, Allah cares for all the worlds He has created and likes to bring His creatures to maturity by evolution from the earliest state to that of the highest perfection and completion. In a training process if the teacher or the trainer is strict and hard on the trainee, even if he doesn't find the reason behind this strict behaviour, at least he knows what the trainer does is for his own good. In a larger scale, we may not know Allah's intention behind different happenings, still we shouldn't doubt that Allah has arranged them to do us (particularly *Mu'minin*, because they have accepted the idea of Divine Guardianship) good. This idea of Divine Guardianship (*Wilayat*) is the belief in the fact that Allah has taken it upon Himself to manage *Mu'minins*' affairs and look after them and the fact that Allah wants nothing but good for them.

When you go to a dentist for a filling, he removes the decayed tooth material, cleans the affected area and fills the cavity. But do you ever complain if the process hurts? You will thank him even though he prescribes some bitter medicine because you know he intends no harm. A believing Muslim knows whatever happens to him has been part of a plan on the part of Allah to make him spiritually perfect and prepare him for the World to Come, so he grins and bears. This belief that the ultimate cause of all things is

Allah, that whatever He causes to befall us is absolutely good with no tint of evil in it, is a very important belief.

$$\text{«مَّا أَصَابَكَ مِنْ حَسَنَةٍ فَمِنَ اللهِ وَمَا أَصَابَكَ مِن سَيِّئَةٍ فَمِن نَّفْسِكَ...»}^{1}$$

"Whatever good, (O man!) happens to thee, is from Allah; but whatever evil happens to thee is from thyself."

Allah does not permit anything evil to come down. Whatever He issues is good, pure and holy. He doesn't step in to stop pain and suffering, but He sure stops evil. If this notion is deeply ingrained, you will reach the high level of contentment. In that case any kind of bitterness will taste sweet to your palate. In relation to this statement Amir al mu'minin, peace be upon him, has said:

$$\text{«وَ مَن رَضِيَ بِرِزْقِ اللهِ لَم يَحْزَنْ عَلَى مَا فَاتَهُ»}^{2}$$

"He who feels happy with the livelihood with which Allah provides him does not grieve over what he misses." Because he knows what he gets is good for him, and what he misses is also good for him ultimately. In donating blood and bloodletting some blood is withdrawn from you. However, this reduction not only doesn't endanger your health, but it also reduces risk of a number of health problems including cancer.

A friend once said that somebody who frequently suffered splitting headaches had an accident in which he received a deep cut in the forehead. As a result, the mucus, which had caused inflammation and headaches, through the nasal passages and sinuses oozed out. While sewing the wound together, the doctor told him, "You know what? God has treated your headaches." Sometimes we don't know why things occure the way they do.

---

[1] An-Nisa, *Ayah* 79
[2] Nahjul Balagha, wise Saying 349

Under Allah's protective care or Divine *WilAyah* (Guardianship) nobody suffers imperfection. In the eye of a believing Muslim nothing is imperfect, even if he gets wounded or killed in the way of Allah. This is the secret of suffering. Other complicated solutions to the problem of suffering serve only as a pain reliever.

An Important Point

Divine *WilAyah* is always conveyed through a perfect man. People are allowed to be connected to Allah by being connected to him: In the time of the prophets (AS) the duty of the guardianship was undertaken by them. After the end of prophethood it came to the infallible Imams (AS). As the Prophet (pbuh) said in the *Moustafid* related by both Shi'a and Sunni: Islam is constantly exalted in might by twelve Imams (AS). The word "constantly" in this statement clearly shows at no period of time is the earth void of Imam (AS). So unlike prophethood, guardianship is never disconnected: at the time of the absence of the Imam (AS), a religious jourist who is most similar to a prophet in terms of his knowledge of *Shari'ah* will undertake to see to *Mu'minin*'s affairs, so that they have somebody to follow, be under his leadership in all aspects of life, and reject *Taghut* (any tyranical power) as a focus of obedience and worship.

If a pond is connected with the ocean, it is no longer a pond. If a limited man is connected with the Divine *WilAyah*, he won't be a small man of no account. He will be one like Salman Farsi of whom it was said, "He was abounded with rich knowledge and deep wisdom." His imperfections will be compensated for, he will be like *Mu'minin* in *Ziarat Jamia Kabira*: through our loyalty to your leadership (Divine *WilAyah*) Allah has taught us the features of our religion, and has set aright the spoiled items of our wordly lives..., and saved us from the brink of the pit of perdition.... It is exactly right, (and for which there is enough evidence), to say that all the shortcomings in life and all the problems we face are due to some flaw in our loyalty to the Divine *WilAyah*. It is said in a *Hadith* that Salman Farsi had a misgiving about *WilAyah* for a moment, and he got neck pain immediately. So what the whole book boils down to is this single statememt:

MU'MIN'S STRICT ADHERENCE TO *WILAYAH* ABSORBS ALL THE BOONS AND BLESSINGS AND DRIVES OUT ALL THE AFFLICTIONS AND INDIGNATION.

These groups of Mu'minin are those about whom Imam Sadeq (AS) has said: There are some servants of Allah who live a life of comfort and joy Here, and in the Hereafter they live a life of bliss in Heaven.

Therefore, instead of asking Allah to remove suffering in all degrees of intensity, from mild to intolerable, we'd better narrow all the petitions down to one, and ask Him to confer on us the highest degree of *Wilaya*, which is the panacea for all corporate ills. This string, of course, has two ends: one end is in Allah's hand; the other endpoint is the *Mu'min*'s efforts in achieving that degree. As the doctor's skill is not enough in treatment, the patient should take what is prescribed; as the availability of a savior over the pit into which somebody has fallen is not enough, the victim should take hold of the other end of the rope (or in Hafiz's words: keep your oath such that the chain won't come undone); the *Mu'min*, too, should ask Allah to help him but do his best at the same time. Now think! Is the essance of the book anything more than this?

Hafiz, if ever in thy head dwell union's wish serene,

Thou must become the threshold's dust of men whose sight is keen.